PENGUIN BOOKS

COMING CLEAN

David Kinnersley gained his good degree in economics and several prizes at Cambridge after the war, learning almost as much from a remarkable farmer near Worcester with whom he worked each vacation. After experience in the Coal Board for much of the 1950s, he helped to shape and manage the policy transition in the 1960s to far more use of canals and river navigations for recreation. The award in 1973 of a Winston Churchill Fellowship to study citizen participation in river basin agencies began his enjoyment of North America and long-distance working travel elsewhere which still continues. He was then appointed chief executive for one of the new water authorities serving a region of seven million people. More recently he has been an Oxford college fellow and an adviser to Ministers, overseas governments and the World Bank. A renowned authority on water, his first book *Troubled Water* was published in 1988.

David Kinnersley has been a board member of the National Rivers Authority, the Public Finance Foundation and WaterAid, a voluntary body helping poor communities overseas keen to improve their own water supply and sanitation with their own effort. WaterAid was formed in 1981 after the Thirsty Third World meeting in London which he convened.

He is married with three grown-up children and lives in the Chilterns close to the river Chess.

David Kinnersley

COMING CLEAN

PENGUIN BOOKS

PENGUIN BOOKS

Published by the Penguin Group
Penguin Books Ltd, 27 Wrights Lane, London W8 5TZ, England
Penguin Books USA Inc., 375 Hudson Street, New York, New York 10014, USA
Penguin Books Australia Ltd, Ringwood, Victoria, Australia
Penguin Books Canada Ltd, 10 Alcorn Avenue, Toronto, Ontario, Canada M4V 3B2
Penguin Books (NZ) Ltd, 182–190 Wairau Road, Auckland 10, New Zealand

Penguin Books Ltd, Registered Offices: Harmondsworth, Middlesex, England

First published 1994
10 9 8 7 6 5 4 3 2 1

Photoset by Datix International Limited, Bungay, Suffolk
Printed in England by Clays Ltd, St Ives plc
Set in 10/12 pt Monophoto Sabon

For Barbara,
with much love and thanks

Ye nymphs that reign o'er sewers and sinks,
The river Rhine, it is well known,
Doth wash your city of Cologne;
But tell me, nymphs, what power divine
Shall henceforth wash the river Rhine?

Samuel Taylor Coleridge
(1772–1834)

Contents

Acknowledgements

In the 1990s, those who work in water and river basin agencies hardly have time to read books about their situation. They are mostly having a rough time as many communities try to regain some sort of balance amid forces that for decades have led them to put an overload of claims on the water environment, and still tend to do so.

Yet in writing mostly for the many others now taking a more positive interest in water and how people share it, it is my water colleagues I need to thank. In my writing and much other work, they have helped me more than they recognize, though what I have made of that help is my responsibility entirely. These colleagues, in many different settings overseas and at home, have repeatedly given me personal friendship as well as professional support before I had done much to earn them. It is very reassuring to find this spirit still prevailing as strongly as ever amid so much change and strain in the agencies they work in.

One sadness at this time is that Nicholas Ridley has recently died. As Secretary of State for the Environment and accomplished fly-fisherman who understood rivers, he made a distinctive mark on some of the policies this book discusses, while being involved in so many other issues at the same time. Far more than his public reputation sometimes suggested, I found him and his ministerial colleagues always considerate and constructive to work with as heads of a very demanding department.

I should specially acknowledge here the attention that the *Economist* and the *Financial Times* have been giving to water issues in the last few years. This is not only helpful to my work and interesting in itself: it signifies and reinforces the way regard for natural resources and the water environment is becoming a regular concern of decision-makers in industry and agriculture, no longer some exceptional alien burden. I have also relied on the

ENDS Report for regular briefing and analysis. Among other organizations, I am grateful to the World Bank, the Department of the Environment, the Overseas Development Administration, the National Rivers Authority, the Water Services Association and Water Companies Association, General Utilities plc, WaterAid and the Water Research Centre, and many individuals in them. I also owe John Briscoe and Sheila Quennell special thanks for the speed as well as the quality of their help at a late stage.

Any list of others who have helped me here or overseas would quickly become both too long and yet still incomplete. So I must limit myself to thanking those without whom the writing would not have gone forward at all. My wife, Barbara, has been, as ever, full of understanding. Mary Gray has been enthusiastic and excellent in her secretarial support. Tony Lacey, Janice Brent and Kate Parker have made producing this book for one of the great publishing houses of the century nothing of an ordeal. I hope they may all find the result worthy of such generous encouragement.

David Kinnersley
Chesham, Bucks., 1993

Introduction

The politics of water and the environment is a theme at once age-old and very up to date. In this context, politics has the older and broader sense of civic affairs that concern the community as a whole in addition to a wide range of individual interests, rather than that of party politics (despite a controversial privatization, described in detail in Chapters 5 and 6). The ways in which people and communities get and share water are currently subject to much questioning and radical change, after a long, settled period when such matters were largely left to water engineers and town hall bureaucrats. The citizens and water users are engaged in these changing attitudes as much as the professionals, public agencies and businesses directly involved. The spirit of change is manifest in the water sector in many countries besides Britain, and in international agencies such as the World Bank and the European Community. Water has, so to speak, come out of the closet into the headlines.

There is a paradox here, because using water is still largely a matter of unthinking habit for most people for whom fetching it first is not a time-consuming daily chore. Yet the deeper changes now unfolding are almost certainly irreversible: they are part of an uneven and slow adaptation in the relationship between communities and the water environment on which they depend. These changes are comparable, say, to those that arose as industrialization and urban development spread and gathered pace in Europe and North America for a century or more from about 1800.

The activities under review include the getting and use of water for many diverse purposes in the home and work place, in the town and countryside; the disposal of human wastes, all sorts of effluents, waste water and provision of rainfall drainage; guarding against flood, pollution and drought, and fostering the natural ecology of rivers and lakes for their own 'health' and for the fish that live in them; dealing equitably and openly with claims for access to river basin resources, endeavouring to keep them within sustainable limits; and, by no means least, the many activities for recreation and relaxation that people take on and around water in the open landscape. As well as a human habitat and a rich and endlessly renewed natural asset, the river basin is a sort of playground. Chapter 9 acknowledges this all too briefly, noting signs in England of congestion even in claims on water 'space' for leisure.

The management of water requires a large technical input for which the skills of engineers and scientists are still crucial. But the conspicuous change in the last fifteen years or so is how prominent and compelling economic, social and legislative, or regulatory, issues have become. This reflects partly the increasing claims that are pressing more intensely on limited resources, and partly the greater public interest. Water serves such diverse purposes that almost everyone is likely to be not only a habitual user, but, from boaters and bird-watchers to industrial chemists, farmers and voluntary campaigners, a sharp-eyed specialist. Chapter 7 gives some indications of how public attention to the affairs of water has grown, and Chapter 1 describes the influences that have generated it.

These changes are specially striking in Britain. The English live in the drier parts of the island, but even they have long believed that, whatever other deficits they may have to face, they would always have plentiful water within easy reach at a cost they would hardly notice. Now that they are more alert to the issue of water quality, and are grasping the detrimental effects that sewage disposal and intensive farming can have on this, they are beginning to realize that in a small, crowded island, with about twice the population of Canada, such assumptions are becoming unrealistic.

But administrative and political influences have contributed to change as well. One mark of the old regime was that for more than thirty years up until 1985, Whitehall insisted that details of authorized effluent discharges made by businesses and local councils should be concealed from public knowledge. Save for special purposes such as court proceedings, it was illegal for the authorities that gave out the permits to publish information about who held the permits, what effluents they discharged, or how far they complied with the obligations and limits which the permits specified. Potentially the greatest threat to sharing river capacity well for different purposes was kept strictly under official wraps.

Now this concealment is ended; the details are in the open on public registers that anyone can study. To motivate a serious reduction in pollution by all sorts of dischargers, it was essential to 'come clean' with this public information. The degree of current public interest in water pollution shows how mistaken it was to have concealed it in the first place. Chapters 10 and 11 outline the many sources of water pollution and the task of protecting water quality, including that of underground water.

The moves to privatize the regional authorities providing the water supply and sewerage services in England and Wales were an even sharper change, turning the old order on its head. As Chapter 4 describes, these agencies had been brought together only by a radical reshaping in 1974, and could not be privatized in that form. But from 1985, preparations were made, including separating the river basin functions from the utility services, for these ten regional units to be floated as commercial water utilities, and extreme monopolies, in late 1989. Chapters 5 and 6 discuss these processes, including the tensions inherent in the government's several roles as seller of public assets, would-be protector of consumer and tax-payer interests, and guardian or trustee of the community's common property in river basin resources. The river basin functions – such as flood defence, water resources, pollution control and the care of fisheries – were brought together in a new National Rivers Authority (NRA), which quickly gained respect for its positive response to changing public attitude, despite an awkward launch briefly described in Chapter 7.

Privatization of the water companies, unlike that of the other utilities, did not go beyond the Scottish border. The latter part of Chapter 4 gives some account of the very different situation in Scotland. In a vivid illustration of how water institutions are still conditioned by local circumstances, Mr Major's government has decided again (in July 1993) not to carry the English and Welsh model for water privatization into Scotland.

That model's design reflected experience gained from the other utility privatizations, including price-cap regulation (such as in the case of telecommunications and gas) and the special feature of water services as a little-growth business requiring huge investment to achieve improvements. Thus price increases above the rate of inflation (rather than below it, as in the case of most other utility companies) had to be provided for, and a new office established to regulate these monopolies. As Chapter 12 describes, this system is approaching its first major test, probably in July 1994. Then, limits to each company's price increases will be newly set for a further five years, a real opportunity to moderate the balance between investor interests and consumer interests settled for flotation in 1989. On the evidence of water company share prices, the investors seem to have been more comfortable with the regime to date than some consumers have been. This issue, and the question discussed in Chapter 8 of moving from taxation-based charges for domestic water supply to usage-related bills, has to be tackled even if many companies seem reluctant or uncertain about sorting it out directly and positively. In this and perhaps other ways, old attitudes seem to prevail to a larger extent in the new private companies than might have been expected some four years after the great change that privatization was claimed to bring; but a monopoly rarely changes its spots.

How effective a role consumer interests can play in such necessarily standardized services as water supply and sewerage remains, however, an awkward matter to assess. Given that municipal administration was unaccustomed to consumers defining the standards of service that really suited their needs, the consumer lobbies that have been influential in the high street and the supermarkets over the last thirty years may still be confused about what they should aim for and hope to achieve in the water sector. They may be at risk of seeming so narrowly consumerist as to take little or no account of environmental issues that bear strongly on water services. Indeed, the standards settled for the sewerage service – which is essentially a collection service carrying wastes away from customers rather than a delivery service bringing water to them – have to be related to river capacity and the maintenance of water quality; for most consumers, such processes are literally out of sight, and at risk of being out of mind too (less so in France:

in Paris, remarkably, part of the sewers have been open for visits since 1867). With regard to river basins, even the most rational and articulate consumers may still need some assistance in grasping fully the nature of the relationship between upstream and down-stream communities: that it is essentially one of neighbours who, in effect, have to share discharged waste water as well as natural river flow.

But far and away the greatest change affecting water agencies and professionals since the early 1960s has been the world-wide surge in concern about the impact of human activities on the natural environment. In the pollution of English and Welsh rivers and beaches (tending to worsen through the 1980s) and in the over-pumping of some vulnerable river catchments (subject to a more intensive review by the NRA than such a matter had been before), the water sector readily provides examples of how nec-essary it has become to moderate the demand for water more effectively. But environmental issues go beyond just the water sector, as indicated by the proposal to form a new environment agency (see Chapter 11) to achieve integrated pollution control across land, water and air. Moreover, it is not only Britain or Europe that is preoccupied with these issues. The increase in concern is global, and it is striking that, in matters of water and the environment generally, many industrialized countries, despite their prosperity, are as perplexed – in their case, about the real scope for and cost of sustaining their comfortable life-styles – as countries still struggling in the earlier stages of economic development.

The themes of this book can thus be put into a wider perspec-tive. In the closing years of this century, following the collapse of the Soviet system, the market economy is seen as the most likely route to effective economic development. Yet this is also the period when its major deficiency is being revealed: the fact that it makes so little provision for the costs and side-effects inherent in use of the capacity of the natural environment and its resources, often called market failure.

Rather more constructively, one can suggest that a long, slow process of adaptation to repair this, begun in the 1960s, has become irreversible. Nevertheless, this process is still at an awkward stage: the outcome is still not clearly enough foreseen, even in theory, for widespread practical policies to be implemented with confidence. Even if some adjustments to the conventional market economy may bring about most of the reorientation required, other changes in legislation and regulatory mechanisms will have to be settled and made effective.

The new-style market economy has to find ways of making it a matter of routine for environmental costs to be fully reflected in the prices of everyday transactions. That we can organize and operate a very sophisticated, world-wide financial system and yet not know how to safeguard adequately the natural resources that we and future generations will depend on is a direct challenge to our current attitudes, and a disturbing irony not to be shrugged off.

The relevance of this to water is as follows. First, as was demonstrated in the nineteenth century, building the capacity to organize and operate basic services for expanding urban communities is itself a practical step towards making the most of human talents and resources that other business also requires. Secondly, water, despite being an essential and valuable commodity, has on the whole not been incorporated into conventional markets as an economic resource because its very character resists that over-simple categorization. Thus the water sector is now a sort of test case for working out how market mechanisms and frameworks can be adapted to deal with water and waste disposal more appropriately, especially as scarcity and competing claims on access to the relevant river basin capacity become more acute. The recent work of the NRA in introducing charges for effluent discharges to inland and coastal waters is at once encouraging and yet inadequate due to the lack of more positive legislation. Comparable schemes in France, the Netherlands and Germany have been operating successfully for 10–20 years (see Chapter 11).

More broadly, in the long process of adaptation, several activities or industries that are highly dependent on the environmental capacity for renewal may be seen as likely to suffer particular strain up until the middle of the next century. This applies especially to the disposal of waste water and other wastes, as well as to the energy industry and mining, agriculture and forestry, transport and vehicle manufacture. Several of these industries have already recognized that problems lie ahead.

Chapter 14 touches on how industries besides the water sector are adapting, seemingly faster – perhaps because their direct dependence on environmental capacity is lower. One closing assessment of that chapter is that even now water agencies in Britain are making only very patchy and half-hearted progress in establishing more effective economic mechanisms and incentives to promote essential changes in the patterns of water usage and effluent disposal. This is disappointing, but consistent with the perspective suggested here.

What water privatization has achieved so far must therefore not be regarded complacently as some kind of triumph. It has done little more than increase the pace of capital investment, important though that is. The proposed further reshaping of agencies concerned with environmental protection is probably not as urgent as the need to create stronger incentives for users of river basin capacity to moderate their claims on it. It should be a mark of confidence in the market economy for it to hasten the process of its adaptation to incorporating environmental costs and constraints as a matter of routine: this should be one of the most powerful ways to drive forward changes that could be as significant as those generated by the early stages of industrialization itself. If Adam Smith had not lived in the more spacious age of the eighteenth century, he might have given more guidance on how to deal with the pollution and congestion that have devalued so much of the gain in productivity and prosperity since his time. Now, a substantial adaptation of the market economy has become no longer optional.

Only one other comment remains to be made by way of introduction. Chapter 13 and the appendix linked to it dwell only briefly on matters that deserve far more attention and discussion. That access to a safe water supply and healthy sanitation is so inadequately provided for millions of people, with such harsh consequences in the form of high infant mortality, adult disablement, waste of human potential and sheer drudgery, is a specially bitter contrast with the ease of access experienced in Britain and many other places – some of them in the very same countries.

Yet the obstacle is not just poverty. The capacity to organize and operate community-run water services, political will and leadership with a different set of priorities are all relevant factors. A number of countries continue to press for costly and often inefficient irrigation projects instead of first improving the basic water supply and sanitation facilities for their people. International data repeatedly show what a large share of water and financial resources irrigation absorbs, in addition to much political and professional attention. Too often in countries not really short of the necessary competence, this demonstrates the politics of water gone wrong, but it would take far more than one chapter to do justice to this theme. Consider the main focus of this book to centre on the hazards of sharing water in a country where it is accessible for many purposes to almost everyone and they are all, in global terms, relatively rich.

Chapter 1

Not Taking Water for Granted

Soaps for delicate skin, shampoos for every type of hair, washing powders and floor cleaners are all the subjects of perennial promotion by the companies that make them. Yet water, the basic cleaner on which they each depend, is hardly advertised at all. Among the reasons for this is that for tap-water there is locally no choice of quality or of supplier. Also, it seems plentiful: the typical British attitude to water is that there is always more where the last lot came from. Moreover, the way people mostly use water is a matter of habit; not something to think about, let alone advertise.

Yet there is one point that deserves more notice than it gets. Water is a very convenient cleaner because it not only removes dirt but holds it in suspension. When dirty clothes are washed, the dirt ends up in the water, no longer on the clothes. Water has a great natural capacity to collect dirt or contamination, and to carry it away: in rivers water can also purify itself to some extent as it does so. So much is indeed so familiar about water that people need hardly give it any thought. But two questions arise. If water has a natural inclination to gather dirt, and people add a good deal of their own dirt and wastes to it, at work and home, what of the task of cleaning up water as the basic cleaner of most other things? More specifically, if people expect an endless supply of clean water, within easy reach at the tap or sparkling in local streams, where is this to come from when the rivers are heavily used as waste-disposal channels?

In a sense these are very old questions that communities in Britain and elsewhere have had to deal with down the centuries in their social arrangements, even if they could not spell out the scientific hunches on which they relied. There are records, for example, of English villages five hundred years ago having local rules or laws about the times when wastes from middens could be discharged to the stream. European towns had rules to keep

1

water-supply fountains free of contamination: only clean vessels were to be used to draw water.

Today such questions become more difficult to address. Now we understand the medical and scientific implications of good water quality, and have the technology to deal with most of the hazards of which we are aware. But can we cope reliably with the hugely increased volumes of effluents and wastes that modern communities want to eject into inland or coastal waters? Can we even measure how much pollution is now reaching rivers or underground aquifers from diffuse sources such as accidents to road tankers carrying chemicals, the use of pesticides and fertilizers, and other industrial or agricultural procedures regarded as necessary nowadays to achieve greater efficiency or productivity almost regardless of their consequences?

These questions, it should be noted, are not primarily technical. They assume technology is in use producing or applying the pollutants, and they ask in effect if and how the cumulative results of that can be coped with. The underlying issue is how to share water as a natural resource when the uses to which it is to be put are partly as a life-support system requiring high standards of purity, and partly as a waste-disposal system where the wastes may be getting, singly or together, more hazardous. Modern technology has great potential for waste purification; but even well-designed sewage works that are not overloaded will produce residual sludges in addition to treated effluent. How then to dispose of sludge – to land, sea or air? The broader social and economic issue, with political implications too, is how modern, industrialized communities are to relate reliably and sustainably to their water environment. The European Community has been agreeing over the last fifteen years or so a whole series of Water Directives, which member states can hardly find straightforward to implement, even in the long time-scales agreed upon.

Sources of the World-wide Concern about Water

The Industrial Revolution and everything that has followed it since – in terms of financial and business organization as well as technological development – has hugely increased human ability to make major interventions in natural resources and regimes. River flows can still cause great destruction when in flood, but nowadays they can be harnessed and tamed and diverted or stored on a scale impossible to achieve in earlier centuries. The use of water in development programmes has proved a powerful influence: the western United States, for example, would almost certainly have fallen well short of its present levels of prosperity but for the provision of huge volumes of extra water being made a major feature of government action and funding.

In global terms, a second influence arises from the fact that the pressures of greatly increased world population are being added to aspirations for economic growth. These larger populations not only need water for domestic purposes: the increased demand for food they generate prompts planning for more intensive cropping over wider areas, often depending on irrigation. Two types of conflict may arise from this. The needs for water of rapidly growing towns and cities may come to clash with the commitment of water resources to irrigation. At least as threatening, the sharing of rivers between sovereign states may become unsettled from its past patterns. At present, anxieties are evident about possible conflicts over, for example, the flow of the Tigris and Euphrates, the River Nile, the River Mekong and the Danube. People and their needs for food or new energy sources are pressing very hard on water availability in more parts of the world than most people in well-watered countries such as Britain may realize.

A third major reason for water now taking so much attention is that the capital spending required to supply water for most kinds of usage is very large and has to be provided 'up front'. In cities, networks of supply pipes and sewers have to be put in place, in addition to purification plants and maybe reservoirs and dams where underground water is not plentiful. The system has to be complete, at least for some areas, before anyone can get service. Water infrastructure is essentially collective in the benefits it offers. Again, the facilities required for irrigation, and for hydro-electric power stations, can be very costly to construct, even if their advocates emphasize the many long years of service they will provide once they are operating.

A special difficulty with all such debates and decisions is how to assess the benefits and consider how lasting they may be. In developing countries, an estimated value can readily be placed on increased food production from irrigation, assuming the forecasts of crop yield and market price are well judged. The benefits of water-supply networks or projects to improve sanitation do not lend themselves so readily to pricing. The value of better health or lower mortality, even if it can be assessed, may not be dependent on safer water supply alone. The benefit of people (usually women) having less drudgery to bear in the daily fetching of water from sources an hour's or more walk away is yet more open to dispute in terms of national economic priorities. Even in Britain, one of the Thatcher Cabinet's main reasons for privatizing water utility services was the agreed assessment that £24 billion had to be invested in them in ten years, to catch up on arrears after years of restriction on capital spending. Ministers insisted that water investments were getting too costly to be financed through government borrowing.

Finally, and most generally, the world-wide concern about taking better care of the natural environment has grown powerfully in recent years from its start in the early 1960s, as the range of political leaders attending the Rio de Janeiro Conference on Environment and Development in 1992 demonstrated. However much or little this achieved in policy terms, the significant thing was that it encouraged increased commitment from leaders throughout the world. Even an obviously reluctant President Bush did not dare to stay away. Although this concern includes complex and remote issues such as global warming, such changes, if they can be reliably measured at all, are occurring only very gradually. The state of the water environment is something people feel is much closer to home. They are correct in two senses: they do indeed inhabit their local river basin, and so are personally involved in some of the impacts on it. More compellingly still, the water environment provides vital parts of their own life-support systems.

Change in the Structure of Water Agencies

Water is essentially a local resource. Once the sharing or distribution of it is to be organized collectively, no matter how flexibly or patchily, it becomes a matter for the community. At that stage also, or later, the significance of water-supply networks to the spread of housing and other aspects of urban development will gain attention. Water will come on the agenda of civic leadership and organization, with little likelihood ever to be completely dismissed from it. The concern of local government with water supply and drainage, housing and highways will continue to be a major influence in countries at many stages of economic development. In communities at advanced stages of industrialization and prosperity, the concern of local government about water may nevertheless become diluted. Man-made and natural influences may contribute to this. The safeguarding of public health becomes more routine. Urban development may also be a less pressing priority. Local authorities find other services repeatedly calling for extra finance – to improve roads and public transport, for example. The costs of congestion begin to work against further city expansion. Moreover, when the impact of water supply and waste-water disposal within the local river basin becomes a larger issue, the individual local authority may be ill-placed to handle it effectively. Water resources from further afield may need to be drawn on; effluent disposal may have to be dealt with in a broader context. In this setting, elected authorities may be slow to accept obligations defined by non-elected environmental or river basin agencies. On the other hand, the European Community has had a very positive influence on the adoption of higher standards of water quality.

Thus, more 'utility-style' agencies may be formed in water supply and waste-water services as in the distribution of natural gas or electricity. It can take various forms: in France, for instance, some two-thirds of water supply is provided by the local authorities setting up operating contracts or franchises with private operators, which may include financing investment and collecting charges. These franchises are widely held by only three or four companies, so the system offers economies of scale, with continuing control remaining locally with the mayor or a consortium of neighbouring municipalities. This is a very robust structure, having been already established for more than a century.

In the United States, the US Army Corps of Engineers has an important role in controlling rivers, in flood alleviation, navigation and other aspects of water management. This has a historical origin, and may seem to have little modern justification: on the other hand, it works well and proposals to change it radically have been put forward but have never made much progress. A different format is seen in South Africa and other places where bulk-supply boards develop major water resources and aqueducts, and municipalities buy water from them and manage local distribution and the collection of charges. This pattern clearly fits a particular, relatively early, stage of development. At later stages, the fragmentation inherent in such patterns of multiple operators between sources and users may have several disadvantages, including divided responsibility for costs, water quality and accountability to users. In central Scotland, a special Water Development Board also deals with water resources and bulk supplies of 'raw' water: its future will be one element in the restructuring of water agencies there, and its survival as a separate unit is likely to be in doubt.

In England and Wales, the moves to put the services of water supply and sewerage and sewage disposal into privatized companies during the late 1980s may thus be seen partly as the product of right-wing party-political doctrine and partly as reflecting a trend taking water services away from a locally administered level towards being organized and developed much more as a utility business. This trend, leading as it did to the formation of water services into large private monopolies, called for monopoly regulation to be established to protect the consumer interests – though in effect it would be giving reassurance to investors as well. At the same time, the river basin functions had to be reshaped into the hands of a new National Rivers Authority (NRA), a significant innovation in the progress towards better care of the water environment.

Financing and Monopoly Regulation

Another form of adaptation in water institutions claiming notice here is that older models of financing water investments are giving way to new ones. Far and away the greatest change in industrialized countries is that earlier financial systems, mostly in the hands of local authorities, depended very heavily on borrowing for capital finance. When local authority control of water utility services in England and Wales ended around 1972–4, some 80 per cent of the capital programme was financed by borrowing; only 20 per cent came from internal cash flows, such as depreciation provided out of income from charges paid by consumers. Historically, this was an understandable system when the capital had to be spent early, and there was a reliable source of income which would be available for many years to repay long loans at a comfortable pace. Inflation, however, put this system into disarray. The asset owners would find the loans becoming almost trivial (to the lender's discomfort) compared to the renewal cost which would have to be faced in due course.

The interaction of the capital intensity of water services and long-term inflation made the financing of water utilities much more of a burden for public authorities and the Treasury. They had to borrow even larger amounts of capital to sustain or improve services, where, often, it would not be sensible to hope for greatly increased usage of the service (assuming more or less stable populations). Moreover, it is not politically popular or congenial to keep raising water charges; yet the older tradition of water supply and sewerage services being subsidized out of local or national tax revenues has become less tenable as many other claims on public sector budgeting are also becoming more burdensome.

Two different consequences arise from these influences. One that might be seen as socially unwelcome is that charges for indispensable water services are tending to rise. This may bring difficulty to some families with very low incomes, despite the fact that water bills generally take a far smaller proportion of lower incomes than the cost of fuel or electricity and other necessities. A

7

second consequence is that water is gaining more recognition as an economic resource, which should be welcome in environmental terms. Good water is becoming more costly to provide because pressures of water pollution are making it less available for purposes that require it to be of a high quality, such as drinking water. Water being more highly valued will, in broad terms, support greater effort to protect it in the open environment.

In any event, price increases in the privatized water services in England and Wales will be heavily regulated. The part played by the monopoly regulator, the Office of Water Services (OFWAT), is obviously a key issue on which it is as yet too early to form a conclusive judgement.

Openness and Environmental Regulation

The control of river basin pollution by discharge consents began in 1951, but this did not gain public attention until a few years ago. By law, the authorities operating it were forbidden to publish any details of individual discharges or permits, save for statutory purposes such as court proceedings. Thus both the dischargers who regularly complied with the limits and conditions in their consents and those who often breached them were unknown to the public. Hence the system was hobbled from the start by being deprived of probably its most powerful tool – publicity for leaders and laggards.

In 1951, this concealment had been adopted in response to urging by industry. The fear was that commercial confidentiality would be breached if the analysis of company effluent discharges was open for all to read, though this always sounds a rather thin argument. Keeping the results of sewage-works performance out of sight also suited local authorities as the operators of them. But in 1974, when Parliament voted to establish open registers of discharge consents and sampling results, the main responsibility for the all-purpose authorities then operating the sewage works lay with government ministers – the very ministers who were restricting investment needed to improve the sewage works and other infrastructure. Thus under Labour and Conservative ministers in turn, the creation of public registers was postponed, for no less than eleven years after Parliament legislated for it. In difficult times for government, the politics of dirty water can hardly be expected to be shining clean.

The Need for a New Coherence of Policy

As influences for change, these factors – reorganization in the water agencies or new legislation bearing on them, the pressures to gain more income, reduce operating costs and increase capital investment, and the wider dissemination of public information – have much more impact collectively than they would individually. They emphasize the need for new forms of co-ordination to be developed between the different functions of the water agencies and in the relationships between them, the water users and government, at both local and national levels. In particular, where sizeable subsidies have been involved, maintaining them, and more especially adjusting them to continuing inflation, may prove a great strain and ultimately impossible.

Agencies may be pressed to expand their water services when even their current commitments are less well handled than is fully admitted. The dominance of routine and habit in the water sector makes for inertia if not deliberate resistance, especially where water professionals or politicians see change as threatening their de facto monopoly of decision-making. Especially perplexing are the signs that good-quality water is becoming scarce relative to increasing demands on it for multiple purposes.

Such prospects of scarcity call for a proper assessment in economic terms of the costs involved. Yet realistic pricing has been little applied to water; rarely are serious efforts made to assemble even the relevant cost information or to publicize it. Water has not conventionally been regarded as suited to allocation by market instruments, other ways of sharing being traditional or preferred.

In short, the challenge for water agencies at this time is to make innovations of the very kind that they and the constituencies which they serve have long shied away from. They have to help the community recognize the onset of relative scarcity in the availability of good water, and the need to respond to this more constructively than by calls for yet more enhanced supply or subsidies.

Examples of well-intentioned but ultimately unhelpful policies abound. In the Baltic states under the Soviet system, industrial users of water supply and sewerage services were made to subsidize domestic users. When the industrial collapse came, the appropriate revenue from industrial use would have been a serious loss, but the loss of the highly inflated revenue companies had been forced to pay had particularly devastating effects. In Pakistan, the large irrigation authority in the Indus Valley commendably managed to get its field staff to work closely with local farmers; yet keeping water charges at such a low level that they no longer covered operating costs put this liaison on a false basis. In California, legislation limiting the number of farms eligible for irrigation subsidies has been eroded, to the advantage, for the most part, of large corporations growing and canning fruit in what was naturally a near desert. In Britain, the creation in 1974 of all-purpose regional water authorities in England and Wales was undermined by Whitehall economic policies preventing the authorities from improving their performance by increased capital investment. For nearly ten years, and even as this book is being written, water companies have been hanging back – even in the south east of England where prospects of scarcity are well attested – from promoting the need for much more widespread metering of domestic water usage.

In short, the water agencies are at odds with themselves: they lack a coherent operating policy. A balance of functions and policies that was adequate and defensible in earlier circumstances becomes in a different setting ineffective through mutual frustration. As demonstrated by the dismantling within fifteen years of the ambitious 1974 reorganization in England and Wales, the need to rearrange functions is not as significant, ultimately, as the coherence of policy in relation to new external trends affecting the sector. The pattern established in 1974 took into account the rise of issues of water quality, but responded all too little to the need for economic flexibility to provide for appropriately enhanced investment. Privatization produced a different approach, but in leading consumers to recognize that high-quality water supply and the opportunities for adequate waste disposal are becoming more scarce, and to accept the implications of this, most water companies have so far been moving much more slowly than they might and may need to move in future.

This is not simply an issue of engineers losing influence internally to accountants. It involves changes in the relationships of companies with water users, and in the perceptions of the latter. To achieve this, private and public water agencies have to establish and sustain a new coherence in their own policies. This has to include more attention to economic incentives than was called for earlier in this century, when the water services could be taken for granted without much attention to economics or the natural environment. That can no longer be the case today.

Chapter 2
Environment and Infrastructure

At a time when attention has been focused, rightly, on the great capacity humankind has developed for damaging the natural environment, a good starting-point is to recall how much of a threat that environment has posed, and still can pose, to human communities. This is probably more true of the water environment than that of the air or land, despite the damage that hurricanes and earthquakes do. When extreme storms occur, flooding is often among their most dangerous features and consequences. This illustrates one aspect of the two-edged relationship between people and water: they continually need some of it, but not too much of it, as excess water can destroy or damage their houses, their crops, livestock and other physical assets on which they depend. The scholars and preachers who put the story of Noah and the Ark so early in one of the world's most sacred texts understood this and must have known they were making more than a theological point. In our own day, the Thames Barrier, built to protect the centre of London from the real danger of flooding, represents a similar form of action to that taken by the earliest civilizations to guard against flooding as a risk they could foresee but hardly assess.

The broad term much used today for such investment is 'infrastructure', applied in many contexts besides those related to water. Because the circulation of water can vary so much depending on the level of rainfall, infrastructure, at its most basic level, takes the form of reservoirs to combat periods of drought, as well as defences against flooding. Thus in one way, such as in the physical provision of raised river banks as flood defences, infrastructure can be described as modifying the environment itself – offering some degree of protection for the community against the elements. In another way, infrastructure is directed to providing services and facilities that people want or depend on for public health, productive work and congenial life-styles. This sort of 'service' infrastructure includes water-supply distribution networks, sewers and rainfall drains, and the various kinds of treatment plants associated with such networks.

The Hydrological Cycle

The scope for natural forces to operate for or against human purposes and life-styles is evident in the circulation of water, generally described as the hydrological cycle (see Figure 1). This has four phases:

1. Evaporation from the oceans, bodies of inland water, soil and evapotranspiration from plants continually take water vapour from the surface of the earth to the upper atmosphere.
2. In the atmosphere this vapour is circulated over great distances by variations in atmospheric pressures and winds – droughts in Europe have been associated with anomalies in ocean temperatures in the Pacific.
3. The water vapour then returns to earth as the precipitation of rain or snow. This may include pollution, as when so-called 'acid' rain falls in Scandinavia having been carried from more industrial regions of Europe.
4. This water continues its travels when it reaches the earth, in snow melt and movement through the soil to streams and rivers where it makes its way back to the sea. The evaporation process then carries it round the cycle again.

This circulation is subject to all sorts of random variations in addition to more regular seasonal ones. In some parts of the world, rainfall is consistently very low for months each year; in temperate climates as in Britain, rainfall is more evenly distributed throughout the year. But whatever the average rainfall or its usual pattern may be, marked variations are likely to occur. They will be disconcerting because so many activities depending on water will be geared in practice to the average volume and pattern of rainfall. Some major disturbances in global weather patterns arise irregularly yet as frequently as once in four or five years. They are

Figure 1: The water cycle

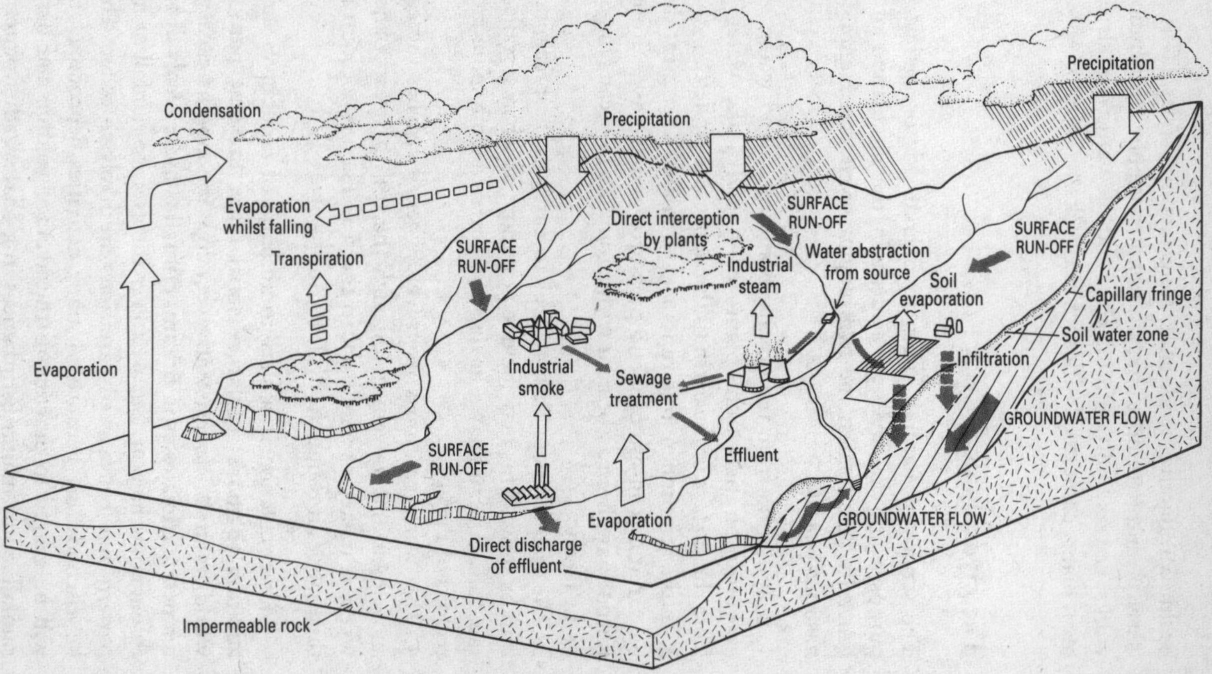

liable to generate droughts in some areas, floods and storms in others. A marked disturbance of this type in 1982–3 caused floods in Ecuador and parts of the western USA and severe droughts in Australia and South Africa, reducing the harvests of some crops by more than 50 per cent.

River Basin Unities and Tensions

A significant feature of the hydrological cycle in its land-based phase is that river basins bounded by watersheds provide a framework within which water maintains a strong natural unity. This framework was itself formed long ago by movements of water, glaciers and disturbances of underground strata. Whether the watersheds are mountain ranges or no more than modest elevations in an otherwise flat landscape, rivers flow within them towards each other and towards the sea. Their course will rarely be direct or straight: the River Severn flowed from Wales on a course that might have led it north west to the sea near Chester (like the River Dee), but changes of geology and contour sent it instead towards the south west. This unity within the river basin is a key point for the organization of river basin agencies: the basin defines a natural area of jurisdiction which it is helpful to have within the coherent control of a single agency, although in practice this is often not possible. While rivers constitute a good natural defence, and often form the frontier of an independent territory, watershed boundaries are recognized or used rarely for political purposes, and many international boundaries have rivers flowing across them.

Whatever the political pattern, this unity of the river basin has the major effect of creating relationships between what may be called upstream and downstream neighbours. When water is abstracted in the topmost lengths of the river, it will be lost to all downstream lengths (unless it is returned), thus reducing natural flow and the volumes available for downstream uses and dilution. In the past, the building of bridges downstream could become (perhaps deliberately) an obstacle for navigation and upstream trading. The building of locks may also obstruct the passage of migratory fish, unless openings are provided for fish to pass through. Perhaps most seriously in modern times, pollution in the upstream lengths of river is likely to be carried along and cause damage to water quality downstream. The communities nearest the mouth of the river are at most risk in this respect. However, all riparian communities have to put up with seasonal variations of flow. Rivers receiving snow melt, such as the Danube, are likely to carry more than half their annual volume of flow in only a few months.

In the use of river flows, very long-term patterns are established, which become the focus of tension and conflict if they are threatened. In south-east Asia, the long course of the River Mekong from China to the coast of Vietnam makes it of huge importance to a number of riparian countries all committed to growing rice as the major food for their people. Rice is traditionally grown in the wet season with the fields flooding easily. But irrigation is of huge importance where rainfall may be inadequate or unreliable, and also for growing 'dry-season' rice, which can produce great increases in total annual production.

Classification of River Uses

Uses of rivers may be classified in at least two ways. A traditional division has been between so-called 'in-stream' and 'out-of-stream' uses. The former include fisheries, navigation and, under some circumstances, the generation of hydro-electric power (where flows are abstracted and fully returned at the same point). Out-of-stream uses include public water supply, irrigation and direct abstractions for industry.

This distinction makes prominent the question of whether volumes committed to out-of-stream uses may be returned to the river, how far away, and at what standard of quality relative to the main flows. The generation of hydro-electric power, which can require storage of water, lends itself to being linked with irrigation systems where these are in use. The loss of return water can then have more serious consequences. In the system of charges for abstractions applying in England and Wales since the mid-1960s, the scale of return water has always been an important factor (the lower the amount returned, the higher the abstraction charge – with transfers out of the catchment treated as cases of nil return).

A second classification distinguishes between uses which are compatible with each other and those which are or may become conflicting or competitive, possibly to the point of being mutually exclusive. In broad terms, all out-of-stream uses threaten in-stream uses to some extent, because they reduce flow. On the other hand, river systems also have great powers of recovery, through the very processes of circulation and renewal that are a distinctive feature of them. Thus there is huge scope for conflicting uses to build up – possibly for centuries – without much sign of stress in the river system itself until some critical threshold is reached. This threshold may be one of low flow, low quality or both.

Side-effects in River Basins

In economic terms, the most common hazard is the way in which rivers spread damage caused at a particular point. Activities that pollute the river or divert part of its flow usually affect water quality or flow for some distance downstream. The water may thus be made unsuitable for other uses downstream, but often without would-be users downstream being able to trace who or what caused the pollution and thereby claim compensation. Thus the polluting upstream activity, assuming it is a business, may be said to be escaping costs of waste disposal and preventive measures against pollution which it should normally have to provide for and reflect in its selling prices. This is an example, in economic terms, of an 'externality'. Whether externalities are damaging or benign in their effect, their costs or credits are not included in conventional accounts. In short, externalities are essentially unintended or indivisible, not part of any conventional market transaction, but none the less able to distort market transactions and prices. While human interactions in river basins are at a low level, externalities may be present but have little effect because the river basin regime can absorb them. When the interactions become more substantial, however, externalities can give rise to much difficulty, because the momentum of the river regime makes the basin with its natural unity a ready arena for them.

Historically, the main reaction to this from communities and basin agencies once they were formed has been to look to legal instruments such as permits to provide a disciplinary framework within which any externalities could be either authorized and limited or excluded. But in the last few decades, this system has been losing effectiveness. The pressures of conflicting uses in crowded river basins have continued to mount, especially from pollution from diffuse sources mostly outside the discharge authorization system. Moreover, that system has been lacking in economic motivation. Thus one modern trend, as will be shown in later chapters, is to apply charges for using the natural capacity of river basins, for discharging wastes as well as abstracting 'raw' water. In effect, this combination of legal and economic measures holds out possibilities of bringing access to river basin capacity into a more constructive relationship with a market economy. But the river basin itself cannot be a conventional market place, because transactions cannot be separated from each other, nor can interactions between each user be completely controlled.

Water and Human Health

The relationships between water and human health are complex but a few points are clear enough to demand more recognition and more action. First, water has the capacity to act as a life-support system and a spreader of infection at the same time, without the difference being obvious. Second, a major global divide is between those with ready and comfortable access to safe water and sanitation and those who have to live without them. This is not just a divide between rich and poor nations: in many urban areas, informal settlements and shanty towns are without services that business and suburban districts take as routine. In Porto Alegre, Brazil, in 1980, a study showed child mortality rates at 42 per 1,000 live births in poor neighbourhoods, more than twice the level in non-poor areas of the same town. Inadequate water supply, sanitation, sub-standard housing and lack of other infrastructure often become the defining features of poor and unhealthy life-styles.

As to water, two issues are repeatedly troublesome. Some diseases largely arise from poor water quality, but others are aggravated and spread by having too little water within easy reach for family hygiene, almost whatever the quality. This latter shortage is worst when families have only as much water as they carry home from sources a long walk away, or as much as they can afford to buy at high prices from itinerant water vendors. The second issue is that, when water is available, it also needs to be drained away after use. Waste-water pools become ready sources of further infection around the home or in the street.

In a classic piece of research,* diseases and disabling conditions linked to water were divided into four groups:

Water-borne: water carries the infection, such as typhoid and cholera.

Water-washed: lack of washing affects skin or eyes, as in scabies or trachoma.

Water-based: via parasitic worms depending on aquatic life-cycles, as in schistosomiasis and guinea worm.

Water-related insect vectors: such as malaria and yellow fever.

This classification helps to show the different character and setting of necessary precautions and remedies. But it also shows the cruel point that having too much water nearby can propagate some diseases while having too little may spread others. Lack of water for washing especially promotes diarrhoea, a great killer of children under age five, as so much of it arises from handling food with unwashed hands.

Thus, water infrastructure provides defence against hazards to human health most effectively when it makes water both easy to use and easy to get rid of reliably after use. A World Bank estimate has suggested that nearly 30 per cent of the global disease burden may be debited to inadequate infrastructure including poor water supply and sanitation. The economic cost of disablement and loss of human productivity is huge, and three to five times as high in India and Sub-Saharan Africa as in 35 prosperous

---

* See more fully, G. White, D. Bradley and A. White, *Drawers of Water*, University of Chicago Press, 1972.

market economies (1993 World Development Report, p. 3). The human suffering is yet more harsh: child mortality rates are central to the family confidence on which plans or hopes of moderating population growth depend.

Since 1950, the trend has been for urban life-styles to benefit rather more than rural ones in these respects, but accelerating urbanization may overtake and frustrate this. Even prosperous cities with good water infrastructure are not free of natural (as well as man-made) threats to their water quality and thus to their public health. More refined monitoring in the USA and UK is picking up evidence of protozoa such as cryptospiridium and giarardia, though definite identification of these is still often difficult. Intensive stocking of cattle and sheep may give rise to heavy local incidence of such hazards, and water treatment works need multiple processes as barriers to arrest them. Disposal of the washwater from treatment works may then still be a further hazard.

How far the incidence of these risks is increasing, or whether they are simply being more often recorded and reported by sharper monitoring, is not easy to say. But at least it is clear that industrial technologies and chemical pollutants are not always the main threat to water quality protected by well-operated infrastructure. Biological hazards from the open countryside still have to be a matter for vigilant concern by those who guard the quality of urban tap-water.

Water Infrastructure

People cannot survive without water, yet they may face a wide and complex range of risks when they use it in its natural setting. For hundreds of millions of families throughout the world, getting water involves more than the daily toil of fetching it: usage for the whole household is confined to the amount that can be carried home by whoever goes to get it, and the hazards of water-linked diseases are additional to the drudgery. The global injustice in this is gross, but hardly remote from us. For many people whose homes are a little more than a night-flight away from Europe or

North America, access to water certainly does not mean a tap within easy reach in kitchen or bathroom. Sanitation for them may be at best a clean latrine of their own, at worst whatever space they can find with some brief scope for concealment or privacy.

The appalling contrasts so inadequately expressed here are the differences between communities with substantial water infrastructure and those without it. The main purposes of networks of water pipes and sewers, water and sewage treatment plants, reservoirs and the like are to guard against all these hazards to public health and, beyond that, to make good water and sanitation accessible to the people for their ready and comfortable use at home and at work. In this context, water infrastructure may be said to have three features relevant to its social or institutional nature.

Water infrastructure becomes collective and standardized within the community as soon as it is made available at all in any organized way. This reflects in large part its distributional character through networks that cannot be individualized or duplicated to offer choice on any economic basis. This indeed explains some of the rise in the popularity of bottled water. The only reasonable alternative to tap-water from the public supply is bottled water from the supermarket – and in that there is abundant choice.

Secondly, the public health considerations lead to public water supply and sewerage being widely regarded as a community or social service. It is expected to be available to all who want it, if need be on concessionary or subsidized terms for those with low income. Thirdly, because of its fixed network, water infrastructure is very capital-intensive. The big spending has to be 'up front', to establish the basic sources, treatment facilities and distribution systems.

As regards financing, water supply is usually given the highest priority. Sewerage is sometimes provided by using rainfall drains to carry sewage flows as well. Adequate treatment of sewage long came a much belated third, and still often does. London only achieved in the 1950s major improvements in treatment sufficient to clean up the river downstream of it. Brussels is only now building its first full sewage treatment works. In many less prosperous countries, it is difficult to foresee when major provision of sewerage and sewage treatment even in urban areas will be able to be reliably organized and financed.

Similar effects arise where the capacity of infrastructure, already in place for water supply and sewage treatment, needs enhancing to cope with overload from increasing population or industrial discharges. Then infrastructure usually reveals itself to be inflexible physically, making improvements costly and slow to introduce.

Many relatively affluent communities are finding it more expensive than they expected to improve their water services in terms of investment in infrastructure. A key point here is that users of these services are not really in the position of conventional consumers, whose interests claim much attention these days. Water services are necessarily collective, standardized services. Those who use them are in a sense involuntary users, tied to the local operating agency and without access to alternative levels of service. Thus the services that water infrastructure provides are apt to show instances and effects of so-called market failure instead of market forces allocating private goods and services to customers who know what they want.

Setting standards to be achieved by water services reaching everyone can thus be difficult. Users may have differing views on desirable levels of service, reasonable charges and the environmental or health protection to be sustained. A monopoly provider may advocate standards that will optimize his business results. Campaigners and committees may be better at ruling out hazardously low standards than at defining obligatory higher ones with some regard for cost. Settling standards turns in the end on decisions about acceptable risks, even to health: and on this, people have different attitudes (as towards smoking). Also, in different settings, exposure to risk and the cost of reducing it vary. But the technical experts, economic regulators, politicians, media and others involved still have to find the means for clearer exchanges with each other as well as with the citizens and users who pay the bills.

Three other influences need to be noted which complicate and reinforce these frustrations. First, far more concern is arising from fuller understanding and assessments of the impact of infrastructure on the water environment. This is a different – and largely new – dimension from issues of service to users for their amenity. Not only do rivers have limited capacity to cope with discharges and pollution from diffuse sources but the marine environment is certainly not a bottomless sink for waste disposal, as the next chapter on the Mediterranean and the Baltic seas indicates.

Secondly, modern industrial communities are widely unable to adapt their water infrastructure as quickly or forcefully as they change the loads they impose on it, for example through growth of housing or new industrial processes and effluent discharges. Because sewerage acts as a gathering system, it tends to concentrate its impact in one geographical area, making any inadequacy in treatment facilities all the more damaging. These effects may be aggravated by the fact that improving infrastructure usually takes the form of substantial, costly capital projects often vulnerable to delay.

Thirdly, professional attitudes may create another difficulty. Planning and design of new capital projects tends to bring prestige to the designers of the scheme. Skilful operation and maintenance of existing facilities reducing costs or improving service may get much less professional recognition. The collective nature of infrastructure has also long worked against water utility services being organized with really effective attention to customer preferences in matters where they are relevant (such as methods and frequency of billing and payment arrangements). The essence of serving customers well with a necessarily collective service is to make them feel they still get individual attention when that is relevant.

At one level then, infrastructure is the instrument through which communities can adjust their relationship to the water environment if collectively they organize to do that and keep it suitably adapted to their needs and demands on it. This can protect them against flood, drought and disease, as it can guard the water environment against degradation by excessive abstraction and pollution. At another level, infrastructure is a collective service to users increasingly led to think their individual preferences should be paramount. The balance is not easy to sustain even in prosperous communities. Public and political pressure builds up in the demand for fuller protection for the environment (as the consequences of past inadequacy become clearer); for higher standards of service to users defined and enforced by more monitoring results on open public records; and for special regulators to discipline monopolistic practices and profits.

These conflicting pressures present an economic problem: that is, a problem in resource allocation, or in scarcity arising from competing claims on finite resources. This is because the resources involved include the water environment which has its own dynamics that are beyond human control. In addition, infrastructure hardly lends itself to market transactions because it is location-specific, is monopolistic in its constitution and used to provide collective rather than individualized services. In short, this is an economic problem for which conventional economic instruments and market forces have important but limited application. Thus for the market economy to take account as a matter of routine of the different impacts on the environment, and the constraints and costs involved, almost certainly entails breaking new ground for the economics of infrastructure too. Communities manage their relationship with the natural environment through their use of infrastructure. However well understood infrastructure is by technical experts, the public's understanding of its implications, political and economic, needs to be enhanced. Later chapters will be discussing many specific aspects of this general deficiency in the economics of industrialized and developing countries alike. The next chapter indicates some consequences of that deficiency as it has prevailed around the Mediterranean and Baltic seas for the last fifty years.

Chapter 3

Regional Seas, Global Reflections

Water is useful to people much of the time because it can hold dirt in suspension and carry it away, as noted in Chapter 1. Its capacity to do this is central to relationships between riparian communities, as the river may be passing the wastes and effluents of those upstream on to others downstream. Even so, another question arises: where does the pollution, including the wastes from the most downstream communities, go to in the end?

It used to be thought that the seas offered such a huge capacity for dilution that the idea of man-made waste having any impact on them would hardly be realistic. Such pollution would in any event arise largely from the limited amount of deliberate or accidental discharges made at sea, for example from oil tankers or dumping of wastes in the sea. In more modern assessments, however, a large share of marine pollution is seen to come from land-based sources. This includes not only coastal discharges but flows from rivers and estuaries and also air pollution (in the perpetual circulation of water vapour that Chapter 2 has already outlined).

Two seas that are close to the interests of much of Europe – the Mediterranean and the Baltic – provide some relevant perspectives on this. Because they are both mostly enclosed, with only limited exchanges of water with the wider oceans, the impact on them of river pollution is more significant. Moreover, they each are bordered by nations and cities at different levels of economic development and prosperity. This makes these seas somewhat like a mirror in which Europe can get an impression of the pollution it is still generating from land-based sources, rather than preventing; that is, pollution not staying where it is caused or deposited. In another view, these seas are like the commons discussed in Chapter 7, where neighbours have some incentive individually to exceed the limits of sharing beyond which they begin collectively to cause damage to each other.

These two seas also each have a distinctive feature. The Mediterranean serves as the holiday playground for much of Europe, including the northern parts of it. Now that travel is so easy, Danes, Swedes and Germans can be found at what have become their regular and favourite resorts in the Greek islands and elsewhere, so they do not depend on the Baltic alone. Most recently, the special feature of the Baltic has become the collapse of the Soviet political and economic system which dominated several littoral states of the Baltic. Soviet doctrines often insisted that, as pollution was a by-product of capitalism, it could not be a serious problem in the USSR. But it is now clear that a different economic order, based on central planning, a command and control economy and backward technology, has not avoided the sort of problems that market economics and up-to-date technology have not yet subdued in western nations.

The Baltic and the Mediterranean seas are each of modest size in global terms, despite the Baltic being the largest body of brackish (low-salinity) water in the world. Yet they offer insights of world-wide relevance. The challenges in the Baltic may be more specifically economic and institutional, but they go to the heart of the economic system prevailing in most western economies. Can the states liberated in economic as well as political terms from the collapsed Soviet system regain their industrial momentum in the style of free-market philosophy, but with greater care to reduce their impact on the environment? Will the more prosperous littoral states such as Sweden and Denmark find their way to give substantial financial support to this recovery? The links between them – in commercial rivalry and occasional invasions as well as in more benign connections – go back to the Middle Ages. At least they have little tradition of ignoring each other. Formal and informal links between Baltic cities are already making the progress they never could in the days when St Petersburg was Leningrad.

The Mediterranean represents even more of a microcosm of the world's tensions. The major contributions to present levels of pollution are coming from the industrial economies along its northern coasts. The major aspirations to rapid economic growth are most evident in the southern lands. To the east, among groups of countries adjacent to and including Israel, Turkey and Egypt, signs of increasing conflict about access to water resources give a reminder that water scarcity is still for some a more pressing issue than loss of quality. All around this sea, ambitions to increase foreign currency earnings through tourism remain strong. In several parts of the region, increases of resident coastal populations almost guarantee more intense congestion and pollution, regardless of the tourists.

Thus coastal areas and river catchments – of the Tigris, Euphrates and Nile, Tiber and Rhone – in which were enacted so many of the world's early adventures in forming and spreading the cultures of successful cohabitation face some bleaker periods ahead. Despite the economic advances of the last two centuries, public health may become less secure due to the combination of more people, less adequate infrastructure and increased mobility of populations. How considerate and imaginative can riverside and coastal communities learn to be as neighbours, amid the pressures on them all to be self-centred and go for short-term gains?

The Mediterranean: The Hazards of Attractive Settings

Some of the Mediterranean's most attractive features in fact add to its hazards. The warm temperatures give rise to high levels of evaporation, only three-quarters of which is replaced by rainfall. In the pattern of hot dry summers and mild wet winters, the south and east of the region have markedly less rainfall. But three-quarters of the increase in demand for fresh water is expected to arise in these areas where it is most scarce. Perhaps remarkably, the climate of the whole region allows the cultivation of wheat and barley, grapes and olives. But the confined channels of entry and exit at Gibraltar and the Dardanelles make this an almost enclosed sea, with relatively little mixing of water from other seas. The deltas of several rivers flowing into it thus have notable significance and influence as ecological systems.

In the land around much of the Mediterranean, water hardly rates as plentiful. Cyprus and Malta already have severe shortages of it, which have driven the latter to rely on desalination for half its supply at some fifteen times the average cost of tap-water in France. For the region as a whole, ground water only provides one-fifth of resources, and in several places this is known to be replenished more slowly than it is being drawn on. This leads to salt-water intrusion and to land subsidence. Across twenty-nine significant freshwater river basins, conditions obviously vary: Turkey, in addition to a number of countries in the northern Mediterranean, has a water surplus, but about a third of the population along the southern Mediterranean coasts is short of potable water, and an even greater proportion without adequate sanitation.

The eighteen countries falling within the definition of the Mediterranean here (Monaco counts as a Mediterranean country for only some purposes) are listed in Table 3.1, with some indications of differences between them, in so far as numbers can illustrate such matters.

Future prospects are more significant than what can be derived from this snapshot of the *status quo*. By the year 2025, resident coastal population is expected to double its present level – from 82 million to 150–170 million. But the tourists are forecast to be doubling also, to something like 260 million by the same date. The distribution of population is also changing. The population concentrated in urban settings doubled between 1950 and 1985. In 1950, hardly a third of the population lived in the southern parts of the region and a full two-thirds in the northern parts. By 2025, that pattern will have been almost reversed, with the generally less prosperous south having some 60 per cent of the much larger total population.

To give one example of how localized this increase of people may be within individual countries: the coastal area of Spain makes up 17 per cent of its land surface, while only 12 per cent of national population lived there at the start of this century. Now 35 per cent lives near the coast, and 85 per cent of summer tourists stay there too. Thus it is no use blaming the congestion mainly on the tourists. They and the residents are drawn in greatly increased numbers to the waters that they are collectively making more polluted: they risk degrading the very attraction

Table 3.1 Mediterranean countries – selected figures

Country	Population (millions) mid-1990	Av. growth Population % p.a. 1980–90	Area (000 sq. km.)	GNP p./capita US$ 1990	Life expectancy Years: 1990	Fertilizer consumption[1]	Annual withdrawal renewable water resources p./c.: m.³: 1970–87 Domestic:	Ind./Agri.
Spain	39.0	0.4	505	11,020	76	1,009	141	1,033
France	56.4	0.5	552	19,490	77	3,192	116	612
Italy	57.7	0.2	301	16,830	77	1,507	138	845
(Yugoslavia)	23.8	0.7	256	3,060	72	1,155	63	330
Albania	3.3	2.0	29	N/A	72	1,506	6	88
Greece	10.1	0.4	2,150	5,990	77	1,752	58	663
Turkey	56.1	2.4	779	1,630	67	645	76	241
Lebanon	N/A	N/A	10	N/A	65	917	30	241
Syria	12.4	3.6	185	1,000	66	454	31	418
Israel	4.7	1.8	21	10,920	76	2,425	72	375
Egypt	52.1	2.4	1,001	600	60	4,043	84	1,118
Libya	4.5	4.1	1,760	N/A	62	367	93	530
Tunisia	8.1	2.3	164	1,440	67	232	42	283
Algeria	25.1	3.0	2,382	2,060	65	283	35	126
Morocco	25.1	2.6	447	950	62	344	30	471
(UK)	57.4	0.2	245	16,100	76	3,502	101	406
Population below 1m.								
Cyprus	0.702	N/A	9	8,020	77	N/A	N/A	N/A
Malta	0.354	N/A	N/A	6,610	73	N/A	N/A	N/A

NOTES

1. The units in this column are hundreds of grams of plant material per hectare of arable land

Source: World Bank: World Development Report 1992 (this source includes technical notes on the figures quoted above)

they seek. Other industrialized nations of Europe besides Spain display around the Mediterranean the tensions that have arisen between their pursuit of economic growth and the greater opportunities for leisure it makes possible. The affluent spread congestion abroad, while those trapped in poverty may add to it at home by tending to have larger families.

Signs and Sources of Degradation

Among the sources of degradation is the provision of an infrastructure not adequately geared to its purpose or the conditions to which it has to relate. Some 70 per cent of municipal discharges in coastal areas of the Mediterranean provide little or no treatment for the waste water they disgorge through outfalls close to the shore. In 1973, a serious outbreak of cholera in Naples was traced to contaminated mussels taken from the sea in the Gulf of Naples. Near some industrial areas, abnormally high levels of mercury have been identified. Tuna in the western Mediterranean carry about double the levels of mercury found in similar fish in the eastern Mediterranean and the Atlantic.

Inadequate infrastructure is by no means to be associated only with poorer communities. The River Po carries drainage from one of the most prosperous regions of Italy, covering a quarter of its territory and just over a third of its population. Some 80 per cent of organic pollution in the northern Adriatic now comes from the River Po, the main source of nutrients such as nitrogen and phosphorus. These give rise to eutrophication and algae blooms in the sea water around the coast of Emilia Romagna, which attracts 40 million tourists a year and provides a fifth of Italian fishery yields. In recent years, the Italian government has been courageously pressing upwards charges for sewerage services from levels that had long been little more than nominal.

But it is a sign of Italy's rigid price-control system that the central government has to do this and take the responsibility for it instead of dispersing the blame among local communes. Moreover, as recently as 1991, almost all capital investment to enlarge and update sewage treatment capacity depended on grants (not loans) from central government because the communes had so little experience or scope to provide such finance more locally. Emilia Romagna has an enviable reputation as among the best-administered regions in Italy, but has still been constrained by the centralization of public finance in Rome. This shows how, even where highly skilled water professionals are available, the obstacles to better relationships between communities and the water environment remain substantial, institutional and slow to change.

Poorly managed irrigation can constitute another type of degradation by reducing the fertility of soils from which it is meant to make possible larger harvests. Poor drainage, waterlogging and evaporation all contribute to the accumulation of salts in the soil. This salinization may be affecting now as much as 5 per cent of the surface area of the Mediterranean basin, and 30 per cent of the Nile Delta and Nile Valley. In a period of increasing population, this represents a severe loss of productive areas for providing food. From farmland, drainage flows carrying fertilizer and pesticide residues is one main cause of eutrophication. Estimates suggest that 550 tons of pesticides are reaching the Mediterranean each year. One of the strongest influences making it difficult to moderate the drive for more intensive crop production is that the spread of urbanization repeatedly puts at risk the amount of agricultural land available.

The direct pollution of the sea by shipping remains significant. Three-quarters of oil pollution is attributed to the deliberate discharge of ballast and bilge waters. The volume of hydrocarbons released each year is equivalent to the spill from the *Exxon Valdez* in Alaska occurring every three weeks. Air pollution, moreover, adds to the load: about as much chromium and mercury reach the sea from the air as from rivers; and, of the lead in the western Mediterranean, up to 90 per cent reaches it by air. One consequence of all this pollution from marine and land-based sources is that in many areas of the Mediterranean fish stocks are estimated to be reduced to one-fifth of natural levels. The region is becoming, most ironically, a net importer of fish. In a 1988 sampling, a quarter of beaches, including Spanish, French, Italian and Greek ones showed pathogens exceeding safe levels: the signs of degradation in the natural resource which gives the whole region a coherent identity are painfully comprehensive.

Underlying Causes and Remedies

Just as the damage that pollution brings becomes pervasive, so the deeper causes of this degradation stretch into the very structure of public finance and administration and other institutions of the countries which contribute most to it. This is not a poverty-related issue. The northern Mediterranean is the scene of much of the pollution: 23 per cent of the total (by one estimate) can be seen as arising in the north-eastern sector of the sea (from Spain, France and parts of Italy) and more than that again (35 per cent) in the Adriatic, mainly from Italy. Four underlying causes may be identified.

1. Economic policies and influences do very little to motivate companies or municipal authorities to reduce pollution; in fact they often have opposite effects.
2. Regulatory systems for environmental protection are poor or non-existent, and arrangements for public finance and administration are weak. They are not effective in providing for the enhancement of infrastructure capacity or even for the better use, operation and maintenance of what is already in place.
3. There is a considerable lack of popular interest and awareness, despite the striking rise of public concern about matters environmental further north and west, in Europe and North America. This tends to weaken the political will to tackle problems that are complex and multi-national in their implications.
4. Increases in coastal population are likely and have already occurred in some areas.

These causes show that the underlying problems are attributable to institutions that are not well shaped for delivering service to users of water and dischargers of wastes on a sound financial or technical basis. They are unlikely to provide or operate infrastructure adequately, and even less to bring communities into less damaging and more sustainable relationships with the freshwater or marine environments on which their welfare substantially depends. Indeed, the very concept of providing water supply or drainage as business-like services is not widely acknowledged by civic leaders. Infrastructure is generally thought of as more static than that; as something that may bring some betterment to an uncomfortable or harsh collective life-style, but often as a political act – like the imperial Roman 'bread and circuses' – rather than as a continuing utility service for which payments by users should provide much or all of the necessary finance. This is not to say that user charges will solve all the problems. Real protection of the environment needs much more than that, but finance is one crucial ingredient in getting better facilities for the people and in protecting the environment.

Moves towards this have been in progress for almost twenty years now, in respect of the Mediterranean. An Action Plan was adopted at the Barcelona Conference in 1975, and, with co-ordination by the UN Environment Programme and substantial support by the European Investment Bank and the World Bank, understanding and awareness of problems and remedies have been advanced. The initiatives of the EC in committing member states to enforce agreed standards of bathing waters and municipal waste water (to give only two examples) have also been pushing forward remedial action that as yet still has a long way to go.

The most difficult point remains that, as the changes required are institutional (implementation of the relevant structures, policies, legislation, financing by local services and the overseeing of these by central government), much of the reform must be internal to each country. Deciding on the necessary changes and building the sustained political commitment to make them effective has to be each country's responsibility. Collective improvement cannot come without that. The tireless apparatus of the EC or the UN cannot be a complete substitute for it. The welfare of the Mediterranean is now at risk because so many people want to share it on terms that suit themselves. An adaptation of economic signals to make them recognize environmental costs has to be a major objective.

The Baltic

The Baltic is a much less inviting sea than the Mediterranean, yet it has long been a profoundly valuable natural resource for the communities that dwell and earn their living around it. In the

Baltic, like the Mediterranean, there is a low level of intermixing of water due to the presence of basins of various depths divided by sills or shallow areas, and to the fact that there is only a narrow link with the North Sea. Throughout this century major inflows have occurred at intervals of about eleven years, but these may be becoming more infrequent still. Without intermixing, the deepest layers of water can become anoxic as all their dissolved oxygen is used up, creating conditions that are toxic to marine organisms.

Nine countries share the coastline of the Baltic: Sweden and Finland to the north; Russia, Estonia, Latvia and Lithuania to the east; Poland to the south; Germany and Denmark to the west. The coastal population of the Baltic is some 16 million, but the catchments of rivers flowing into the sea stretch into the Ukraine and the Czech and Slovak Republics, with a population of about 80 million. Again – applying the example of the commons outlined in Chapter 7 – a relatively small sea is like an area of common land with a substantial population having a significant impact on it, though some of these people no doubt hardly think of themselves as living anywhere near it. Others closer to it, however, remain very aware of it. The number of people travelling on ferries between capitals such as Helsinki, Riga, Tallinn and Stockholm is high relative to the level of population.

This makes it the more ironic, however, that the main deterioration in the condition of the Baltic Sea has occurred in our own time. As recently as 1950, it could still be described as 'environmentally healthy'. Industrialization, intensive agriculture, forestry methods dependent on use of fertilizers and pesticides were only in their early stages. Now there is not only substantial pollution from coastal discharges and the many rivers flowing into the Baltic, but much air pollution as well. About half the total nitrogen input to the sea comes from air pollution. The hydrological cycle described in Chapter 2 thus becomes a circulation of pollution as well as of water, across the land and the sea.

Pollution and Remedial Action

A great array of chemicals and other pollutants have been finding their way into the Baltic, many of them highly toxic and with an accumulative effect. Restrictions on the use of mercury in the very significant paper and pulp industries and reductions in discharges from the chlorine-alkali industry have begun to slow down the deterioration, but severe contamination in many coastal areas still persists. Throughout the Baltic during this century (and mostly in the last fifty years), the nitrogen loading has increased about four times and that of phosphorus by eight times. A greater intensity of algae blooms shows more eutrophication in some parts of the sea. Generally, coastal conditions reflect the impact of land-based discharges, and some of the bays close to Poland, Lithuania and Latvia have become very polluted, with recreational beaches having to be closed for several years. In the 1980s, Danish waters were also suffering stronger, more frequent and longer-lasting depletion of oxygen than before.

Much of this pollution and its effects are little different from those arising around the coasts of other industrialized nations, including Britain, though the natural features of the Baltic Sea may aggravate some of the consequences. Moreover, as early as 1974, the coastal states agreed a Baltic Marine Environment Protection Convention (the 'Helsinki Convention') which came into force in 1980, with a commission to steer it. Backed by the relevant international agencies and banks, notably the Nordic Bank, this has promoted and co-ordinated programmes for reducing pollution and giving the Baltic more protection from abuse by the millions of people who depend on it.

A Whole Economic System Crumbles

For almost fifty years, however, an important set of countries bordering the Baltic were enclosed in the Soviet political and economic system, looking inwards and eastwards and committed to central planning that was showing increasing signs of strain. Now, that system may be described as collapsing into openness. The openness is very welcome, but the economic collapse is very harsh for the people involved. All sorts of distortions are appearing. Unemployment, which notionally did not exist before, is very high, and wages very low.

In practical routine matters, for example in Latvia's capital city,

Riga, most people until recently had access to hot water only two days a week, and, for those living in high buildings, even the water pressure from the cold-water tap remains unreliable. One manager of water supply for another city was only paying his staff half wages early in 1993 as his unit did not have the cash flow to pay more. Another manager whose unit had the benefit of good and plentiful underground sources nevertheless feared that his funds would not be sufficient to pay the electricity bill as pumping costs were high for him.

The collapse of industry was hitting the cash flows of water-supply units particularly hard because, under the Soviet system, industries using only about 30–40 per cent of water utility services were made to pay charges that covered three-quarters or more of total costs. This cross-subsidy kept charges to domestic users much lower than the actual costs of serving them. These charges were widely included, moreover, as one of half-a-dozen items on monthly bills including housing rental, so the whole matter of water supply and waste-water services, how adequate they were and how much they cost, received little exposure and even less attention. As later chapters will discuss the concealment of pollution control in Britain, it needs saying here that this Soviet system involved a great deal of economic distortion. Its concealment of pollution was severely destructive of public awareness of matters central to good co-operation between communities in sharing infrastructure and environmental resources in constructive ways.

Since the collapse of the Soviet Union, the governments of the separate states and many national and international aid agencies have been trying to establish new systems for orderly services and to help employment recover. There is a difficulty and an opportunity in this for water management. The difficulty is that, since the previous system has been so distorted by the central government then in power, decisions on its reshaping and refinancing are not easy to resolve quickly. In Estonia, for example, there is at least one organization providing water supply for most smaller towns, as well as another one for the capital. But in Latvia, where water services in the capital are strongly managed, the government hoped to leave water supply to be dealt with as a municipal matter. No government ministry has any role in this, one was told, although one department was trying to deal positively with environmental matters. The economic uncertainties are of course awkward for utility managers: until industry regains some level of more or less stable activity, neither water consumption nor potential income can be reliably foreseen. Many households cannot readily pay bills reflecting even basic costs until wages and levels of employment become more settled.

The opportunity, nevertheless, is that, if water services can be restructured on a basis that is effective for operation, finance and, over a period, essential investment, a better service to water users and effective reduction of pollution to arrest the deterioration of the Baltic Sea may become objectives that can be achieved together. The route towards this does not have to involve water services becoming private monopolies along English lines, but it may need imaginative leadership and substantial finance, beyond what a series of middle or small municipalities could each be expected to handle on their own. Indeed, one of the necessary features is that international aid and lending should be used to the full, and the agencies providing this normally insist on dealing through national governments. This is desirable, moreover, for any coherent sorting-out of what it is most urgent or rewarding to improve first. The volume of potential projects has to be put in some sort of sequence that local communities can handle with the relevant skills and physical resources. The story of recovery from the Soviet collapse, indeed even understanding fully the consequences of that collapse, is still only in its very earliest stages.

Thus in the Baltic and the Mediterranean alike there is an awareness now that the working of modern economic systems in industrialized nations has not been going well for the water environment. This is in some sense true for the market economies, the ex-Soviet ones, and those in earlier stages of industrial development. Moreover, the action required to set a significantly different course has to be a matter of international programmes for relevant projects and, more deeply and uncertainly, for the reshaping of internal institutions and social attitudes. The next few chapters discuss the efforts taken in this respect in England and Wales over more than forty years in total, but most significantly since the mid-1980s.

Chapter 4

British Water Institutions

One reason for turning now to Britain is that many radical changes have been made in its water institutions in recent years, and there are striking contrasts in these changes. But another reason is that, in the context of water, taking Britain (that is, England, Wales and Scotland) as the main basis of discussion offers some simplifications. There are no 'international' rivers divided between British and other jurisdictions. Irrigation and hydro-electric power generation, major and often dominant activities in many overseas river basins, are of little significance here. Indeed, by European standards the rivers of Britain appear almost as replicas on a 1/10 scale or less, as Table 4.1 shows.

On the other hand, Britain does have, especially in England, one complication that many other countries do not suffer so intensely. It is crowded even by world standards, as indicated by Table 4.2.

This crowding may indeed be more intense than figures suggest, because, in England especially, agriculture is very intensive. Relatively few large areas are empty of towns and villages, business activity and traffic, as they are in many other countries. At least Britain has a temperate climate, with the benefit of rainfall spread through all months of the year to meet the needs of this crowded population, but different parts of Britain differ notably in their average annual rainfall, as shown by Table 4.3.

Residual rainfall is total rainfall less evaporation; that is, rainfall effectively available for uses of all sorts as well as flow sufficient to maintain the ecological health of the river. As Table 4.3 shows, regions differ in their losses by evaporation: the North West has about twice the total rainfall that the Anglian region has, but, with lower evaporation losses than Anglian, it has five times Anglian's residual rainfall. Between these two regions, however, the North West has more than double Anglian's density of population, so both end up as middling regions in terms of the proportions of

Table 4.1 Sizes of some European rivers

River	Length[1] (km.)	Mean flow[2] (m.³/sec.)
Volga	3,690	8,000
Danube	2,850	7,000
Rhine	1,320	2,000
Loire	1,012	6,500
Rhone	800	2,000
Severn	345	86
Thames	328	67
Trent	274	93
Great Ouse	251	16
Wye	190	72
Tay	185	175
Dee	163	35
Clyde	130	46
Exe	106	17
Tyne	100	48
Forth	89	51
Great Stour	64	3
Itchen	62	6

NOTES

1. The length is the distance (estimated where necessary) from the source to the mouth

2. Flow rates are measured in cubic metres/second (m.³/sec.) at the tidal limit. Where there is no gauging station close to the tidal limit, the figure is an estimate

Source: RCEP, 16th Report

Table 4.2 Population, area and density

Country	Population (millions)	Area (km.²)	Density (per km.²)
Netherlands	14.9	37,000	403
England/Wales	50.8	152,000	334
Japan	123.5	378,000	327
Belgium	10.0	31,000	322
India	849.5	3,288,000	258
UK	57.4	245,000	234
Italy	57.7	301,000	192
France	56.4	552,000	102
Spain	39.0	505,000	77
USA	250.0	9,373,000	27
Canada	26.5	9,976,000	3

Source: World Bank (excluding the figures provided for England and Wales)

Table 4.3 Residual rainfall (annual averages) and abstractions

Region	Average annual rainfall 1941–70 (mm.)	Average annual residual rainfall (mm.)	% Residual rainfall committed to abstractions	Density of population (per km.²)	Population (000)	Area (km.²)
Thames	704	225	55	836	11,500	13,750
Severn-Trent	773	300	37	383	8,300	21,650
Southern	787	310	25	411	4,300	10,450
Yorkshire	818	380	23	338	4,600	13,600
Anglian	611	150	18	204	5,600	27,500
North West	1,217	750	14	471	6,800	14,445
Welsh	1,334	870	10	145	3,100	21,300
Northumbrian	879	450	9	276	2,600	9,400
Wessex	864	410	9	250	2,500	10,000
South-West	1,194	680	3	138	1,500	10,880
England & Wales	912	460	16	334	50,800	152,000
Scotland	1,431	–	–	65	5,100	77,750

Source: Waterfacts, 1992, and other sources

residual rainfall committed to annual abstractions. They are close to the 16 per cent average for England and Wales.

By contrast, the Thames region has over half its residual rainfall committed to a population which is twice as dense on the ground as the next most densely populated region (the North West). Such figures are, however, less than satisfactory indicators of demand pressing on naturally available water as they do not show how much water is returned to rivers after use, and thus available for re-use subject to its quality being suitable. The River Thames is well-known for carrying large volumes of purified effluents from towns such as Oxford and Reading to London to meet the public supply requirements of the capital's large population. This volume of waste water flowing down the river probably improves in quality as it does so (assuming there are no severe incidents of pollution) and makes it much more acceptable to the public. There is less occasion to wonder how much of it has graduated earlier through Oxford or other sewage works.

One reason why equivalent figures cannot be readily presented for Scotland is that the system of licensing water abstractions which has applied in England and Wales since the mid-1960s has not been regarded as necessary in Scotland. Rainfall there is higher, evaporation lower and population less dense on average: all this adds up to less strain on naturally available water in most of Scotland. The Royal Commission on Environmental Pollution (RCEP) has recently completed a study of freshwater quality which now recommends the application of a water resources licensing system to Scotland, a change that may also be necessary as the government consider options for the restructuring of water utility services in Scotland.

In hot dry weather, evaporation increases and rainfall is below average, so resources and storage systems come under strain, which increased usage may aggravate further. At such times, unless restrictions are applied, usage in residential garden watering and irrigation for agriculture may be notably increased. Some periods of below-average rainfall may continue significantly through winters as well as summers, as Table 4.4 shows (with a repetition of one key column from Table 4.2).

Over a period of two and a half years, the Thames region,

Table 4.4   Main dry spells, 1988–91

| Region | Percentage of average rainfall | | | Percentage of average residual rainfall committed to abstractions |
	5/89–9/89	3/90–5/90	11/88–3/91	
Thames	52	36	81	55
Severn-Trent	41	39	88	37
Southern	41	39	80	25
Yorkshire	27	45	82	23
Anglian	56	52	81	18
North West	23	63	88	14
Welsh	45	41	87	10
Northumbrian	27	59	86	9
Wessex	66	33	88	9
South West	59	36	90	3
England & Wales	48	45	85	16

Source: Waterfacts, 1991

already committed to abstraction of more than half of average residual rainfall, had rainfall about one-fifth below the long-term average. Shortfalls were widespread through all regions of England and Wales; the South West was the only one to have the benefit of rainfall as high as 90 per cent of average.

In the face of much uncertainty and variation in water supply, sharing water and setting allocations of it are essential. As final witness to this, consider the figures in Table 4.5 for some of the same periods as the figures for rainfall deficiency in the previous table.

The question that arises for a small, densely populated country such as Britain is how these fluctuations in the water supply, and the hazards of there being too much or too little, are to be combated. In some situations, storage for flood alleviation can also provide storage for water supply, but the levels must be lowered again before the next flood occurs. Generally, institutions managing water in Britain have tended in the past to give far greater priority to meeting demand than to encouraging economy in use. But in the allocation of river basin resources, the control of river pollution and supervision of other basin functions, moves towards establishing more coherent policies, including the use of permits, have been developing for almost fifty years.

Table 4.5   Liability to flooding in England and Wales

Region	Flood warnings issued to police 1988/89	1989/90	Major flooding incidents (rivers and coastal) 1989/90
Severn-Trent	102	296	5
South West	20	146	26
North West	96	145	12
Anglian	85	95	1
Welsh	68	76	67
Southern	N/A	53	1
Wessex	4	41	14
Thames	27	28	8
Yorkshire	15	17	2
Northumbrian	5	2	1
TOTAL	422	899	137

Source: NRA Facts, 1990

River Basin Controls United and Extended

Apart from special initiatives taken in the nineteenth century, such as the formation of the Thames Conservancy, river boards covering all parts of England and Wales were not created until 1948. These were an amalgamation of the Fisheries Boards with the catchment boards, which had long dealt with land drainage and flood alleviation on the basis of watershed boundaries. Both types of board were under the influence and oversight of the Ministry of Agriculture, Fisheries and Food (MAFF), though there was little centralization. Finance was partly raised by local taxation and fishing-rod licences, and partly provided by central government grants. Governing boards were nominated partly by elected local councils, partly by ministers in Whitehall departments. A combination of interests was thus included, even if some of the more modest of the thirty-four river boards still had upwards of fifty members.

Once formed, the river boards were soon seen as suitable for carrying out new functions. In 1951, pollution control was made far more effective by the requirement for effluent discharges to be subject to individual consents setting limits and conditions related to the receiving waters at each location. Previously, causing pollution only led to criminal proceedings if it were noticed and traced to its originator, who was then prosecuted. Civil actions could be taken by downstream businesses that had suffered damage, but it was often difficult to identify and prove who was to blame. The new system applied in 1951 only to new discharges to non-tidal waters, but was extended in 1960 to estuaries and coastal waters, and in 1961 to discharges which had commenced before 1951. The river boards set up monitoring systems accordingly, and an unpublished survey of river-water quality in 1958 became in 1970 a regular five-year event in which comparative results were published.

Organized control of water resource development and abstractions was also seen as necessary in the early 1960s, following the severe drought of 1959, and due to competition between water companies and anyone else (such as farmers and industry) who wanted new major supplies of raw water. Reservoir projects could make better use of suitable sites by being designed to meet various needs at the same time, including supplementing river flows if further abstractions from them were proposed. This supplementation (often called river regulation) would not be necessary in periods of high or even average flow; thus it made economical use of reservoir capacity, saved on the cost of pipelines, and could keep river flows at levels beneficial to the biological health of the river and of fisheries. The control of abstractions by licences – also applying to ground water – was legislated for in 1963, and was clearly another new major function for river boards, which were renamed river authorities at the same time and slightly reduced in number from thirty-four to twenty-nine.

The abstraction licensing system was launched without the phasing-in period for existing and new installations that had applied to effluent discharge controls. But existing abstractors were granted licences of right to take volumes of water which later turned out to be more than some smaller rivers could sustain. Thirty years later, the NRA is now struggling to correct those misjudgements, as reducing licensed volumes is beset with the difficulties of finding replacement sources for the licensees.

The introduction of pollution control by discharge consents combined with the supervision of abstractions by licensing enabled

the river authorities to allocate and protect the river basin resources of England and Wales in a coherent fashion. In the detail
of these changes, there are two points that are very significant for
the future. The abstraction licensing system had annual charges
associated with it (as a sort of rental for access to resource
capacity). These charges, related to volumes authorized, were set
in order to produce enough funding for the river authorities to
enhance resources, and were rebated where abstractors provided
substantial capital investment themselves. Such charges were also
beneficial in promoting economical use of a natural resource. In
practice, charges soon became higher in eastern England, where
far more enhancement was required, than in Wales.

The much-needed equivalent of applying charges to discharge
consents was not put in place till the early 1990s. Worse still, as
mentioned earlier, the discharge consent system of that time was
committed by law to the concealment of all details of individual
consents or sampling results, save during court proceedings when
a prosecution had been made. Thus it was impossible for other
businesses sharing the river to get information about the scale of
discharges, the make-up of effluents, or how far relevant limits
and conditions were complied with or breached and by which
public or private dischargers. Occasional official reports showed
that non-compliance was widespread, but gave no details. In
short, the consent system was hobbled from the start, deprived of
potentially its most powerful tool – exposing the identity of the
polluters. This secrecy was advocated by industrial interests as
being necessary to avoid details of commercially sensitive production processes being revealed when effluent flows were analysed,
but it was hardly a convincing argument for universal concealment. One result of it was that many local councils providing
inadequate sewage treatment escaped the exposure they deserved,
and all those dischargers taking care to control their effluents
missed receiving credit for their responsible behaviour. Remarkably, the secrecy that started in 1951 lasted till 1985, ultimately
because it suited both government, wishing to restrict spending on
sewage treatment, and industry. By contrast, the abstraction licensing system was open to scrutiny from its launch in 1963. Applications for new abstractions had to be advertised, were then open to

objections, and subject to public enquiry procedures when objections were substantial.

In a similar vein, a contrast may be drawn between the organization of water supply compared with that of sewerage and sewage disposal. Proceeding largely by mutual agreement, with no major legislation or comprehensive restructuring, the thousand or so water-supply units operating in the mid-1950s under local government or statutory company control had reduced themselves to some two hundred larger units by 1970. This was achieved, moreover, with little or no political argument about whether the new units should be in the municipal format or the private-investor one. This contrasted with almost complete inertia in sewerage and sewage disposal, operated by some 1,300 local councils, nearly all of which hung on to this function and neglected it at the same time.

The 1960s can be seen as a period when river basin functions were on the whole being developed more positively than utility ones (especially sewage treatment). This was the last decade before water quality became a more dominant focus for policy and public concern than water resources. The Water Resources Board (WRB), a planning agency created by the legislation of 1963 and generally considered a disappointment, was intended to plan water resources strategy but in fact had no powers to address issues of water quality. The next radical change, bold in conception but inadequate in practice during its first ten years from 1974, illustrates how water quality rose to become the key issue, and how the situation was unintentionally created in which privatizing water services despite their extreme monopoly nevertheless became a plausible proposal.

Ambitious Restructuring Turns Sour

The trigger for the next, much more ambitious, change lay outside the water sector. Local government units outside London were being substantially reshaped in the early 1970s, and their functions in water supply, sewerage and sewage disposal had either to be provided for in the new structure or taken out of local government control. The rationale behind adopting the latter format was the development of river basin functions since 1950 (just described), not any concept of utility organization in principle, and certainly not nationalization (a Conservative government was in office at the time).

The essence of the reshaping was that utility and river basin functions should be brought together into ten regional authorities (subsequently the ten regions controlled by the NRA – see Figure 2, p. 82), their boundaries defined by watersheds. This gained much support from water professionals, in addition to strong commitment by relevant civil servants as well as ministers. Its advocates saw the regional authorities as each reflecting the unity of river basin resources from source to tap and back again to the river. A handful of critics – seemingly opposed to far-reaching change – urged that combining utility and basin functions was like expecting one agency to be poacher and gamekeeper combined. A few voices even suggested that the new structure could be a model for the rest of the world in its respect for the unity of natural resources and the hydrological cycle.

Yet that was quite unrealistic. Most of the world has river basins far too large to be controlled by even regional water utilities, and many are divided between different nation states. The deeper point was that the new structure should enable an all-purpose water organization to moderate the external damage it generated from sewage disposal, as its own water supply sources would otherwise suffer. This could work well, but could also be more valid in theory than in practice. In any event, the form of restructuring could only be applied to countries like Britain, in that it reflected the dominance of utility functions as abstractors and dischargers in small, densely populated river basins. This model would hardly be plausible in any country where irrigation was a major influence on water resource development and the institutions relevant to that.

The new structure might perhaps have made sustainable progress under less difficult conditions. It coped very well with the severe drought of 1976 – so well, indeed, that integrated management of basin resources and water-supply services seemed justified, reducing worries about water resource adequacy. But its weakness turned out to be that, although regional water authorities were not really a nationalized industry, the Treasury wanted to limit their investment spending as if they were. Moreover, the mid-1970s to the early 1980s was one of the British economy's periods of severe strain. As the capital spending on sewage works came to be severely limited, their performance deteriorated. This in turn discredited the other role of the authorities as controllers of pollution and protectors of basin resources. The 1985 River Quality Survey showed the number of lengths of river downgraded in quality overtaking those improved in quality for the first time since surveys started in 1958.

In broad terms, the new-style, all-purpose water authorities turned out to be failing in what was becoming clearly their key mission – the protection of both tap-water quality and river-water quality from increasing pollution by industry, agriculture and discharges from sewage works. The ambitious reshaping, moreover, had taken water utility services out of local government control (though until 1983 local councils nominated somewhat ineffective majorities of members to each regional authority's governing board). But this reshaping had not turned water supply or sewerage services into a recognized or single-minded utility. No serious effort was put into moving domestic water charges from the old property rates used by local councils to the metered charging used by other utilities such as electricity, gas, or telephones. It was found convenient to use local councils generally as sub-contractors for sewerage services. The progressiveness that river authorities had shown in the 1960s was smothered by the problems of managing water supply and sewerage services under the direct constraints that Whitehall wanted for macro-economic reasons.

Ironically, this restructuring went sour just as environmental concerns were gaining great momentum in the 1970s and 1980s. The all-purpose water authorities were quite unable to respond to this. They either lacked public recognition – being seen as hardly different from their local authority predecessors – or gained public opprobrium through failing in their environmental responsibilities. Yet, as ideas of privatization began to be hatched in 1985, the notion of hanging on to power over river basin functions became very important to those water authority leaders most keen to shed the financial harness of Whitehall. Before the next chapter takes up this episode, however, some brief description of the situation in Scotland is already overdue.

A Different Case in Scotland

The key feature of Scotland is that its river basins are generally under much less strain than those south of the Border. This is due to higher rainfall, less evaporation, fewer people and less intensive agriculture, as well as, sadly, the decline of much of Scotland's heavy industry.

Thus an early move to take water services out of local government control was reversed in the mid-1970s. The upper tiers of regional councils then being formed were judged suitable for water supply and sewerage services to be included among their directly operated functions. No system of controls over abstractions has been applied in Scotland, though the RCEP has recently argued that one is now needed. Pollution is dealt with by river purification boards operating as single-purpose agencies in the local authority mould but for river basin areas.

Water institutions in Scotland not only stood apart from the establishment in 1974 of all-purpose regional water authorities in England and Wales. They were left untouched by Mrs Thatcher's thrust to include water among her privatization programmes. Unusually in the case of water, this accepted Hadrian's Wall more or less as their boundary. (Other privatization programmes, such as gas and telecommunications, had included Scotland.)

In late 1992, however, the calm was disturbed by plans to reorganize Scottish local government again, with a preference for unitary authorities. This pattern would hardly be suited to direct operation of water utility services, though it could provide for various forms of franchising or sub-contracting. The major fear was nevertheless that the Conservative government would press for the kind of privatization they promoted in England and Wales. The Conservatives have much less support and representation in Scotland, while other parties taken together are much more influential.

The Scottish Secretary of State therefore published a consultation paper which offered no less than eight options. Called *Investing in our Future: Water and Sewerage in Scotland*, this placed a heavy emphasis on finance, noting the average household bill for water services in Scotland (£102 in 1992–3) as about 40 per cent more than in 1989–90, and stating that bills 'will continue to rise in future, whatever new structure is chosen'. The range of bills is in fact quite wide: charges in the Western Isles are some 50 per cent above the average, while Fife and Central Regions have charges some 15–20 per cent below the average. Future investment needs are put at £5 billion over fifteen years. This is a much lower total than the £24 billion projected for England and Wales at the time of privatization, but a considerable figure for a population of only 5 million. About half of the financing is for maintenance and renewal of existing infrastructure and services to new development, and the rest for new work to achieve upgradings of service, but the projected total is not a precise forecast.

The eight options consisted of three that suggested retaining significant local authority roles, three recommending private-sector participation, and two maintaining that the utilities should remain in public ownership, either as a single organization serving all of Scotland or several for the different regions. The consultation process gained a strong response. Opinion was said to be widely hostile to privatization: even the Scottish Landowners Federation was reported to be against it. The Scottish Office received 5,000 written responses, four-fifths of them from private individuals. Scottish local authorities reported 89 per cent of respondents to surveys as very or fairly satisfied with present water services, though generally local authority services do not find it easy to work in ways that are sensitive to individual consumer concerns.

At the time of writing, the Secretary of State has declared his decision as preferring the utility format in the public sector to be divided into several units, but looking for scope to provide for private investment. One real test of that approach will be whether it may tend to confuse managerial responsibility by fragmentation or keep it coherent by confining the private involvement to financing arrangements. The river basin functions in Scotland will remain in some uncertainty until proposals for a Scottish Environment Agency become clearer.

Chapter 5

Taking Privatization to Parliament

No one planned water privatization from the start. Indeed, those involved were remarkably vague about it to begin with. In January 1984, for example, the secretary of the Water Authorities Association (WAA) told *New Scientist*: 'Water Authorities are exploring between themselves a wide range of possibilities, including whether or not there would be any advantage in changing the status of the authorities as a whole. They are a long way from reaching any conclusions.' More than a year later, in March 1985, Sir Peter Harrop, one of the most senior officials at the Department of the Environment (DoE), was giving evidence to the House of Commons Public Accounts Committee when he was asked about the effects that privatization might have on the financing of water authorities or the cost of water supplies to their customers. He replied: 'The Minister announced that the Government would be examining a measure of privatisation for the water authorities, and this we have started to do. But it is too early to suggest what form might be considered, *certainly too early to consider what the effects might be*'* (emphasis added).

Following that vague, if honest, reply, it was not surprising that the DoE circulated in April a discussion paper that asked more questions than it answered. In this situation, the water authorities continued to persuade themselves that privatization could mean carrying all their functions together into a setting where government control of them would be minimized. That could retain their monopoly in utility services and add a new private grip on river basin resources. In a more sober written response to the government discussion paper, the WAA saw some of the hazards: 'The main community services (fisheries, land drainage, recreation and navigation) raise difficult issues ... there could be a risk of

* Committee of Public Accounts, Minutes of Evidence for 4 March 1985, p. 9.

conflict between the interests of shareholders and the discharge of their community service functions.' But the main theme of the response was nevertheless that the combination of utility and river basin functions should be sacrosanct.

In February 1986, a White Paper was issued, which tried to show that the all-purpose authorities were excellent and, simultaneously, why they had to be privatized. The *Economist* got to the heart of the matter in its headnote of 8 February 1986: 'If you can privatize the water industry, you can privatize anything. The government reckons it can (at least in England and Wales). A year ago, it issued an unusually honest discussion paper examining how, and this week produced its answers. They are not convincing.'

By May 1986, Ken Hill, chairman of the WAA and one of its most experienced members as chairman of South West Water Authority, was saying publicly that the preparations for privatization were in danger of being too rushed. By June, Nicholas Ridley had become Secretary of State for the Environment in place of Kenneth Baker. On 3 July 1986, at the unusual hour of 10 p.m. on a Thursday evening, Mr Ridley was making a statement to the House of Commons that there would be no Bill to privatize water authorities in the next session of Parliament. He said more time was needed to prepare legislation, and further powers might be necessary even to allow the water authorities to prepare themselves for it.

This early episode in the long process of water privatization, which took until late 1989 to complete, is significant in several ways. It shows how unfocused the early moves were among ministers and civil servants, and misjudged among water authority chairmen. The concept of the great 1974 reorganization – all-purpose authorities including river basin controls and major water utility services – was still an important influence, although, in the context of privatization, open to strong objection in principle, and likely greatly to reinforce monopoly.

Utility Privatization Alone

Nicholas Ridley restarted the privatization process as abruptly as he had interrupted it, though he had consulted the Cabinet in advance. As the 1987 general election opened in his Cirencester and Tewkesbury constituency on 22 May, he used his adoption meeting at Chedworth Village Hall to announce his new proposals. With scrupulous propriety, the press release came not from the DoE but the Conservative Central Office, at 7.30 p.m. on a Friday evening:

In our consideration of the future of the water industry, we have been increasingly concerned by the role of the water authorities as both poachers and gamekeepers in this field. They are responsible for controlling discharges from industry and agriculture; but they are responsible for sewage treatment, and are major dischargers in their own right . . . Last year's White Paper suggested that the privatized authorities should be responsible for substantially the same range of functions, executive and regulatory, as the water authorities themselves. We have reappraised these proposals. We have decided that we should transfer to the private sector only the functions of water supply, sewerage and sewage disposal . . . The regulatory and river management functions of the water authorities will remain in the public sector . . . We shall set up a new National Rivers Authority to discharge these functions.

In political terms, this was a striking moment. A new agency specifically to guard the water environment was to be included in the Tory election manifesto. A notoriously right-wing minister, a chief proponent of the doctrinaire school of privatization, in the view of many people, was insisting that the functions of governing river basins were not for privatization, despite earlier proposals that they could be thrown in alongside the utility services. In his autobiography, Nigel Lawson claims some of the credit for also recognizing this change from the earlier proposals to be essential, but Mr Ridley carried more clout with the hard right of the Conservative party. As a civil engineer and a fly-fisherman, he also understood rivers.

Headlines such as 'Thames Water to attack sale plan' (*Financial Times*, 3 June 1987); 'Fight over water sale plan' (*Daily Telegraph*, 26 June 1987); and 'Most water authorities oppose flotation scheme' (*Financial Times*, 10 September 1987) showed that the water authority chairmen had learned little from the year's interval for reflection that Mr Ridley had provided. It took most of the chairmen most of the next six months to adjust to the realities of the new-style privatization respecting the water environment as the concern of the whole community.

Meantime, the DoE published in July a consultation paper on forming a National Rivers Authority (NRA), inviting responses to its proposals by mid-October. By mid-December 1987, a further publication confirmed its proposals. Yet the chairmen were still trying to keep their rearguard action going. As the *Independent* reported, the chairmen were refusing offers that NRA functions might be sub-contracted to the new companies for operational purposes. They still wanted these statutory powers for private businesses and believed they could get them.

But this was not on offer. From early 1988, the shape of the intended privatization (confined to water utility services and related assets only) and the formation of the NRA began to unfold. The river basin functions would no longer be lacking in independence or overshadowed by utility managers.

Which Format to Adopt?

A Case of Extreme Monopoly

This is not the place for an essay on different objectives and formats for privatization, but three demarcations might apply in the case of water utility privatization. The first relates to the availability of competition. Across western Europe, and especially in eastern Europe and the former Soviet block, governments have come to control, own and operate many industrial activities and units that could readily be conducted as private enterprises in a competitive market. Where that market already exists, with some private companies active in it (as it often does, for example, where multi-national companies have a significant presence), it should be straightforward in principle to sell a government-owned unit to private investors and management and let it find its place in that market.

However, some of the industries in state ownership are monopolies. In some cases, this is the reason they are in state ownership: they have been seen as too important to the community for private control of them to be acceptable, and utility services such as water supply, electricity supply, telecommunications are often in this situation. Yet this point can be reversed: such industries may be monopolies because they are in state ownership. The state often finds it helpful and profitable to exclude competition, perhaps in the name of better economic planning and industrial development where these are important political objectives. Thus one key question on any privatization programme is whether the unit to be privatized is foreseen as going into a robustly competitive setting. If not, another important question must be why a private monopoly should be created in place of a public one; and how secure or illusory are the arrangements for disciplining it. It is mere rhetoric, and sometimes misleading or dishonest rhetoric at that, to insist that private enterprise management will always be more efficient than public agencies in serving customers' interests, even in the absence of competition.

In this perspective, water utility services have to be recognized as extreme monopolies. Providing water pipes and sewer networks is so capital intensive that no community could expect several competing networks to be available in the same district to provide either service. So water utility privatization has to be about creating some form of private monopoly in place of some form of public one. This is not so true of telephones, as the emergence of the Mercury service, albeit slow in spreading, shows. In electricity, it is possible to provide for competition in generation if not in local distribution: electricity is the opposite of water in being impossible to store but cheap to move about. But water supply tends as infrastructure to monopoly from source to tap. Sewers (which rely on gravity mostly, while water supply operates under pressure) offer no choice of which sewage treatment works they lead to. These are part of the community's basic services; passing them out of public ownership or control must be a matter for special questioning, though it can be observed that, under competition, other basic commodities such as bread are reliably provided by private companies.

The Asset-sale Format

The second important demarcation is between two main categories of privatization format. In many cases, the national government, or a public agency in a provincial or regional setting, may decide to retain ownership of the assets, but under one or another form of contract or franchise to involve private management and investors in partly or wholly operating the business. This may include financing investment, collecting income and setting charges with only limited reference to the public agency. This broadly is the system under which nearly three-quarters of water supply in France is organized, and just under half its sewerage services. The customers' interests are essentially represented and exercised by the executive mayors of municipalities, who control the granting and renewal (or not) of the contracts or franchises. At each termination, all assets, even if financed by the contractor/operator, revert to public ownership in the hands of local government.

The other format is where the government or public agency sells the assets wholly to the private company, which replaces the public body as owner, investor, operator, setter of prices and everything else. This is generally the better form of privatization where there is active competition, or where international business is involved. Thus the British government adopted the asset-sale format for telecommunications, British Airways and many other cases. For asset-sale privatization, there obviously has to be a sale, but it does not have to be by flotation of shares on the stock exchange: it may be by a process of tender or auction, or by negotiation. Quite often, governments want to privatize an industry because they have come to regard the activity in question as a liability, calling for frequent injections of capital or not making profits. Thus buyers should beware: assets may be offered for sale, but the business may still be a liability. The government that sells it can often make it, deliberately or accidentally, even more of a liability in future.

Dividend Control or Price Cap?

The final demarcation to be noted here applies only to cases of monopoly privatization, because in the absence of competition there has to be a discipline to guard against monopoly abuse due to excessive prices or poor levels of service (or both). A widespread traditional form for this control, especially for private utilities in the USA, has been dividend limitation. The operators have no incentive to set prices too high, it is said, because they cannot pass more than a defined dividend to their shareholders. But an opposing argument is that, under this system, the operators have little incentive to cut costs of operating or investing in new facilities. The limitation on dividends puts a cap on profits, but not on costs. The customers may still have to pay higher charges than a really efficient service would require.

Thus the British utility privatization programmes came to rely on a different form of monopoly discipline that was first used in the case of British Telecom, where competition was foreseen as developing after a few years. This involved price-capping, where the company is left to make as much profit as it can, subject to not raising prices beyond specified limits for levels of service which are also defined and monitored. This method, it is argued, provides the very incentives to efficiency that dividend limitation fails to offer. It has two other effects: it makes for share prices that are more prominent and more variable in a sophisticated stock exchange where utilities can compete for capital by offering better rewards to investors. It also requires more complicated and intrusive regulation than plain dividend control.

New Tasks and Hazards

The significance of these three demarcations in water utility privatization is as follows. There would be virtually no scope for competition between the ten privatized companies because generally in England and Wales all but a few properties already have public water supply and all but 5 per cent also have a sewerage connection. The privatization of multiple monopolies by the asset-sale method would require the organizing of ten flotations, either separately or together. A price-cap method would have to be developed for a group of companies, taking account realistically of the differences in the large investment programmes each would be committed to carry out. On this last point, of course, there was scope to argue that regulation of a group could be more effective than of a single monopoly, because the performance of different companies could be compared, and they would be competing in the same capital market for investment finance.

Sorting out these complexities, which are in principle different aspects of the same basic conflict between the community's interests and private interests in the absence of competition and conventional market forces, could be quite an intellectual challenge in theory. Resolving them in a practicable fashion was to be a very difficult assignment indeed. The purpose here will be no more than to illustrate some of the main considerations involved in that process, for the effects they had either in the process or on its outcome. At the start, it is worth identifying three hazards which arose as a result of the format of privatization adopted – an asset sale of ten companies – despite the advantages of that format.

Usually the aim of ministers and civil servants is to prepare legislation and get it approved by Parliament with little or no amendment, so that they can implement it on lines they have confidence in, in order to bring about the beneficial results regarded as the purpose of the whole process. Government departments not only have much skill and influence in these matters, but also real power at the implementation stage, which the detail of the legislation may amplify in what it explicitly leaves to ministerial discretion. However, in a privatization which is to involve a share flotation, some of the greatest uncertainties arise not in Parliament but after the legislation is completed. Then the financial centre becomes the critical arena for implementation: all the perils of the London stock market and international markets become relevant, and the government's City advisers have far less control of the situation than the party whips have in Parliament. This is a major hazard for this type of privatization, especially because timing is so important. The whole market mood may change after key decisions are taken, even though they have been left to the last possible moment. In late October 1989, for example, Nigel Lawson resigned as Chancellor of the Exchequer, and the FTSE stock market index fell 60 points just as the pathfinder prospectus was to be published. 'Lawson crisis jitters will hit water sell-off price' was one headline.

But in terms of preparation, the flotation method has another hazard. For a flotation, the prospectus has to provide a complete and accurate disclosure of all relevant information available to the directors, so that potential investors may not miss anything they might want to know. For many private companies, preparing a prospectus is a fairly routine procedure, because they and their City advisers are familiar with it, and often the company or the industry and markets in which it will be doing business are well-known to investors.

But for the water utilities it was quite different. Such private companies as there were in water supply were regarded as specialized investments subject to dividend control, and suitable mostly for insurance company investments. The City had no experience of commercial sewerage or sewage disposal companies: they are hardly known in North America, let alone in Britain. Moreover, all investment decisions and flotations are heavily influenced by a mixture of views of past track record and future prospects. The water authorities had no track record outside the public sector, where, for example, they were exempt from taxation for reasons related (oddly enough) to their flood defence functions and the way they were financed. So the task ahead of flotation was to secure the passage of legislation so that it would be as little altered as possible, and then to prepare ten prospectuses for companies in a utility service industry that few people in the City or anywhere else had seriously thought of as a commercial business.

But underlying each prospectus was a deeper hazard that would be difficult to surmount. The success of the flotation depends essentially on the offer price of shares and the prospects investors see for good and growing profits in the future. To maximize the proceeds of sale for the Treasury, the offer price needs to be as high as these prospects will support. Yet those prospects will be threatened the more the government indicates that, to protect consumers, the charges that the monopoly utility will be allowed to apply will be rigorously regulated. So the regulation on which consumers will depend has a negative influence on a share price that the flotation would aim to maximize. Unless investors believe that profits can grow, the flotation might really flop.

The Real Liability

The conflict of investor objectives and consumer interests was specially acute in the water utility flotation for a reason that was central to the whole process. As a result of the limits that Labour and Conservative governments had placed on capital investment in water services since about 1976, the ten companies would have to invest the huge total of £24 billion in the first ten years of their operation as private businesses. This is equal, in effect, to about £500 for every man, woman and child using water in England and Wales, or to adding over £1,000 to the debt of most households, whether they already have a mortgage or not.

Yet, in another sense, water and sewerage services are an industry nobody really wants to see growing in terms of volume. With nearly every property already provided with both services, there is little sign of growth by population increase in total, though some regions need more additional house-building than others. The construction of new reservoirs is still resisted where these are proposed; people will hardly go to the toilet more often, which constitutes much the largest use of water in the average household. So in business terms, an extra £24 billion would have to be invested in a service where the growth would be in upgrading quality more than volume.

This explains, first, why the government was so determined to privatize this unlikely candidate by asset sale. Whether or not it had other, doctrinaire reasons, the government wanted this huge financing of additional investment to be taken out of the public sector, even though no grants or subsidies were involved. The part of it that would come from borrowing, the government wanted to be private borrowing; the part that would come from price increases, the government wanted not to be the responsibility of ministers.

But, secondly, this format provided a contrast between the water privatization and that of the other utilities. In telecommunications and gas – both businesses with great prospects of volume growth – the price-cap formula was to be in the form of annual increases below the rate of average price inflation, to motivate the perennial drive for efficiency gains: Retail Price Index (RPI) minus X, as it was expressed. But because of the capital intensity of the water industry, the price-cap formula would have to be annual increases above average rate of inflation: RPI + K, as it came to be referred to.

In terms of the wider themes of this book, this is one detailed example of government adjusting to the limits of what the natural environment and the community's dependence on sharing it could stand. Once it took the view that public finance could no longer stand the strain of investment that had already been held down far more than it should have been, the government had to devise some other economic mechanism suited to the situation. Water utilities are especially exposed to environmental pressures, since the water environment is both source of water supply and sink for waste-water discharges. This is why the water utility privatization in England and Wales was different from its immediate predecessors: the environmental constraints on a densely populated island produced the RPI + K formula as much as did the government's need to attract investors to finance capital spending of £24 billion within ten years in a non-growth industry.

The Intended Structure

Removing the river management functions from each authority disrupted such track record as the accounts for their public sector activities provided. But, ambitiously, it was decided to allow for something to be added on as well. The companies had ideas of themselves diversifying into all sorts of other business, at home and overseas, that might or might not be related to their water utility interests.

The government was to provide for so-called enterprise activities by proposing for each privatized company a structure comprising three elements. At the top, the company quoted on the stock exchange would be little more than a holding company for a group. Below this would be the water supply and waste-water service company subject to detailed regulation as a monopoly, often called the core service company. At the same level, there could be any number of subsidiaries, so-called enterprise activities, free of regulation save for the laws applying to all commercial companies. These enterprise activities might have been only allowed to be started several years after flotation, so core services got a period of undivided attention in the new set-up. But if this was the initial approach, it was changed in favour of all activities of the new companies being allowed to start together. The core services may have lost something from that change.

Regulating the Core Business

The obvious question here is how the core service companies alone would be regulated when none of their assets or shares might be held by government. The answer reveals an artificial combination of the asset-sale approach and the contractual or franchising method mentioned earlier. Each private company was to hold an appointment, for twenty-five years in the first instance, as provider either of water-supply and sewerage services (in the case of the ten newly privatized companies following the regional authorities) or of water supply only (in the case of the older statutory water companies long financed by private investors). As these latter companies served territories within the larger regional ones, most privatized companies had different service areas for water supply from their (regional) area for sewerage service. There are no 'water only' companies, as the older statutory companies are now called, in the North West and South West regions.

For all these companies, there was to be an instrument of appointment, or licence, as it was often called. In essence, this conferred and confirmed the territory in which the company had a monopoly, but it also committed the company to all the regulatory conditions and arrangements that would be applied by the new regulatory agency, the Office of Water Services (OFWAT). It was essential for this licence to be very robust: the health and life-styles of the whole community could be threatened by a signifi-cant failure of water and waste-water services. Therefore the licence had to provide for OFWAT to have full data on levels of service, and to regulate them as well as water charges. In this, it would have the advice of customer committees which it would organize in each area (in contrast to consumer bodies, set up under the 1983 legislation, which had been organized by, and largely under the thumb of, the old regional authorities themselves).

The licence had to provide, of course, for the private water company going bust, unlikely as that would be when the regulator was given an express duty in setting price caps that would always allow investors an appropriate return on the capital they put in. One special feature here is that, if receivers were to be appointed, they would have express duties to keep the water services going while they did whatever else might be best for the shareholders. As the company would be owning all the relevant assets, it seems highly artificial to talk of scope to revoke the licence for serious failure of service. Yet clearly that is relevant.

In July 1988, at Camelford in Cornwall, an exceptional 'poison-ing' of the tap-water supply occurred when, at a treatment works left to run automatically to save manpower, a relief driver from a chemicals supplier let himself in with a key and misunderstood which tank his 20-tonne delivery of aluminium sulphate should go into. As a result, 20,000 people were reported to have become ill and bands of aluminium were found in the bones of one of the worst-affected victims ('like rings in a tree trunk', commented the *Sunday Times* on 18 June 1989), who had died later from other causes. Some Camelford residents who wanted private health insurance were denied cover for any treatment related to the aluminium poisoning. This incident actually happened under public ownership, in mid-preparation for private ownership. The government chose to do nothing in such a period which might have sharpened criticism of company management, for example by insisting on resignations. But if such a calamity happened under private ownership, would it be acceptable to leave the licence comfortably in place for the monopoly to carry on? Competition would certainly not allow the company to carry on as before: consider how Perrier's market share was disrupted when it had to withdraw supplies of its bottled water due to chemical contamination. Since the Camelford incident, a Drinking Water Inspectorate (DWI) has been established (though it does not cover bottled water).

OFWAT is asking for fuller and clearer information on the boundary between the core business and enterprise activities. The scope for overlap may be seen, for example, in the case where a commercial company with large volumes of effluent to dispose of discharges them into the sewers, which forms part of the regulated core business. But if, instead, the discharging company asks the water company to operate treatment works on site at the end of the manufacturing process, that will be part of the unregulated private business. If anything proved the need for pollution control to be fully and openly separated from the utility service business, this sort of overlap, small and artificial detail as it may seem, clearly does.

The French are Welcomed

From mid-1987 onwards, three major French companies much involved in water management under the franchising system in France began to intervene in the British water arena. By agreement, they were purchasing shares in the so-called statutory water companies financed by private investors and subject to dividend limitation. Under the 1974 reorganization by Mr Heath's Conservative government, these companies had been allowed to survive in their own right, although the logic of that reshaping favoured their inclusion in all-purpose authorities as for other similar units.

With privatization in prospect, the water authorities would obviously want to tighten their grip on the territories of these statutory companies, where the regional authorities provided all sewerage services. However, the water-only companies were keen to resist this, and the French interest provided them with a great chance to do so. Generally, the French companies (to one of which the author of this book acted as consultant) were insistent that they would only buy shares where the companies did not oppose this and would not exceed limits in share ownership that the companies asked them to observe. On this basis, the French purchases were repeatedly found to be congenial to the statutory companies. The share prices rose in some cases to ten times the level at which their shares had stood before the French arrived.

This intervention by several large companies strong in water utility services in France was helpful to the British government too. It showed investors that the water business need not be just the sleepy backwater they had seen it as. Three French companies as rivals for stakes in the English water companies demonstrated that a sort of competition was really possible.

Hardly any British companies in other industries showed any interest in buying seriously into the water businesses. Trafalgar House – which incidentally partnered the French company SAUR in the first French purchase of shares, in the Rickmansworth water company – was said to have been warned off by Mrs Thatcher personally. A company called Biwater, involved in making water treatment plant and interested in cutting a bolder figure overseas, also bought smaller statutory companies, in East Worcestershire, Hampshire and Dorset (and has recently sold the first of these to Severn-Trent with OFWAT's consent).

The big regional companies being privatized were protected, in any event, from complete take-over by a golden controlling share to be retained by the government until 1994, even though earlier ideas of its selling less than the full amount of other shares on initial flotation were changed in favour of a complete sale. All ten companies were to be floated at the same time, not in sequence as first contemplated. The anxieties of the water authority chairmen about where each company might be in the sequence of sale (with wide preference for Thames not being first) was one reason for this change. The desire of the Cabinet to complete the water flotation within the financial year 1989/90, and shorten the gap between completing the legislation and flotation, was another reason. Amid so many conflicts among the different parties, the occasional coincidence of interest deserves recognition.

Issues of Land and Development

Unlike the French intervention that started more than a year before the main privatization Bill was submitted to Parliament in November 1988, the strong influence utility companies would have on access to open land and future building development got little exposure until the Bill went into Parliament. The Council for the Protection of Rural England (CPRE) published a report, *Liquid Assets*, which focused attention on what was to happen to the large land holdings (much of high scenic value in the uplands) that the privatized companies would inherit. These had survived from the days when municipalities purchased large parts of the catchments around their major reservoirs to guard against pollution of drinking-water sources. They set limits to what tenant farmers could do, and sometimes to public access too.

The CPRE report showed that the water authorities owned some 455,000 acres of land, nearly two-thirds of it in three regions, North West, Yorkshire and Welsh. Clearly the prospect of activities in these areas falling into the category of enterprise business outside the regulatory scope of OFWAT was specially disturbing.

It showed very forcefully, to MPs in particular, that the environmental threats of the water and waste-water companies were not just related to the damage they might do to rivers if the NRA was not fully effective. Despite land-use planning controls, ownership is a huge source of power, in the control and use of land and the direction of its disposal. The support that *Liquid Assets* attracted led the government specifically to put forward a Code of Practice for Conservation, Access and Recreation, and gave the future companies a striking warning that they had better watch their step. Additionally, the legislation was amended to create obligations for the companies to disclose land sales to OFWAT, and in certain cases for a proportion of the proceeds to be credited to reducing water charges to customers instead of increasing profits for shareholders.

In July 1989, the Water Bill completed its Parliamentary passage – not a moment too soon for the government – and received the Royal Assent. As an Act, it occupied 419 pages and cost £20 a copy. Yet, as noted earlier, this was by no means the end of the main privatization process. Water still had to be taken to the market. The pathfinder prospectus for that was to occupy more than another 600 pages.

Chapter 6

Taking Water to Market

Preparations for the final act of flotation gathered pace while the legislation was still going through Parliament. From February 1989, the spotlight moved from what concerned the politicians to what would worry the investors. This focused on the central issues of the privatization, the form of price control and the effect of environmental obligations, together constituting for investors a powerful source of anxiety that profits and dividends might be severely squeezed between these two forces.

The first real sign of rising tensions for investors arose in crossfire between ministers and the statutory water companies which would not be involved in flotation. While these were free of the perils of flotation, at the same time they would have to enter the price-cap regime without the balance-sheet reconstructions and debt write-offs that would make the big regional companies far more attractive to investors ahead of flotation. Thus their last round of price increases before price-cap regulation started was virtually their only chance to prepare for it.

In February 1989, the water authorities showed that their price increases would be just under 10 per cent on average, though in some regions about 13 per cent. Within days, price increases by statutory companies were being announced as probably averaging 30 per cent and reaching in several cases as much as 50 per cent. Chairmen of companies going over 10 per cent were summoned to the DoE to explain themselves. At one level, this row was only a minor distraction. The *Independent*'s Jeremy Warner reported that companies understood the politics but were confused as they felt prior consultation with the DoE indicated that 'large tariff increases had the tacit approval of Ministers' (*Independent*, 8 February 1989). At another level, it showed the special complexity of putting public authorities into a price-cap regime after privatization, while driving already private companies straight into it from a different regulatory regime that was meant to limit reserve-building as well as dividends.

At this stage, the *Independent* (on 9 February 1989) took the opportunity to make a broader and very penetrating comment, still relevant four years later:

The theory behind the Water Bill ... is simple, but it implies hard choices. The government ... intends to sell off the water authorities while keeping the regulatory powers in public hands. In practice, however, this leaves the government with a very difficult balance to strike. It has to decide how much importance to give to each of three factors: raising environmental standards, keeping down prices, and making the industry attractive to investors. The row about the prices charged by the existing private companies, although a side-show, is a foretaste of things to come.

This comment is both topical for the mid-1990s and close to the themes in this book. It is observing that a special feature of privatizing the water utility services lay in the direct impact they have on the natural environment, and the additional exposure to regulation that this makes inevitable for them. At one level, investors would hardly be comfortable with this until they could see how it worked out. More deeply, the community's use of the water environment and that environment itself each have their own dynamics which are partly independent, partly in endless interaction with each other.

European Neighbourhood Watch

The pricing row led to sharp words from Mrs Thatcher, and, more generally, it shaded into longer-running tensions about environmental standards and obligations for the water utility companies. The NRA would be the main regulator here, of polluting discharges and of abstractions from surface and underground sources: the NRA Advisory Committee (NRAAC) was already at work. But, with its Water Directives, the EC is also a major setter of standards, all achieved by consultation and ultimately by agreement between governments of member states. These separate governments, including the British one, each have the task nationally of enforcing the standards they agree upon at Brussels.

Neither Mrs Thatcher nor Mr Ridley were notably pro-European, and they might draw comfort from the fact that Britain is still an island, not obliged to share its rivers with anyone but its own densely packed citizens, agriculture and industry. Yet, increasingly, the sharing of seas has been recognized as more a link than a divide. The North Sea has become – like the Baltic – the focus for current conferences and international programmes, largely because the quality of the rivers flowing into it (much influenced by the effectiveness of upstream pollution control) is recognized as among the greatest influences on the pollution of the sea as a whole.

Thus the EC has a valid role of neighbourhood watch on the water environment of member states, whether or not they are active and careful in keeping their own 'doorsteps' clean. The worry here for investors in British water companies was that some of the water authorities were already lagging behind in their compliance with EC standards. The government had committed itself to enforce these, even if the new companies were guaranteed an easier ride for their early years by the way their discharge consents had been made less strict.

These problems were awkward in two ways. The necessity for the flotation prospectuses to be complete, open and accurate in the information that directors of each company would sign was never a mere formality. But could it go so far as to confirm that the company was regularly breaching tap-water or other quality standards that were binding by law? Might the directors be prosecuted before their companies were privatized?

Secondly, the setting up of new Water Directives, or tighter standards in some existing ones, could not be too far away in the future. These might call for further investment, which investors might worry about if the price cap were not adjusted to allow an adequate return on it. Economics and stock markets are often said to be all about coping with uncertainty and risk, but investors dislike lack of certainty, and are forever analysing and trying to reduce the risks to which they may be exposed.

To get round these difficulties, two main devices were developed. First, the Whitehall bureaucracy carried through intensive negotiations with the (smaller) Brussels bureaucracy about the belated end-dates when compliance would be achieved, and moved to put these dates into the legislation. Despite Brussels being often accused of interference, the House of Lords on at least one occasion rejected the dates agreed for compliance with EC drinking-water standards (September 1993) in favour of a much earlier date, such as the end of 1989. The House of Lords was more keen than the government to see British water companies achieving full compliance as early as possible.

The second device to calm investors' anxieties went deeper and would be longer running. The price-cap formula for water services was to be RPI + K, where K was a series of annual figures set in advance for ten years, unless OFWAT altered them at a five-year review. As outlined in Chapter 5, this was in contrast to RPI – X for other privatized utilities, which could even generate price reductions once the rate of inflation fell below the X percentage. But K was seen as potentially inadequate if environmental standards were changed in ways that generated cost increases beyond anyone's predicting. So scope for another addition was provided, often called 'pass-through', whereby a company could make a case for an increase larger than the pre-set K, and OFWAT could grant it if convinced of its merits. This was a notable, and perhaps unnecessary, concession that the companies bargained out of a Whitehall too nervous to refuse it.

Moreover, the director-general of OFWAT was being given a duty by the legislation to ensure that the companies could achieve an appropriate return on capital to sustain the services they were appointed to provide to their designated areas. Although there was scope in the legislation to make appointments where service was required in no-man's-land areas served by no existing companies, few such areas existed in reality and generally each monopoly was being made even surer of its income.

Towards the Finishing Line

Thus all points in a triangle of conflict were being reconciled yet also reinforced. The prices row showed the strength of the consumer interest; the DoE was going a long way to reinforce the power of each company as a monopoly, in the duty it put on

OFWAT to sustain company finances and the scope for the regulator to go beyond the pre-set K figures; the water environment with its own dynamics could always be, ultimately, a more powerful force than the NRA or the Brussels Water Directives. But the investors' interest was evidently strong enough to carry the stress that flotation would put on it.

In early July, when the legislation achieved the Royal Assent, the privatization still had not gained much acceptance, let alone support, from the wider public, according to polls such as that published in the *Observer*. The *Financial Times* had an editorial on 6 July headed 'Few cheers for the water sale'. The earlier arguments about taking care of the companies' land assets launched by CPRE's *Liquid Assets* were still rumbling on.

By the end of July, within a fortnight of the legislation being complete, Nicholas Ridley was moved from the DoE in the sort of reshuffle Margaret Thatcher liked to make before the holidays rather than after them. There had been a sign of difficulty between them in early March, after the price-increase row, when Mrs Thatcher said openly to a Conservative Party audience that water privatization 'has not been handled well or accurately'. This was widely seen as a crude attack on Mr Ridley and Mr Howard at an awkward point in mid-legislation, despite Mrs Thatcher's also stating that Nicholas Ridley was 'the best Environment Secretary we have ever had'.

The difference between them, in the author's view, was that Mr Ridley did grasp very fully the environmental dimension that was special and awkward in this privatization, where Mrs Thatcher, who had long put the environment near the bottom of her priorities, possibly did not. On the other hand, it was thoroughly helpful that much of the time she had such confidence in Mr Ridley. This was evident in his getting acceptance for the concept of the NRA as a new substantial body in the public sector. Possibly Downing Street intervened less in the DoE's work on this than it is said to have done with some other ministers and departments.

Some of the newspapers recognized the different threads in Mr Ridley's personality. Richard Evans (in the *Financial Times* of 13 February 1989) referred to 'his laconic, couldn't-give-a-damn manner' and his brimming confidence. On 10 March, in the same newspaper, when talk of Nicholas Ridley being replaced by Chris Patten was already being reported, Joe Rogaly wrote: 'Civil servants and others who have worked closely with Mr Ridley praise him highly. His immediate associates are remarkably loyal. They appear to have a strong personal regard for him.'

The affectionate regard for Mr Ridley implicit in these comments – amid more widespread dislike by those who had little direct contact with him – is worth recalling now since his recent death in 1993. At policy meetings, he was notable for seeking real solutions to difficulties rather than simply applying political sticking-plaster, and he was a good listener. The author came to share this regard for Mr Ridley after working with him as an adviser during the period when legislation for the NRA was being prepared.

As well as being more patient in discussion than his public style often suggested, he could be relaxed and amusing too. In a proposal that the NRA should have advisory panels involving local people, these were temporarily given the acronym RENPANS ('River Environmental Panels'). Mr Ridley conducted the discussion (with a dozen or so officials) calling them 'Bedpans', but it was clear he favoured the proposal. Due to professional discretion, civil servants usually say little about their ways of working with ministers, and a well-known television series may have inclined them to be even more reticent. But it seems worth saying in this context that the working day of ministers is part political and media limelight, part departmental treadmill backstage. When massive and complex legislation has to be prepared and various interest groups consulted, Whitehall does a remarkable job in providing ministers with the necessary information, and, despite other claims on their time and attention, most ministers respond by participating to the full. Mr Ridley and his Ministers of State dealing with water legislation (Lord Belstead and the Earl of Caithness in turn during the author's period of involvement) were always ready for thorough but concise discussion. All three of them fostered open comments unconditioned by preconceptions of their own, and their consistent attention and courtesy, despite a heavy workload, was a notable encouragement to everyone involved in the consultation process.

Making Companies Fit to Float

By the time Mr Patten replaced Mr Ridley, he could largely concentrate on the mechanics of the flotation and the final critical negotiations with the companies. Some of the decisions had been taken as the preparations advanced. The settling of a common price would simplify publicity and procedures for investors, as well as making it easier to oblige institutional investors to buy packages of shares in all ten companies. In the advance publicity, no figure such as the imaginary 'Sid' of the British Gas flotation was created, but there were various printed slogans about 'H_2 Ownership' which the newspaper headlines could easily adopt with variations.

The financial analysts of course provided endless figures and commentaries. This material needs no discussion here, and the prospectuses are now only of historical interest. But two main points are worth illustrating with detailed figures (see Tables 6.1 and 6.2): one is the differences between companies being made less obvious by the common share price, and the other is the range of figures that would apply as price caps, especially between the privatized companies and the statutory companies. These figures represent, as it were, the tips of ten icebergs for the privatized companies, because they arise from the massive amount of work done out of sight in projecting capital expenditure and reconstructing balance sheets. In this, there was much sophisticated modelling and some hard bargaining. Is perhaps this sort of privatization only possible with modern computers as well as political will?

The K factors for the statutory, water-only companies are more varied between companies and between years. All the companies, including those privatized, can set increases below annual limits and retain a carry-forward potential, so the figures for each year are no longer exactly as shown in Tables 6.1 and 6.2.

Although the stock market was somewhat disturbed by the resignation in late October of Nigel Lawson as Chancellor of the Exchequer, it was soon recovering its enthusiasm for a new utility flotation. In the event, the offer (at 240p per share, but only 100p to be paid in the first of three instalments) was 2.8 times

Table 6.1 Look-alikes look different – company line-up for flotation

Company	Anglian	Northumbrian	North West	Severn-Trent	Southern	South West	Thames	Welsh	Wessex	Yorkshire
Populations (millions)	5.4	2.6	7.0	8.3	4.0	1.5	11.7	2.9	2.5	4.5
Turnover 1988/89/£m.	357	142	458	476	204	106	558	220	131	308
Pre-tax profit (£m.) forecast to 31.3.90	136	350.3	172	208	81	82	178	93	54.5	96
Market capitalization £m.	707	157	854	849	393	293	922	346	246	472
Yield %	8.51	8.91	8.73	8.25	8.35	9.68	8.10	9.31	8.45	8.57
Dividend cover	2.3	3.6	2.3	3.0	2.5	2.9	2.4	2.9	2.6	2.4
Capital expenditure 1990–95 £m.	1,470	540	2,220	2,330	830	765	1,890	880	650	1,210
1995–2000 £m.	1,990	345	2,060	1,750	500	525	1,920	875	625	1,210
K factor 1990–95%	5.5	7	5	5.5	5.5/3.5	6.5	4.5	6.5	4.5	3
K factor 1995–2000%	5.5	3	5	2	0	5	4.5	5.5	4.5	3

NOTES

Population for sewerage service (including areas of statutory companies)

Profit forecast as if new capital structure in place all year

Market capitalization at share price of 240p

Yield is for year to 31.3.90, notional dividend on 240p

Capital expenditure projected at 1989 prices

K factors are price increase limits above inflation, subject to five-year interim review. The two figures for Southern are for 1990–93 and 1994–5

Source: Various publications

Table 6.2 Statutory water companies' 'K' factors (as set in 1989–90)

Company	1990/91	1991/2	1992/3	1993/4	1994/5	1995/6	1996–2000
Bournemouth	18.5	18.5	15.0	0.0	0.0	0.0	0.0
Bristol	5.0	5.0	4.0	4.0	2.0	2.0	2.0
Cambridge	12.0	10.0	8.0	0.0	0.0	0.0	2.0
Chester	4.5	4.5	4.5	1.0	1.0	1.0	1.0
Cholderton	6.0	6.0	6.0	6.0	6.0	6.0	6.0
Colne Valley	10.0	10.0	10.0	7.5	7.5	1.0	1.0
East Anglian	19.0	13.0	13.0	13.0	3.0	1.0	1.0
East Surrey	16.5	16.0	2.0	2.0	2.0	2.0	2.0
East Worcester	25.0	11.0	11.0	11.0	−1.0	−1.0	−1.0
Eastbourne	20.0	20.0	2.5	2.5	2.5	0.0	0.0
Essex	5.0	5.0	5.0	5.0	5.0	4.5	4.5
Folkestone	18.0	8.0	8.0	8.0	8.0	8.0	0.0
Hartlepool	3.5	3.5	3.5	3.5	3.5	3.5	3.5
Lee Valley	7.5	7.5	7.5	7.5	2.5	2.5	0.0
Mid Kent	9.0	9.0	2.5	2.5	2.5	2.5	2.5
Mid Southern	11.5	11.5	10.0	4.0	4.0	4.0	4.0
Mid Sussex	17.0	16.0	13.0	3.0	0.0	0.0	0.0
Newcastle	8.0	8.0	8.0	2.0	2.0	2.0	2.0
North Surrey	8.5	8.5	8.5	8.5	8.5	2.0	2.0
Portsmouth	5.5	5.5	5.5	5.5	2.0	2.0	2.0
Rickmansworth	9.5	9.5	2.0	2.0	2.0	2.0	2.0
South Staffordshire	5.0	5.0	5.0	3.0	3.0	2.0	2.0
Sunderland	7.5	7.5	7.5	5.0	5.0	2.0	2.0
Sutton	12.5	10.5	8.5	8.5	3.5	3.5	3.5
Tendring Hundred	22.5	22.5	13.0	13.0	2.5	2.5	2.5
West Hampshire	7.5	7.5	7.5	7.5	5.5	5.5	5.5
West Kent	20.0	20.0	4.0	4.0	−1.5	−1.5	−1.5
Wrexham	15.0	15.0	15.0	0.0	0.0	0.0	0.0
York	3.0	3.0	3.0	3.0	3.0	3.0	3.0

Source: Waterfacts, 1991

over-subscribed after a claw-back of shares from the institutional market. Remarkably, Northumbrian, in an area of economic decline and strong water-only companies, was nine times over-subscribed. No ordinary applicants would get more than 2,000 shares; those who applied for 4,000 upwards would get none. To spread share ownership (or windfall gains), the meek were to be

Table 6.3 Share prices of water companies

Company	1989		1991		28/9/93		1993 High*	Low*
Anglian	148	(4)	330	(7)	535	(9)	553	455
Northumbrian	157	(1)	344	(4)	629	(2)	661	547
North West	135	(9)	334	(6)	519	(10)	537	431
Severn-Trent	131	(10)	306	(9)	539	(9)	564	439
Southern	141	(6)	305	(10)	556	(5)	583	454
South West	147	(5)	307	(8)	571	(4)	586	465
Thames	136	(8)	340	(5)	543	(6/7)	563	454
Welsh	141	(6)	345	(3)	609	(3)	639	506
Wessex	154	(2)	381	(1)	630	(1)	661	536
Yorkshire	149	(3)	351	(2)	543	(6/7)	593	475

*To 28/9/93.

Source: Water Bulletin, and financial press.

given a brief priority. Some 2.7 million applications were received in total for the ten regional companies. The public incredulity had finally abated: sewage disposal as a traditional Cinderella service in the public sector had finally got to the ball, even if Mr Ridley was no longer the minister to escort her there.

The stock market had achieved in this period an 180-point rise in the FTSE 100 Index, so there was talk of the new water shares going at a 30 per cent premium when dealings opened. Table 6.3 shows the prices on the day dealing began (on the basis of 100p paid); those in December 1991 (on the basis of 240p paid) and the pattern of prices in 1993 up to 28 September. Two of the three highest-priced shares on the first day were still in the top three in 1993.

How Much Did It All Cost?

How much it all cost is a difficult and open-ended question. The long-term consequences cannot yet be known or assessed. The short-term costs depend on what costs are counted in or lost in other figures. But at least one tradition of British government is occasional open self-criticism by Parliamentary scrutiny of expenditure. Two admirably clear reports on the sale of the water authorities were published in 1992, one by the Committee of Public Accounts of the House of Commons and the other from the National Audit Office.* The serious student of privatization on the asset-sale/flotation method should probably get both: one includes the Commons Committee examination of civil service and other witnesses, and the other shows what Whitehall's own internal auditors made of their behind-the-scenes review of the way the DoE handled the sale. The Commons Committee conclusions are more concerned with lessons for the future than are those of the Audit Office report, but the latter includes appendices on K-setting methodology, and proceeds and costs of other recent government share sales.

On the cost of all this a distinction needs to be made between the cost of the privatization process and the issue of how much the government received for selling the assets. Taking the former, net costs to the DoE, excluding departmental staff costs, VAT and stamp duty, were £131 million, some 2.5 per cent of gross proceeds. The costs to the water authorities and companies, again largely excluding staff and other internal costs, were £176 million. The external costs to the DoE and the water industry were thus in excess of £300 million, and there is no knowing the scale of the internal costs that were involved.

On the broader issue of how much the government received from the sale, the 1988–9 accounts of the water authorities show the net book value of assets at £8.7 billion in terms of historic costs and £34.5 billion in terms of current costs. There is a significant contrast between the lack of clout the water authority chairmen had through 1985–7, and the very strong position that the actual approach of flotation put them in. They not only pushed ministers into conceding scope for 'pass-through' beyond the plain price-cap formula of RPI + K. They also gained: tax allowances of £7.7 billion for the new companies; write-off of £5.2 billion of National Loans Fund (NLF) debts; and a cash injection of £1.5 billion.

* 7th Report (1992–3 session of Parliament), *Sale of the Water Authorities in England and Wales*, and *Department of the Environment: Sale of the Water Authorities in England and Wales*.

Questioned about these arrangements, the DoE said that the cash injection was necessary to make the industry floatable at all due to its capital investment commitments. The debt write-off was said to be required because NLF loans cannot be made to private companies. On the tax concession, the Exchequer might get back in future more than this amount in tax revenue, but the Inland Revenue would not get any tax for about seventeen years.*

Thus the final net proceeds were £3.6 billion, notably below the £5 billion or more often mentioned earlier as estimated or expected. The negotiations with the water authority chairmen contributed to this:

By the time their final week was reached, the Department [DoE] had still not settled terms with the chairmen and the 10 new companies, who knew the deadline to which the companies were working. In this final week, the cash injection rose to £1.1 billion, and the illustrative net proceeds fell from £5.7 billion to £4.4 billion . . . the Department had not been able to set any benchmarks for what they were aiming to raise by the sale. They told us that 'illustrative net proceeds' which they had calculated were not meant to imply that this much money could actually be raised. And in the event it was not . . .†

Both the Audit Office report and that from the Commons Committee of Public Accounts draw attention to the several different objectives that government had in this whole process of privatization, some of them conflicting at times. They also recognize the unprecedented nature of the task, with ten utility monopolies to float together after years of restricted investment, with obligations now to spend £24 billion in ten years in order to catch up.

So, in one way, the flotation was the end of a heroic effort, and in narrow terms, it had a successful outcome. The companies were all floated. But, in another way, it was just a beginning, both in terms of all that the companies still had to do, and of their relationships with the NRA, OFWAT and the DWI, as these regulators took up their tasks too.

---

* Commons Committee, 7th Report, op. cit., p. ix.
† Ibid., p. x.

Chapter 7

New Agency, New Setting

The launch of the NRA was very different from that of the privatized utilities. For the utilities, the single dramatic event of flotation of the shares of each company on the stock market was the key hurdle. Once that was passed, a sort of honeymoon period began. Ties to the Whitehall financial constraints were all ended, yet the economic regulator, OFWAT would take time to get into its stride. Indeed, the important price-cap numbers, the so-called K factors, had already been set by ministers for at least five years, and provisionally for ten.

Moreover, the utility companies were in significant ways much as they were before. They might see themselves, or wish to be seen, as embodying a new spirit of commercial drive or devotion to consumer satisfaction, but in practice they had some four-fifths or more of their previous personnel still working for them, at much the same tasks. They would be still serving exactly the same regional areas as before, mostly from the same buildings, largely perhaps without even moving their desks. Repeatedly in this book the influence of continuity is stressed: that is what is expected of utilities, so it is no criticism here to recognize how it prevailed after flotation. As with the upheaval of 1974, water users who did not read the newspapers would certainly not know of the change from any sign of it in their kitchen, bathroom or high street.

The situation for the NRA was, however, quite different. This was to be a new body, with previously regional river basin functions merged into a new, single national organization that had to cover all of England and Wales (including, for example, pollution control in coastal waters and some defences against coastal as well as inland flooding). The ten units coming together to form the NRA (see Figure 2) each had much the same administrative functions, but both their localized form of governance and

Figure 2: The NRA regions

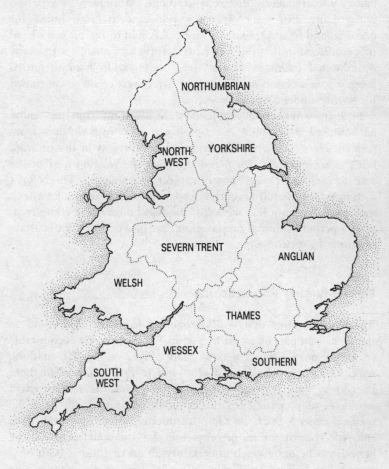

NOTE

Regions under the NRA in 1989–92. Mergers of Wessex and South West regions, and of Northumbrian and Yorkshire regions, have since been carried out during 1993.

the physical differences between the regions (in rainfall, degree of industrialization, mix of farming, and population density, for example) made them individualistic in style and tradition. Posts in charge of the same kind of work tended to be given different names and frequently different gradings. Moreover, in a period when many staff were especially reluctant to move house for personal and financial reasons, the NRA had to recruit for a head office in London that did not exist before, and move staff to new or inherited buildings as the new organization became settled (even if some services such as use of computers could be continued for a while under contract).

In some ways, these problems were more difficult than those encountered in building a completely new organization from scratch. Here, the work demanded continuity, as in the utilities, but the arrangements for achieving it or the relationships of the staff to each other were mostly subject to reshaping. The NRA's assumption of its full executive responsibilities was to take effect, moreover, within a few weeks of the legislation being completed, after a period of formal preparation that proved less than satisfactory in at least two ways.

Unsatisfactory Preparations

The regional units that would together form the NRA had to spend the best part of a year in a sort of limbo, not yet accountable to, or supported by, any new head office, yet finding that the regional authority leadership who still formally controlled them were losing interest in them ahead of the separation amid the extra workload of preparing for flotation. In one sense, this gave the regional units a brief, *de facto* autonomy which they may have enjoyed, at least for its novelty; but, for the staff involved, the period was beset by much uncertainty about the future, both on a personal and group level. The NRAAC was set up about a year before the 'real' NRA could take over; it could not take control of regional units, as already noted, although at a distance it approved organizational proposals for each region.

Among these various issues, the advance planning that was

least well handled – as it seemed at the time and by its consequences – was creating the new head office. One key problem was
how to provide for the NRA's diversity of roles within the
compass of a core HQ of only some 50 posts: yet this limit was
hardly debated in terms of tasks to be covered. The functions to
be developed in policy terms and co-ordinated in managerial and
financial terms included water resources, pollution control and
water quality, flood defence, fisheries and some aspects of recreation, amenity and navigation. But in the event, only two directors
and six senior support staff were appointed (as part of the fifty
members of staff) to handle all technical and operational matters,
including information technology.

About a year later, it was necessary to plan a new structure
with just under 160 staff, coupled with a proposal that the
main head office should move to Bristol, leaving a *pied-à-terre*
in London, as Whitehall would hardly accept that a unit of that
size should be based in London. Needless to say, for such a
significant change of plan, Whitehall called for a very penetrating review by independent consultants (though some extra finance staff were agreed). This review looked at links with regional units as well as the head-office role and workload itself.
The final outcome was approval for all but about three of the
new posts.

Some detail of this episode has been given because it shows the
conflicts involved in government wanting to establish new agencies yet being reluctant to provide them with adequate human or
financial resources. At much the same time, Her Majesty's Inspectorate of Pollution (HMIP) was suffering similar strains. In
the case of the NRA, staffing strains and shortages probably
contributed to the mishandling of purchasing for the move to
Bristol, which became the subject of a highly critical report
from the House of Commons Public Accounts Committee. Thus
in the first two years of the NRA's existence, the executive
directors could hardly settle down as a coherent team either
among themselves or with the regional managers. In stages, two
directors of finance and the chief executive resigned, followed by
the director of corporate affairs, who had been much involved in
the transfer to Bristol.

High-profile Independence

The difficulties just described make the progress achieved in several main policy areas the more remarkable. Following chapters will discuss aspects of this progress, but two features of it need to be mentioned now. First, the river basin functions had taken second place in the all-purpose regional authorities for much of the previous fifteen years, especially because of the secrecy covering pollution control and the complacency about water resources following the successful handling of the drought in 1976. The NRA under Lord Crickhowell's leadership gained new attention for these functions, emphasizing their need to be coherently handled in relation to the water environment. Moreover, the NRA's 'mission' statement and developing house-style committed it to be open in all its tasks as guardian of that water environment. The regional advisory committees were given constructive, positive roles, and Lord Crickhowell drew them into regular regional meetings with the national board. The risk of the NRA seeming a remote body compared to the previous regional units was generally well resisted.

Secondly, the NRA established at once widespread recognition of its independence, both from the privatized companies with which its regional units had been associated in the all-purpose authorities, and from Whitehall. Much of the credit for this must go to Lord Crickhowell, and to his close and confident relationships with Nicholas Ridley as Secretary of State for the Environment, and to other ministers. He showed many signs of using these links fully without being inhibited by them when needing to press necessary, if unwelcome, points.

The establishment of the NRA, however, took place when the climate of opinion was very favourable, giving impetus to the aims it courageously set out to achieve. It was the first environmental agency to be set up at national level since the great surge of public concern about the natural environment gained such spread and influence through the 1980s, following remarkable progress in the 1970s. Probably no one – least of all those most involved in the detailed preparations – really foresaw the implications of this transformation in terms of workload for an agency claiming a role explicitly as 'environmental guardian'. Week by week, committees of Parliament, trade associations, voluntary groups, interests linked to several water sports were making requests that could not just be left without a response. Yet for much of the first eighteen months or so, the material to respond with positive new policies, let alone the time to consult and take account of comments about them, was hardly available. This explained, among other things, some early signs of friction between the NRA and the economic regulator, OFWAT: the NRA was not able to work out all the new strategies and policies for which the need was so pressing. Moreover, work in the ten regions could not stand still.

Public Attitudes

The great increase in public interest in matters environmental is not easy to measure or to evaluate. It may have arisen in part as a result of wider and fuller education, and in part from people having more leisure to devote to the natural scene as the setting for highly energetic or gentler forms of recreation. It may have developed in part from a sense in Britain that congestion was increasing in cities and on motorways and beaches around the coast, with some recognition that pollution tends to build up from it, or that pollution may in turn increase congestion because it makes some natural resources unfit to use. But one rough measure of the growth of public interest is the scale on which the relevant voluntary bodies increased their membership in this period. People were prepared to pay membership fees, however much or little else they contributed in participation and attention.

The older voluntary bodies registered great increases through the 1970s, but then in the 1980s newer ones grew very fast almost from scratch. The older ones, however, were unbowed by this competition and added further to their large gains of the 1970s. Whether there is much overlap in the figures shown in Table 7.1 is hard to assess, but by any standard these voluntary bodies achieved remarkable feats of membership administration as well as of environmental advocacy.

As a shorter indication of the same trend in the USA, the National Wildlife Federation had 2.6 million members in 1971,

Table 7.1 Membership of selected voluntary bodies (000)

Voluntary body	1971	1981	1990
National Trust[1]	278	1,046	2,032
Royal Society for Protection of Birds	98	441	844
Royal Society for Nature Conservation	64	143	250
Ramblers Association	22	37	81
Council for Protection of Rural England	21	29	44
World Wildlife Fund for Nature	12	60	247
Friends of the Earth[1]	1	18	110
Greenpeace (UK)	–	30	372
TOTAL	496	1,804	3,980

NOTE
1. England and Wales only: separate organization for Scotland
Source: The UK Environment

when the Sierra Club and the National Audubon Society had about 220,000 members between them and Greenpeace was just going forward. By 1990, the Wildlife Federation had climbed close to 6 million, Greenpeace to 2 million and the other two organizations to nearly 1.1 million between them: over 9 million in all.

Growth on this scale must reflect among other things the wide range of interests recognizing links with or dependence on the natural environment even within one country. Television and schools were both important additional influences. The environment lends itself to visual presentation in familiar and exotic settings. Teachers grasped the scope that field trips offer even locally to present conventional syllabus subjects in a new way and to point out connections between them. Where better to observe chemistry and biology interacting than the local stream, and then consider what wider influences, from urban development or intensive agriculture, are also reflected in that small stretch of water?

Water Pollution Top of the List

Yet the wide range of professional disciplines, government departments and other interested parties potentially involved in environmental issues has become a source of some hindrance as well as of help. If fewer were involved, they might be easier to consult or co-ordinate, even if the conflicts remained acute. But at least opinion surveys have been helping to indicate how the broader public recognizes the issues deserving priority. The government's own publication, *The UK Environment*, gives for England and Wales diagrams showing the results of surveys in 1989. One sought opinions about the most important environmental problems and the other asked for views concerning where scope for improvement was most needed. Out of thirteen issues presented in both studies, pollution of rivers and seas was placed second, and sewage in seas or beaches fourth in the survey on the 'most important problem', with drinking water seventh. But in the 'scope for improvement' survey, these three issues were placed first, second and third, ahead of all the others.

Some other figures also from *The UK Environment* are relevant to the interpretation of these attitudes. In a survey investigating the reduction of environmental problems through the personal behaviour of individuals, water got no mention save for using phosphate-free washing powder and fewer pesticides in the garden. Thus people see better protection of the water environment as calling for more organized collective effort rather than individual action. Moreover, concern about 'industrial waste in rivers and the sea' was regarded as a serious environmental threat by around 60 per cent of respondents to surveys made between 1983–7 (close to, but usually below, the rating given to waste from nuclear power stations). By 1989–90 it had risen to nearly 80 per cent, the highest rating, and well ahead of nuclear waste.

At much the same time, estimated expenditure on pollution abatement in 1990–91 for the UK was £3,200 million for water, more than spending on reducing air or land pollution, though each of these was over £2,000 million. One reason why this scale of expenditure was not doing more to offset public concern about water in particular must have been that the results take time to come through and gain recognition. These 1989 surveys may have been influenced also by the concentration of critical comment in the privatization debate.

More up-to-date results are available from a survey in September

1991 conducted by OFWAT. This concentrated on opinions about levels of service provided by utility companies to their customers, with some high 'satisfaction' ratings (80 per cent overall, though ratings for reasonable cost and satisfactory taste of tap-water were lower, at 50 and 57 per cent respectively). But it included questions about paying more to achieve environmental improvements.

In the words of the OFWAT summary: 'Customers' views about paying more for improved services are complicated by their attitudes and political views (e.g. "water should be free", and attitudes to privatization, profits and monopolies). There seems to be a greater readiness to pay more for improving rivers and beaches than there is to pay more to improve the appearance of tap water.' Half the people questioned said they would be prepared to pay more to improve rivers and beaches through better sewage treatment. Of those with household incomes over £20,000, 70 per cent said they would pay more; for those with incomes of £10–20,000, the proportion prepared to do that was still 60 per cent; and for households with very low incomes (below £5,000), it was still almost a third, at 32 per cent.

Imaginatively, respondents were also asked about whether they had in the last year walked by rivers, lakes or canals, or swam or engaged in other activities in inland or coastal waters. Two-thirds had been walking by water, though only 16 per cent had been actively involved more directly in or on it. The results showed the more involved as more willing to pay: 62 per cent of the occasional swimmers were ready to pay more, against 47 per cent of the non-swimmers. An age difference may have influenced these figures too: 58 per cent of customers in the survey aged 35–44 were willing to pay more for improving rivers and beaches, compared with 35 per cent among the over-65s. Those buying their homes by mortgages were also more willing than local authority tenants by a similar margin (59 per cent against 39 per cent).

These figures have been quoted in some detail because they illuminate a point where there is often confusion. It is said that the would-be improvers urge improvements with no regard to the consequences in terms of cost. These results show that substantial proportions of customers are prepared to face the costs when the point is explicitly put to them. As one would expect, the responses vary according to the age and economic status of the respondent, but the fact that the positive responses from those with lower incomes were so steadily at or above one-third is also very striking. The increase in public concern about the environment that has grown over three decades is showing real depth and staying-power even if there are still some troughs and peaks from time to time. If the severe recession of the early 1990s has reduced the level of concern again recently, new evidence of natural resources being under strain will soon rebuild it.

The Environmental Movement

Despite the common concern, there have been and still are among environmental groups notable differences of approach to achieving similar objectives, and these differences have themselves been changing. One division, for example, is between the radical and campaigning elements who promote a life-style that is unlikely to recommend itself to more than a small minority, and others who devote most of their effort to persuading others and the building of consensus. Another distinction is how far activists focus on government or the EC as the main engine of change through legislation and its enforcement, or how far they become distrustful of government. In the USA, the environmental movement experienced some changes of attitude in response to lack of confidence in the Reagan administration helping to protect the environment or even taking environmental matters seriously. On this point, some would no doubt regard the formation of the NRA during the Thatcher years as shining like a good deed in a naughty world.

What unites environmental groups and official agencies is the need for efficiency in handling the huge quantity of data that accumulates from any monitoring system that has wide coverage over long periods of time (which systems monitoring water quality or rivers certainly need to have). Friends of the Earth are developing a geographical information system capable of relating a mass of data to the relevant places and activities, and it is working with

the NRA in optimizing uses of this system. Friends of the Earth
are also quite reasonably making the point that, for the public to
gain any benefit, data need presentation and commentary or
explanation to make them into digestible information. A hazard
here, however, is that converting data into information almost
certainly involves selection and omission. How is this to be done
with evident transparency and lack of bias, deliberate or uncon-
scious? Will the availability of all the raw data be enough to build
confidence in what will be, inevitably, an editing process? Much
may depend on the attitudes other voluntary groups besides
Friends of the Earth take about this. In one sense, the environmental movement should not be expected to be tidily co-ordinated:
however, if groups press for different policies in a practical matter
such as public information (and legal requirements still have to be
met), confusion may be wasteful of official and voluntary effort.
Friends of the Earth have helpfully organized one recent meeting
on the 'right to know' in a European context, recognizing that
concealment still has attractions for bureaucrats of all sorts.

The Tragedy of the Commons

In theoretical terms, the problem to be addressed in limiting
environmental damage is how to find long-term methods of sharing resources or natural capacity under conditions in which exclusion (by private ownership, for example) is not readily applicable.
In a celebrated article called 'The Tragedy of the Commons',*
Garett Hardin, a Professor of Biology at the University of California, discusses this situation in relation to population and pollution,
among other instances. He describes it as a problem which has no
technical solution, defining a technical solution as 'one that requires a change only in the techniques of the natural sciences,
demanding little or nothing in the way of change in human values
or ideas of morality'. He contrasts the dominant idea, stemming
from the works of Adam Smith, that an individual who seeks his

---

* In *Science*, vol. 162, December 1968, from an address to the American Association
for the Advancement of Science, Utah State University, June 1968.

own advantage is often 'led by an invisible hand to promote the public interest' with a category of situations where individual interest and public interest are much less likely to coincide.

In Hardin's view, when common pastures were shared, although each commoner might aim to keep as many beasts as possible on the common, constraints such as poaching, disease, shortage of personal capital and even wars usually inhibited the level of actual grazing below the carrying capacity of the common. But any time the situation reached the stage where claims equalled carrying capacity, it would inevitably become unstable, with excess claims in the ascendancy, thereby causing damage by over-grazing. Hardin's proof of this, in bald summary, was that each commoner who could add one beast to graze would do so because he would gain the whole proceeds of rearing and selling that beast while the feeding of it on common pasture would be a cost substantially falling on the other commoners whose cattle would lose some grazing. Thus the individual's calculation of the benefit/cost to him of adding further beasts would be favourable to adding beasts when (and essentially because) much of the cost of keeping them was falling on the rest of the community, though with cumulative damage to the resource capacity of the common through over-grazing.

Hardin's article gives several contemporary applications in the form of free car-parking, over-fishing and the case of the US National Parks where, in the manner of over-grazed commons, excess visitors can ruin the usefulness of the resource they seek to share. Then he turns to pollution:

Here it is not a question of taking something out of the commons, but of putting something in – sewage, or chemical, radioactive and heat wastes into water . . . The calculations of utility are much the same as before. The rational man finds that his share of the cost of the wastes he discharges into the commons is less than the costs of purifying his wastes before releasing them. Since this is true for everyone, we are locked into a system for 'fouling our own nest,' so long as we behave only as independent, rational, free-enterprises.

In Britain we are not exactly in the position that Hardin identifies, but still at risk of slipping back into it. The deterioration in river-water quality through the 1980s was the evidence that the discharge consent system that had applied for some thirty years was no longer enough on its own to limit excess claims on river capacity. As Chapter 11 will show, this inadequacy arose only partly from a lack of clarity and rigour in the consent system itself: another increasing influence was the scale of pollution from diffuse sources less open to control by consents or market instruments than effluent discharges are.

Using the river capacity for waste disposal and other purposes is the equivalent of grazing, an activity which it is to the community's benefit to continue indefinitely but only within well-defined and monitored limits. It would be perverse not to make use of the endless renewal of river flows and the regeneration which the common pasturage offers, but folly to exceed the limits.

One of the differences, of course, between modern water pollution and historic grazing of the commons is that the villagers sharing the commons could readily see who had put beasts to graze on it, and how near capacity this number of beasts was at this or that season. Pollution of rivers is more difficult to limit because its effects are less visible (some of the most harmful effluents do not show up, and some of the less damaging are more conspicuous). Moreover, when overload occurs, it may be virtually impossible to trace all the sources contributing to that, some of them perhaps miles upstream and others more local.

This is why openness and vigilance are crucial to the good operation of sharing within limits. Without these, those who stay carefully within their allocation will not get credit for that and – unless enforcement is vigorous in publicity and prosecutions – those who exceed limits may be hidden from public disapproval.

Finally, the incentives to over-graze the commons as analysed by Hardin show the extent to which sharing river basin resources is not just a matter of curbing externalities which the momentum of the natural regime is always distributing to others. That is, so to speak, an issue special to river pollution. As the discussion in the next chapter turns to water resources, more conventional problems of too many claims pressing on a resource not well enough recognized as subject to scarcity.

Thus the NRA found itself to be a new agency in a new setting where earlier assumptions and policies were less tenable than they had been for their predecessors ten or twenty-five years earlier. Not only had public attitudes changed out of all imagining; so had the pressures of modern communities on river basins, and not just in Britain.

Chapter 8

Water Resources Under Strain

Repeatedly in recent years the spotlight has been on the many forms of water pollution, but equally compelling is the issue of conserving and enhancing natural water resources and river flows: each issue impinges on the other. For the NRA making its first assessment of water resources at the end of the 1980s various factors had to be borne in mind. The adequacy of usable water resources – from surface waters and underground sources – is obviously the foundation on which the multiple uses of water by a community depend. The piped supplies provided by utility companies serve much of these needs but the direct abstraction of raw water by users – for industry, farming, for cooling purposes in electricity generation, and so on – is essential too. Equally, making sure that river flows are sustained at suitable levels is important: the whole ecology, appearance and well-being of the natural environment depend very much on this.

The use of water at work and at home is largely conditioned by habit and the routine operation of plumbing or other fixed facilities. In the home, for example, toilet flushing constitutes, on average, the dominant use. At 32 per cent of domestic usage, it takes nearly double the 17 per cent of water used for baths and showers. The average daily consumption is 140 litres per person, but people living alone may use rather more than this, and each person in a larger household rather less. Clothes washing constitutes about 12 per cent of usage (of all homes some 85 per cent have washing machines), and miscellaneous usage in kitchens and elsewhere accounts for about 35 per cent. Use of water outside the home, such as for car washing and garden watering, is on the annual average hardly more than 3 per cent of the total, but more significant in dry, warm weather, when water is at its costliest to provide.

For two people living in one house, 140 litres each is equal to 60 gallons per day, which, in terms of non-metric weight, is equal to nearly 2 tons a week. This emphasizes the extent to which water supply is essentially a task of transport and distribution – and what a burden fetching this amount of water would be if industrialized nations had only the facilities of many developing countries. It also gives some idea of the volume of waste water to be carried away every day by sewerage. Domestic users may simply not realize the scale of the operation that their water bill has to cover – supplying and collecting a quarter of a ton of waste water every day, providing for the drainage of rain-water, in addition to all the necessary purification processes. Imagine the size of the traffic jam if all this delivery and collection had to be done by road tankers.

With regard to domestic demand for water, especially in view of the increasing strain on water resources, it is worth noting the forecasts and trends in consumption over the past thirty years. British water engineers, perennially fearful of drought or shortage for which they would be blamed more than the weather, have long expected demand for water to go on rising. Logically, household usage could go on rising because, without metering, increased usage costs no more than stable or reduced use. Yet in recent decades total demand has in fact been rising only slowly, and less than the engineers of the 1960s expected.

The WRB, the main agency for monitoring water demand in England and Wales in the 1960s, forecast that, from 12,000 megalitres* per day in 1961 and 15,000 Ml./d. in 1975, 1991/2 consumption would be 21,000 Ml./d., rising to 24,000 Ml./d. by the start of the new century. In the 1970s, the National Water Council lowered these forecasts. But we now know that 1991/92 consumption was hardly more than 17,000 Ml./d. Despite this general slowing of increase in demand, there is a sharp contrast between domestic and industrial usage. From 1975 to 1990, unmetered demand (mostly from domestic usage) did indeed increase by about a third – from around 9,500 Ml./d. to around 12,500 Ml./d. By comparison, the demand from industry and other

* One megalitre is equal to a million litres or a thousand cubic metres, or 220,000 gallons.

95

metered users virtually stood still for fifteen years. At around 4,600–4,800 Ml./d. a year or so before the severe drought of 1976, it fell below 4,000 Ml./d. in the mid-1980s, and by 1990/91, after some upward movement, was still below 4,300 Ml./d. A fall in raw water abstractions by industry was also evident in the same period. From 6,600 Ml./d. in 1974, this volume was down to below 3,700 Ml./d. in 1990/91.

An explanation for these contrasting trends lies in the tendency for industry to recycle water in response to its increasing cost, and, sadly, in the decline of manufacturing generally – perhaps more marked among those businesses that happened to be heavy users of water. But the essential point is that decline in metered (non-household) consumption has been offsetting much of the increase in demand in household usage.

Complacent Attitudes and Excessive Abstraction

One consequence of this apparently lower increase in water demand than had been projected by the engineers and planners was, understandably, a certain complacency. The severe drought of 1976 caused, nation-wide, little of the disruption it brought to South Wales and the south west; recent droughts, more affecting the south east, have led to reservoirs being drawn down and to restrictions on usage, but not to stand-pipes in the street. The current focus on reducing pollution has been helped by the fact that water resources generally have been causing less anxiety.

But within this comforting overall trend, the NRA, as it made its own assessment, identified more serious localized strains on resources. Despite licences for abstraction issued in the 1960s, and not much increased since, it was clear that some rivers had become seriously over-pumped. The early licences had been allocated on the basis of limited data, and had made allowances for additional volumes for the future, within the limits specified. Some river catchments – especially the fragile chalk-stream catchments of the south east, more exposed to the growth in housing and less affected by industrial decline – contained rivers that were at risk of virtually drying up, at least at certain times of the year. Moreover, procedures for minimum acceptable flows to be set by the Secretary of State for the Environment (a provision in the initial legislation for abstraction licensing) had never been called into effect. Individual licences could incorporate limits related to particular seasons or to volumes of river flow prevailing, but these procedures gained almost no public attention compared to more high-profile procedures involving the Secretary of State.

To refocus attention on this neglected issue, the NRA identified twenty rivers whose flows were considerably depleted as a result of grossly excessive abstraction, and twenty more under excessive strain (see Figure 3). One striking feature of this assessment is that more than half a dozen of these rivers are on or around the Welsh border, and about as many again are north of a line from the Wash to the Mersey. So while the south (including Dorset) and east (including Lincolnshire) contain the majority of catchments seriously over-committed by excess abstraction, neither the north nor Wales is wholly free of such problems.

The powers of the NRA to change this situation are limited by law and by practical considerations. Unlike permits for effluent discharges which can be altered or revoked without compensation when two years' notice is given, abstraction licences are seen more as an indefinite property right. They do not guarantee the availability of the volumes licensed, but they can only be varied by negotiated agreement, subject to compensation. In practical terms too, where the excess abstraction is for public supply which consumers have come to rely on, substantial alternative sources have to be found if reductions are to be significant. Transfers of water have their disadvantages (despite the long aqueducts supplying Liverpool, Manchester and Birmingham).

Transfers of sewerage flows can also aggravate problems of low flow locally: in the valley of the River Misbourne, one of the 'top 20' rivers over-committed (by pumping of ground water in this case), waste water from Amersham and several adjacent areas is all carried to a distant sewage works in another catchment. Maybe the people of Amersham might not welcome a sewage works of their own. But, on the other side of the hill, the town of Chesham enjoys a good flow in the River Chess supported by sewage works discharges now upgraded by recent capital spending.

Figure 3: Location of 'top 40' low flows

The Chess and the Misbourne are the only two Chiltern valleys which have sizeable rivers, so taking care of them is all the more important. Sewage treatment is a vital process for putting water back into rivers, but of course the returned water must be of a high quality. Taking less water out of catchments from the outset is an even better policy where the flow is so low that it becomes potentially harmful to people and the ecology of the river.

In a 1993 report on low flows and water resources, the NRA discussed remedies in general and ones that could be applied specifically to the affected catchments in each region. Defining effective remedies within limited areas depends on detailed studies of local hydrology; in some cases, moving existing abstraction points within the same catchment may ease or even solve the problem. Other technical devices such as lining river beds, despite the disruption to the water environment, may prove worthwhile on balance, after a thorough investigation. But in all these cases, achieving a moderation of consumption that enables abstractions to be reduced without requiring large replacement supplies may be the option that offers best value and most benefit for the environment.

Before considering this further, the link between enhancing water resources and making more provision for water-based recreation is worth noting. In the 1950s and 1960s, taking land for new reservoirs usually attracted much opposition. In lowland areas, farming interests often led the resistance and were supported by other local people who disliked major artificial interference in their landscape. In upland areas, objections from amenity groups tended to be strong. Yet with increasing time for leisure and greater personal mobility through car ownership, new reservoirs could be presented as giving more scope for water recreation. Fuller provision of water treatment capacity was replacing the older tradition of buying not only reservoir sites but huge surrounding areas of land in order to exercise control over any activities, including public access, that might generate pollution. Indeed, this is why some water companies are still among the largest land owners in Britain. In the same spirit, the network of narrow canals gained in the 1960s a new future as a facility for recreational boating, as well as retaining their appeal for coarse fishing.

But even proposals for additional water recreation had their opponents – in the wild upland areas especially. The wilderness loses its select appeal as it becomes more accessible to more people. A scheme by South West Water to take water from the River Axe for reservoir storage in an area known as Higher Buckland was objected to by the official Countryside Commission and the voluntary CPRE. Some local people feared this to be a prelude to a more ambitious leisure-park development. Others perhaps were taking a NIMBY ('Not In My Back Yard') attitude; but why should brightly coloured sails or the roar of outboard motors pulling water-skiers intrude into familiar farming land-scape, especially when the proposed reservoir would mainly be providing for water users over a much wider area than the immediate locality? Local people made the point that by making more effective efforts to reduce leakage from the distribution system, the need for more water to be put into supply might be markedly reduced. As economic regulator of the water utility services, OFWAT has been pressing that point too. Even with farmers now being paid not to grow more food and land being 'set aside', a new surge of reservoir building is an unpopular and unlikely prospect, as well as being a very costly solution.

The Emergence of More Positive Policies

Yet even with the departure from the old-style emphasis on creating more reservoirs and transfer schemes where any prospect of water scarcity arises, it took the NRA professionals time to adjust their ideas. In a 1992 discussion document, *NRA Water Resources Development Strategy*, they predicted that most regions would have ample margins in some thirty years' time, but four of them would be on the verge of deficiency, as Table 8.1 shows.

If transfers from regions with surplus to ones with shortage were to be adopted, the NRA discussion document proposed that Wales might help Wessex and Thames. The Vyrnwy reservoir might not be needed to provide extra water for the North West,

Table 8.1 Surplus resources in 2021 as
a percentage of average demand in 2021

Region	Surplus/Deficiency
Northumbrian	62%
Welsh	25%
North West	24%
Yorkshire	15%
Severn-Trent	13%
South West	11%
Thames	1%
Southern	0
Wessex	0
Anglian	1%

Source: *NRA Water Resources Develop-*
ment Strategy, 1992

whereas if it could add to flows in the River Severn, these might
in turn be lifted east to go into the upper reaches of the Thames.
But the control of flows and water quality and the level of re-use
there are already intensive. Possibly some of the central canal
network could help supply the needs of the Thames region too,
even if the Kennet and Avon Canal is likely to remain chronically
short of water. On the eastern side of England, two existing
transfer schemes, one between the Ely Ouse and rivers in Essex
and another between the rivers Trent and Witham, might be
linked into a yet more complex pattern. But making water go
where it is not naturally inclined to go is hardly ever cheap or
without adverse consequences – as underlined by the experience in
southern California to which water is transferred over vast
distances.

Surprisingly, the NRA discussion document went to great
lengths to leave no old idea on the shelf. Transfers by ship were
referred to as having been useful for Gibraltar. Desalination and
the towing of icebergs got a mention, as if they were not complete
fantasy in this context. Possibly the purpose was to show that
nothing had been forgotten (or learned, either); or perhaps it was
to make a set of costly and environmentally questionable transfers
look more plausible than any serious talk of moderating demand.

The document spoke of 'urgent consideration being given to major inter-basin transfers *to satisfy the demands of southern England*' (emphasis added). More confidently, it went on to reassert old attitudes and proposals in defiant fashion:

Major development is expected to be inter-basin transfers where river and/or canal networks are used as much as possible to move water from areas of surplus to areas of need. It is perhaps not surprising that most options are based on those already considered by predecessor bodies but not implemented because anticipated demands did not materialise.

The determined presentation of exclusively supply-side strategies in this NRA discussion document represented a recycling of old thinking that a body claiming to be a guardian of the water environment had no cause to be pleased with. It was ignoring the fact that, if public opinion is to be moved at all towards moderating household usage of water, making it sound as if plenty of water from elsewhere could readily be transferred to the areas of still growing consumption can hardly be helpful. Using water more carefully needs to become a matter which people can see as benefiting their own river basin by subjecting its natural capacity and ecology to less severe strain. Nowadays, that stance can evoke real understanding and support.

There were signs, however, that the backward-looking approach was already losing influence even within the NRA itself. Responding to a statement by OFWAT promoting domestic metering, the NRA had already struck a different note:

The National Rivers Authority today gave its support to the call for metering of domestic water supplies in areas where water resources are under stress and where the development of additional sources of supply would harm the environment. *At the very least*, the NRA would expect to see *a study of the consequences of domestic metering in such areas before being prepared to license new supplies* [emphasis added].*

In a speech to the IWEM in October 1992, entitled 'A Very Precious Resource', Lord Crickhowell, chairman of the NRA, recognized that in some situations new engineering projects such as reservoirs could be beneficial, but he went on: 'Efficient and

* NRA press statement, April 1991.

sustainable water development and use will in future have to take greater account of biological and ecological consequences; and greater emphasis will need to be given to improving the management of existing supplies and infrastructure and to allocating scarce supplies effectively among competing uses.' He reinforced this, moreover, with the direct comment: 'Widespread selective metering is seen by the NRA as having a significant impact on the need for new water resource development and in some circumstances could delay the need for a new project for many years.'

Elsewhere in the same speech he reported that agreement had been reached with Thames Water Utilities on measures to let the River Darent recover its flow (substantial improvements by June 1996; complete achievement of objectives by March 1998). Reducing leakage was also mentioned as a way of helping to protect river flows. Whether or not the water companies liked the main thrust of the speech, it clearly had common ground with similar policies OFWAT was pressing for, despite the impression sometimes given by OFWAT that it is at cross-purposes with the NRA on other issues such as improving water quality.

Further evidence of the NRA's more positive attitude is clearly revealed in *NRA Water Resources Strategy*, which was published in August 1993 along with other NRA strategy documents on water quality, flood defence and several other functions. This identifies the key aim as: managing 'water resources to achieve the right balance between the needs of the environment and those of the abstractors'. Table 8.2 presents the figures on which this aim has been based.

The NRA emphasizes the importance of assessing the availability of surface and ground water in addition to taking account of other uses within the catchment, in order to allocate licences in an objective and consistent fashion. Standards of river flows will be set for environmental reasons and, where necessary, regulations defining minimum acceptable flows enforced. Problems of low flow caused by excessive abstraction already licensed will be resolved by the year 2006, the costs being met by the abstractors responsible, in so far as they can be pressed to do this.

The NRA also commits itself to encouraging water companies to use water sensibly and rationally. This will require, in the

Table 8.2   Uses of the water environment

General

Total abstraction licences in force	48,000
Total water abstracted[1]	59,200 Ml./d.[2]
Approximate number of angling licences sold	1,000,000/year
Estimated number of recreational walkers	20,000,000/year
Number of farming units	186,000
Total number of discharge consents in force	110,000

Key water resources statistics

Demand for water varies for each sector of the economy:	
– Public water supply	17,500 Ml./d.
– Industry[3]	5,500 Ml./d.
– Agriculture (including spray irrigation)	500 Ml./d.
– Electricity supply industry	30,350 Ml./d.
Surface area covered by water-supply storage reservoirs	24,000 HA
Total actual abstraction from surface sources (excluding tidal waters)	32,400 Ml./d.
Total actual abstraction from ground-water sources	6,900 Ml./d.
Total actual abstraction from tidal waters	19,900 Ml./d.

NOTES
1. This figure, when compared with recent publications, is higher due to a re-definition of the calculation
2. Megalitres per day (megalitre = 1 million litres)
3. Excluding electricity supply industry

Source: NRA Water Resources Strategy, 1993

NRA's view, reducing leakage to economic levels and implementing selective domestic metering where resources are under stress. In the new water resource strategy, despite its concern with long-term forward planning, the issue of abstraction charges is given less prominence than in the parallel *NRA Water Quality Strategy* (where 'to ensure that dischargers pay the costs of the consequences of their discharges' is the second of two principal aims) published the same year. But charging gets more attention than it received in the 1992 discussion document on resource strategy. The question of how far the NRA may yet have to contribute to capital spending not wholly financed by abstractors is referred to but not resolved – this was an awkward issue when the basic responsibilities of the NRA and its need for borrowing powers were being defined. A few reservoirs are used wholly or mainly for regulating river flows so they can better support abstractions further downstream, but the NRA does not always have owner-ship of such reservoirs, when arguably it should. The new strategy document also recognizes the government's interest in legislating for incentive charging schemes,* and that these are relevant to abstractions as well as discharges.

As the NRA's water resource planning becomes attuned to providing for multiple objectives and not just meeting projected demand that has few or no economic constraints on it, that planning process will have to deal with both supply and demand, interacting like the blades of a pair of scissors. In that context, the new strategy emphasizes the importance of gathering hydrometric data, the relevance of drought, possible climate change and other environmental uncertainties in the future. As demonstrated by the exaggerated forecasts of water consumption made in the 1960s, future demand for water is subject to diverse social and economic trends. So far, we have little experience of the way in which trends of water usage will move in a community made more alert and sensitive to environmental consequences over several decades. In this spirit, the NRA established in July 1993 in its Southern region a new centre for analysing and responding to changes in the usage of and demand for water across all the regions. Often called 'demand management', this is really more a process of understanding changes in demand and the signals that water users give and respond to in the pricing of water according to varying circumstances at local or regional levels.

While the NRA is the body most concerned with water resource management (NRA expenditure on all water resource tasks was around £80 million per year in the first half of the 1990s), the government still has a substantial interest in this policy area, even after privatization. In July 1992, the DoE published a consultation document with a new and constructive emphasis, entitled *Using Water Wisely*. Some of the points it covered were:

---

* That is, incentive charges which create a surplus beyond the cost of water resource management. (See Chapter 11 for the equivalent on the discharge side.)

Reducing leakage OFWAT promotes this by insisting on statistics to be provided for water delivered rather than for water supplied, the traditional measure, often referred to as 'consumption'. The volume not delivered is assessed as 23.7 per cent. One company calculates that each reduction of one per cent in leakage would save it investment costs of £60 million.

Saving water in domestic usage A shower takes about 30 litres per usage, compared to 80 litres or so for a bath, but only one house in four in Britain has a shower. Showers seem to be fitted less well than in the USA, where they are much used and generally highly efficient.

The role of water by-laws As hundreds or even thousands of separate properties are connected to a single distribution system, some safeguards need to be specified and enforced. The initiative in making and revising water by-laws used to rest with the water boards as public authorities, but since their transfer to the private sector this arrangement has been ended. In matters such as lead plumbing, which can be harmful to water quality and people's health, and more routine matters such as the volume of toilet flushes, it is unrealistic for water policies to be too intrusive into private homes or complex landlord/tenant relationships, yet not safe or satisfactory to regard water fittings within each property (and whatever effects they have) as no concern of public policy. The potential hazards of water are mostly less immediate but no less real than those arising from faulty gas or electricity fittings in the home.

Should We Pay by Meter?

As a final matter, the DoE consultation document takes up – gingerly but bravely – the question of how people should pay for water supply and sewerage services provided by what are now private commercial businesses (and regulated monopolies). Arguably the move towards more usage-based bills will be the central issue of water policy in England and Wales in the next few years, and the most contentious; central because this change challenges the whole tradition of the water professionals in dealing with domestic customers; contentious because it has to be applied equitably, especially with regard to consumers on low incomes. The water companies have little experience of billing householders as individual water users rather than just as entries on a local taxation list compiled for another purpose (and since overtaken by change).

In reality, there is a commitment to change but it is hardly being implemented seriously. In 1988, ahead of privatization, as Mrs Thatcher made her own bed of poll-tax pain in place of the old rating system, legislation provided that by the year 2000 charges and bills for water services must cease to be related to rateable value or derivatives of it. This was not an explicit move to metering, and metering every separate household living in flats and all other forms of accommodation would be quite unrealistic for more than reasons of cost. But it was a commitment to end the link with local government taxation, obviously outdated after privatization. Using the new council tax based on property bands (with rebates for many different categories of people) would be an even worse option than the old rateable values.

In the late 1980s, the way was being paved for change by metering trials to be carried out over a number of years in eleven small areas of Britain, involving some 10,000 households, and on the Isle of Wight (an area of special scarcity), involving about 50,000 households. These trials have provided the data for much detailed and useful analysis, though they have also had two shortcomings. There has been little consideration of what other methods of charge might be suitable for properties such as flats not easy to meter: metering is not worth discussing, let alone researching, as an all-or-nothing system. Secondly, while the trials have proceeded, many companies have seemed very detached from gaining more experience of metering for themselves save in the metering of newly built properties (a scattered handful for whom no old-style rateable values are available). Indeed, as the results of the metering trials are fully published, three large companies in the north and west are saying that they will not opt for general metering, while one or two companies in the east and south have a positive commitment to carry it out.

Motivations are not easy to judge from outside, but the inertia of water companies may be reinforced by self-interest. Rate-based bills are paid (sometimes by instalments) in advance of usage; metered bills largely in arrears. Thus the consequences to cash flow of far more metering could be unwelcome to the companies. Again, metering really individualizes customers and their bills, provoking far more queries. But if a town was served by a single greengrocer, would people accept his selling produce by the sack saying that using scales involved more costs and arguments? Water companies may hardly want to bring more administrative problems on themselves by changing to metering, yet, while insisting how costly metering would be, none the less several of them have invested tens of millions of pounds in new, computerized billing systems with little clear gain to customers.

The costs of water metering in England and Wales are influenced by the fact that frost makes external siting of the meter more costly as a suitable below-ground chamber is required. On the other hand, placing meters inside the house may miss much of the leakage within the boundary that is the householder's responsibility. The average costs of installation for 95 per cent of properties are estimated as £165 for internal and £200 for external siting – but it does not follow that each consumer should expect to pay this full cost on an individual basis or as a crude average. The company would get some benefits from metering as it would provide them with better information for controlling the water-supply system. Operating costs of metered charging are put at £19 per household per year more than the present system; nearly £14 of this is attributed to billing, enquiries and customer services. Any new alternative to rate-based charges could likewise have notable setting-up and other costs. New technology may enable costs to be reduced in the future, as may simple experience. One company is reported as liaising with the local electricity utility, also privatized: in some parts of Canada, water and electricity meters are both read in one visit. Some of the English water companies have had to be persuaded by OFWAT even to reduce the much higher standing charges they apply to metered domestic bills compared to rate-based bills.

As to the influence of metered charging on water usage, a key point to consider is the fact that the meter itself is a neutral measuring device. It is tariffs, not meters, that keep bills rising or steady, and the design of tariffs depends both on policy objectives and on the experience and understanding of customer circumstances and responses. While hardly more than 4 per cent of domestic properties are metered, the water utilities in Britain are still getting very little of this experience (the trials outside the Isle of Wight were on a very small scale indeed). Metering, moreover, is accompanied by specific tariffs, which in areas where water resources are under strain would be expected to be different in their graduations for markedly higher consumption from tariffs in areas of continuing plenty. The smaller trial areas outside the Isle of Wight used differing tariff designs to try out some of these possibilities.

The report on the trials shows, as one would expect, a significant effect of familiarization. Complaints and queries grew less as trials progressed. A 1992 OFWAT survey showed that nearly three-quarters of customers in the trial areas now regarded metering as a reasonable system of charging for water services, though this is not a representative national sample, diverse as the areas were. Moreover, the majority of customers had lower bills following metering. Fewer than a quarter were faced with bills 20 per cent or more above their rate-based bills. A joint DoE/OFWAT survey suggested that about 4 per cent could have suffered social or financial hardship as a result of the change to metered charging using specific tariffs.

The impact of metered charging on consumption as reflected in the trials was as follows:

1. Among the 50,000 households on the Isle of Wight, average demand per head fell by 21 per cent.
2. Reductions of about the same scale were evident in leakage and losses from the system.
3. Since 1989, demand shows little sign of climbing back to former levels as metered bills become familiar (whereas it is common

after notable savings have been achieved by special drought publicity and restrictions for demand to revert to earlier levels fairly
quickly).

The nine companies (including four water-only companies)
who took part in these trials can at least feel that they have
contributed greatly to a better understanding by the industry and
by some households of what is involved in charging by usage.
Here the charge for sewerage services is usually based on the
water-supply reading (and a standing charge) to reflect the related
usage of waste-water and disposal services, though other tariff
bases could be considered.

In concluding a review of how water might be paid for, it is
relevant to note that most business premises (many of which are
shops and offices whose usage is comparable with domestic levels)
are coming to be metered and seeing it as greatly in their interest
relative to the system based on the old rateable values of commercial premises. Moreover, among respondents to a small CBI
survey recently commissioned by the NRA, 69 per cent report
water-supply costs as less than one per cent of total business costs,
and 18 per cent as between 1–3 per cent. Among domestic users,
water bills also take generally a lower proportion of household
spending than do bills for electricity and gas, indeed often little
more than one per cent (compare fuel and power, 4 per cent;
alcohol, 7 per cent and transport, 20 per cent). For water-supply
and sewerage services in 1992–3, the average household bill in
England and Wales was £3.26 a week, or £169.56 per year. As a
measure of regional differences, the lowest regional average was
the Thames company's figure of £138.78 per year, and the two
highest figures (among water and sewerage companies) were the
Anglian company at £227.05 and the South West at £227.84.

However much relative efficiency of operation may be reflected
in these last three figures, other influences of locality also bear on
them. The South West figure reflects notably increased capital
spending on better sewerage and sewage disposal, especially along
an extensive coastline much valued for leisure activities and
holiday-making; yet the South West's water-supply charges are
well below those of Anglian. On the other hand, Anglian's high

water-supply costs are due to it covering an area where resources are under strain and where the density of population is lower than in several other regions. The Thames region, by contrast, is exceptionally densely populated, which reduces the company distribution costs. Paradoxically, the Welsh company, with a huge surplus of water resources, and the Anglian company facing scarcity head the list together of regional-average bills for water supply.

Changed attitudes to metering have also become evident in government. In July 1993, as the outcome of the metering trials became known, Tim Yeo, minister of state at the DoE, observed that

rateable values are not a satisfactory basis for charging for water ... The water industry has not managed to demonstrate why council tax bands are fairer and ... clear undertakings were given that the data collected for local authorities would not be used for other purposes ... My own preference is metering. It's the fairest method ... Where supply and resource issues are a factor, metering makes a lot of sense, as the demand figures on the Isle of Wight show.*

Thus the issue of metering returns constructively to the issues of over-abstracted river flows and catchments that occupied this chapter earlier. We live on an island all of which is relatively well watered all year round by global standards, and the total claims we make on that water can yet be moderated to sustainable levels. Indeed, in the long run they have to be. Water is very costly to move about. Moreover, any systems of charging for it which prescribe a fixed payment (related to bands of property values, for instance) paid in advance mean that the scale of individual usage has no effect thereafter on the user's bill. For the 95 per cent of households not metered, each additional gallon – to water the garden, wash the car or have a bath – is virtually given away, as there is no extra charge for it (until charges to all unmetered properties go up in the next year, on the basis of rising *average* consumption).

This is no way for a modern community to make claims on the

* Interview in *Water Bulletin*, 30 July 1993.

river basin resources it depends on while they are being subject to increasing strains from other influences also. Nor is it the right signal for a forward-looking private company in the water sector to give most of its customers.

Chapter 9

The Pleasures of Water

As the opening chapter noted, people hardly think about water from the tap, from public supply, the water they use most often. About waste water going to the sewage works they think even less. But water in the open landscape – even the small ponds seen in many gardens, and larger ones on village greens – has tremendous attraction for everyone. That this is a very deep feeling is clearly and fully confirmed by all that poets have written about water from Spenser's 'Sweet Thames, run softly, till I end my song' (1596) to W. H. Auden's perceptive 'River Profile' (1969) and Ted Hughes's poems about rivers in our own time. Indeed, the River Thames on its own has more than a dozen references in the *Oxford Dictionary of Quotations*. Pepys often travelled on it to meetings, and one of the most impressive stages of Winston Churchill's funeral was on the river in London.

Such practical and symbolic use of rivers, in real life and literature, is moreover not in any way special to London, Britain or Europe. Many cities were founded by rivers because the water would be useful (often the river was also a good defence), and came to realize how attractive it was in an urban setting. The Parliament building in Budapest stands beside the Danube like the British one at Westminster. Bangkok has among the most fascinating of riverside settings provided by the busy Chao Phya; in Paris, Notre Dame looks all the more striking for being on its small island in the midst of the city; the Nile represents almost the history of Egypt; and India has rivers at the heart of its religion. Indeed, in Roman mythology the River Styx was the boundary of the underworld, and bodies were buried with coins to pay the ferryman to carry them across it.

One of the contrasts, however, between the pleasures of water and the major uses of it discussed earlier is that the pleasures either are less dependent on organization, or they can appear so because participation is more casual, less a matter of habit. The idea of classifying pleasures is hardly congenial, but if it is helpful, one categorization might be between the necessarily organized (in clubs or competitive activities such as canoe racing), the individually active or participatory, and the mostly contemplative.

Yet the difficulty of making any such demarcations is revealed as soon as the most obvious water recreation, fishing, is considered. In one way, the lone angler catching coarse fish is almost in the contemplative category, due to the long periods of peace and quiet. Yet the fly-fisherman could be classified as active/participating on an individual basis; whereas match fishing, with pegs neatly set out along the canal bank and anglers arriving by coach or car is essentially competitive and highly organized with strict rules and conventions.

Angling and the Legal Framework of Fisheries

In terms of the river basin, fishing deserves a special place, however, because anglers relate to the river and its natural regime in a very direct way. Consequently they, and others like them, gain a considerable local knowledge and understanding of that regime. They will be alert to changes of temperature, flow and any incidence of pollution. In England and Wales, they are usually involved in more or less formal arrangements for access to the fishery, because riparian rights provide for ownership of the river bed and the fishing, though the running water cannot be owned.

These riparian rights are significant in two ways. First they become a way in which environmental resources are given an 'instream' market value. Salmon fisheries on the River Wye, for example, are auctioned from time to time, generally fetching prices reflecting average annual catches. From ownership, leasing can also develop, and in both cases the transaction may be individual, for a small syndicate, or by a club for all its members. In addition all the anglers, however they come to have their access, have to pay an annual rod licence fee which goes towards financing the work the NRA does to safeguard and enhance the fisheries – work to which individuals and clubs also contribute by employing their own river bailiffs, often the most knowledgeable people about the ecology of the river and its whole regime.

The second significance of riparian rights has long been, and still is, in the relationships they create between river neighbours. These rights go far back to common law relating to property and the law of nuisance, although various modern statutory provisions have been laid on top of them. The basis of the riparian right – subject to qualifications from cases decided on points that gave rise to conflict – is that the owner of the river bed (to the half-way point, unless both banks are in one ownership) is entitled to receive the flow of the river in its natural volume and quality. Precise definition of these natural and necessarily varying characteristics may not be exact or easy to assess, but the concepts provide a sufficiently strong basis for litigation if an upstream neighbour causes significant pollution or loss of flow (for example, by a diversion for irrigation). But the problem, especially in the event of pollution, may still be how to trace the source of the pollution and discover who directly caused it. The Anglers' Co-operative Association continues to maintain an active and effective role in suing polluters on behalf of anglers, usually getting negotiated settlements out of court because the right to compensation is rarely in doubt.

The greater emphasis these days on statutory control of polluting discharges and enforcement of that has reduced the importance of private litigation based on common law, but it has not made it unnecessary. For one thing, even a successful prosecution will not usually provide compensation directly to the anglers. Secondly, one-off incidents of pollution continue to be a serious threat to water quality even though the NRA's record in prosecuting them has been far more effective than that of its predecessors.

Difficult Conflicts to Resolve

However, while these riparian rights remain valid and able to protect anglers in some situations, they have their limitations too. Poaching of fish remains a serious threat, seeming to become more organized and more aggressive in areas and periods of high unemployment. The cost of NRA work to deter this often pushes the fisheries accounts further towards annual deficits than should be the case. A different conflict may arise where two or more forms of recreation are at cross-purposes rather than compatible. On many rivers there are rights of navigation as well as rights to fish. The occasional passing pleasure-boat may not disturb the fishing that much, but long runs of them on busy summer days can be very destructive of the calm on which angling largely depends.

On lakes and reservoirs, noisier, faster types of recreation such as water-skiing can be even more disruptive of quieter ones such as bird-watching and fishing. If the area is large enough, dividing it into zones dedicated to different activities may be possible (provided controls can be enforced, and access denied if necessary). Otherwise, the only scope for reducing conflict may be by allocating different times to the various activities, thereby lessening the disruptive effect of certain activities.

On rivers, however, it is far less easy to create such zones because the river is essentially linear and boating activities largely depend on travelling along it. A contrast in this is evident between the rivers Severn and Wye, which are often not far from each other or from centres of population. The River Severn is managed in orderly and effective ways, including the issuing by the BWB of licences to travel along it on payment of appropriate fees. The BWB is the inland navigation authority responsible for almost all the canal network and some navigable rivers (as the NRA is for the River Thames above the tidal limit, and for one or two other rivers).

By contrast, the River Wye was once navigable, with a navigation authority responsible for it, but that authority ceased to exist many years ago. The paradoxical result is that, unlike most other rivers, while there are rights to navigate along it, at least upstream to Hay-on-Wye, there is no body with the duty of organizing or controlling boating on the river. Because the River Severn is well regulated, the River Wye thus gets more than its fair share of activities such as rafting and canoeing that can be very disruptive to good fishing. At the same time, the interconnected nature of the water environment makes such disruptions hard to prove. When few salmon are caught along the river, for instance, this may be a natural variation in their long journeys to the ocean and back, or a consequence of their being caught at sea accidentally or deliberately in the nets of deep-sea fishing vessels in pursuit of other fish.

Some voluntary organizations put much constructive effort into moderating these problems and conflicts (notably the River Wye Preservation Trust). In the 1970s and 1980s, the Wye River Authority and the Welsh Water Authority in turn took up proposals to revive in one or another form the role of the long-defunct navigation authority for the Wye. However, the view in the relevant government departments was that, even if they regained some role, they probably could not make by-laws for the navigation or enforce them. The NRA has understandably been treating such a can of worms very gingerly. Some local interests suffer from this; others arguably benefit from fewer restrictions than the new controls would impose on them.

Indeed, perhaps the best example of this type of conflict is one that arose in 1990 on the Basingstoke Canal. The issue here was between conservationists and boaters, the latter group having put a huge amount of voluntary effort into restoring the navigation channels which had been left largely derelict. The conservationists, however, wanted the canal declared a site of Special Scientific Interest, which would severely restrict boating, though not rule it out completely. The intriguing point in this conflict was that the conservationists' case rested on features such as the canal having more than a hundred of the 180 water plants known to grow in Britain, and twenty-seven species of dragonfly, far more in both instances than other waterways (the different types of soil and strata through which the canal passes explains the plant variety). Moreover, the Greywell Tunnel at the start of the canal attracts over two thousand bats as winter residents. The boaters countered this with the observation that the canal and especially the tunnel were clearly items of man-made infrastructure, not part of the natural scene. The plants and bats had colonized them; but why should this be accepted as limiting the very activity for which the canal was built?

Such clashes of interest may seem hardly to be part of the pleasures of water, but they have been included here to illustrate two points of wider relevance. First, such instances emphasize the extent to which the sharing of water or access to it, even in the open landscape, depends on the framework of law. This is so because the points at issue (even in the case of pollution) are those of access or exclusion. Short of exercising violence, exclusion depends on some legal process and its enforceability. The conflict is not open to resolution by financial means – for example, by the party claiming exclusive rights granting paid access, because cutting down or excluding the other conflicting activity is its objective.

Secondly, the framework of law increasingly means, in modern times, statute law or legislation which almost always involves government approval or at least support. Yet legislation about recreation is not an easy or attractive task to address politically. Only called for at the stage when conflicts are persistent and severe, it cannot avoid being controversial if it defines some activities as taking precedence over others, which may be excluded as a result.

Amid such competition for inland-water space – even on an island surrounded by water – should more scope for boating and other water recreation be provided? If this is what people want, why should the demand not be matched by increased supply? For some time measures have been taken to help meet demand. In the 1960s, for instance, a new plan for the canals was approved in which many of them were to be kept going for no more than recreational use. In the same period, no new reservoir project had any chance of approval without elaborate provision for as much multiple recreational use as it could bear. Very recently, Eton College has put forward a project to create a man-made rowing lake for their use because the Thames is becoming too crowded.

Limits to Growth?

However, there are both physical and financial limits to such projects. A vivid example of the former is the Kennet and Avon Canal. Built in about the 1840s using a huge amount of manual labour to provide an east–west freight link before the railways got going, it was short of water from the start. Joining the River Kennet flowing east to the Thames and the Avon flowing west away from Bath involved making water and boats cope with some notable changes of contour. This lovely canal was much neglected until volunteers started to restore it in the 1960s. Remarkably, the task was completed by 1990 and honoured by being re-opened by the Queen. The relevant parts of the canal were filled with water for the occasion, although the informal word from the engineers (amid severe drought) was that the canal might be much less full the following week. Such is the strain on water resources in the south of England now, that providing all the water needed even for full seasonal use of this canal may be no longer practicable, whatever the funds available.

Where adequate water is available, the limited season in Britain during which water recreation is really attractive nevertheless constrains the potential annual income that can be expected from it, and, in the peak holiday months of the summer, aggravates the congestion. Activities such as water-skiing take up much space, and much water recreation suffers from crowding rather than benefiting from it. The BWB has assets the construction cost of which was written off decades ago, but, like other infrastructure facilities dealing with water, it faces spending of nearly £70 million on a backlog of priority engineering maintenance work over four years. With earned revenue of just under £30 million (including nearly £3 million from sales of water), achieving any strong financial success is a remote prospect.

Moreover, maintenance is not the only problem. Despite the pleasures people find in Britain's waterways, they also use them as a dump for every kind of litter. Lord Crickhowell made a publicity point of recovering a supermarket trolley or two from the River Thames. The Tidy Britain group took two barges down the canal route from the Midlands to London and picked up three motor-bikes, as well as breaking a rudder on a discarded sofa. Worst of all, each increment of litter only attracts more.

The pleasures of water are thus subject to congestion and pollution just as are its more dominant everyday uses. Moreover, the property developers and civic leaders do not always appreciate 'empty' space, such as a mud-flat which many birds depend on for a meal. Along the river bank in London, from Putney to the Isle of Dogs, and around areas such as Cardiff Bay, investment is directed nowadays to constructing properties with a view of water. Canute wanted to teach his barons that neither he nor they could stop the tides, but the Cardiff Bay Development Corporation plans to do just that, at least in the area it is focusing on. There could be advantages to some derelict urban areas, but, at a cost of nearly £550 million at 1989–90 prices (or £260 million without the proposed barrage), these would be very costly improvements. Even the number of new permanent jobs to be created by the development seems open to dispute, and the ultimate split of costs between private and public funds can hardly be reliably clear until much later.

Public Roles

The encouraging thing about several of the episodes mentioned above is the scale of private voluntary commitment and effort put into them over long periods. The most perplexing issue is what the role of government and public agencies should be. Ideally, any organization of recreational activity should be low-profile, as people seeking leisure want to experience feelings of freedom and to be given the scope to do their own thing as and where they wish. Yet the conflicts show that access needs to be allocated and sometimes rationed if congestion is not to undermine almost everyone's recreational activity, energetic or peaceful. Like other river basin allocations, this almost certainly calls for clear legal frameworks, some rights of free access, and the use of charges and payments where necessary. The government issued a substantial draft Code of Practice for Conservation, Access and Recreation during the passage of the 1989 Water Act, but this was principally to deal with situations where property rights were clearly defined, mostly in the ownership of water utilities, the NRA, or other bodies affected by the Act. This Code put strong emphasis on the need for consultation and liaison, even if Whitehall is often reluctant to provide the necessary levels of staffing consultation requires.

Chapter 10
Pollution from all Sides

While river basin regimes suffer as a result of people drawing too much water from them, they may be further damaged, ironically, by the way communities put it back – adding sewage and all sorts of other waste and effluent. This is not just damaging locally, because the river's capacity to absorb and break down pollutants is limited (especially by the volume of dilution available). It can be damaging downstream as the water sources and amenity of other communities suffer loss of quality. Moreover, when the river reaches the coast, polluted flows from it may contribute to the pollution of bathing waters and beaches, and the general deterioration of the marine environment, as Chapter 3 indicated in the case of the Mediterranean and the Baltic.

As such pollution increases, it may be described as having two effects. First, it tends to make water 'quality-scarce', in the sense of leaving less volume of flow suitable for other quality-sensitive uses, and eroding the ecological health of the river. The uses of water can be classified in some sort of hierarchy, with use for public supply and drinking water at the highest level of quality required, and, say, navigation as hardly sensitive at all to water quality. Where recreation involving body contact with the water, or operating fisheries for human consumption, are included among likely uses, pollution must be prevented. Water quality may also be relevant to irrigation, for example, if the pollutants would be such as to harm crop growth or contaminate the final product. In these and other ways, therefore, pollution with any tendency to persist and travel downstream can actually make water unsuitable for its intended or potential uses. Such uses will be hindered (with accompanying economic loss and reduction of amenity) or other water resources will have to be committed to such uses.

The second effect arises from the fact that, just as water resources are limited, so is the capacity of inland waters and the marine environment to provide longer-term 'sink' capacity for holding wastes of various sorts, most notably those that are persistent and toxic. The marked loss of quality in the Baltic Sea in the last fifty years and the loss of fisheries in the Mediterranean are each signals that pollution has been outrunning for some time the capacity of these seas to absorb it. The fact that much of the pollution is arriving from inflowing rivers shows both the interconnected nature of the water environment and the scope for communities far from the sea nevertheless to be causing extra damage to it. The notion of all the riparian communities on long rivers being neighbours who interact with each other in waste disposal and other polluting activities is not just a sentimental or theoretical concept: it is often a physical and practical problem, with marked economic and social implications.

Three points follow from this set of physical and ecological relationships that often apply over long distances in ways that people may not be able readily to observe or recognize. First, communities need to monitor water quality in appropriately systematic ways in inland and marine settings. If they can do this to more or less consistent standards and classifications, clearer policies can be introduced and put into action more quickly and more effectively. Secondly, there need to be criteria for deciding the total pollution load to be accepted into the relevant waters. The most regular part of this will come from continuing discharges at known points, or so-called 'point-source pollution'. Damage from such effluents can be moderated by treatment processes and retention in lagoons. Permit systems can set limits to the scale and impact of each discharge.

But much pollution arises from less deliberate and more scattered incidents than regular discharges of effluents: from accidents to transport; from a range of activities connected with mining and agriculture, such as the use of certain fertilizers and pesticides; and, for example, from waste disposal on land that may percolate through the strata to contaminate underground water sources. Such influences – wide-ranging as they are – may be grouped under the general label of diffuse pollution. Their diffuse nature, however, certainly does not make them harmless, despite their sometimes accidental nature. So, as a third point, because people increasingly use materials that can damage the water the whole community has to share, they each need to be well informed and careful about the possible consequences of their activities. It is particularly important that awareness of the need to limit pollution be spread through all parts of the community. In cases of toxic and persistent effects, no increments of pollution, however small, can be regarded as routinely acceptable or insignificant. The accumulation in the water environment of many small amounts of pollution can be as much of a hazard as a few large incidents that attract more censure. This is another reason why the concealment of river pollution control for more than thirty years was such a wrong-headed policy.

Surveys of River Quality

Surveys of water quality in rivers, estuaries and canals effectively began for England and Wales in 1970, though an initial survey was conducted in 1958 and not published at the time. Since 1970, they have been conducted at five-year intervals. The making of these surveys and their publication deserve recognition as one of the more positive steps in the early slow improvement of government policies bearing on the water environment. The 1990 survey attracted special attention as its predecessor in 1985 had been the first since 1970 to show lengths of river degraded in quality overtaking those that had improved. Thus a crucial question was how far this worsening trend has been checked. A second consideration was that the legislation for creating the NRA had provided for River Quality Objectives (RQOs) to be set by the Secretary of State. The NRA would then have a statutory duty to ensure that they were achieved within defined time-scales. This 1990 survey was to be the last one before such RQOs were set for the first time.

The main result of the survey was that, while the proportions

123

of inland waters of either 'good' or 'fair' quality were indeed high (at 89 per cent for rivers), the trend of deterioration in river quality overtaking improvement was still prevailing. The scale of changes in five years was striking: 15 per cent of river lengths had been downgraded, and 11 per cent upgraded, so more than a quarter of all lengths registered a change in category of quality (leaving aside changes within each category). Also, in eight out of ten regions, the net changes were relatively small, though about equally divided between four regions improving, four deteriorating.

Against this background of small changes, however, there was marked deterioration in two regions, Thames and South West. Interpretation of this is not easy, as methodology influenced the results in both cases. In the Thames region, over half the changes of category reported are attributable to more extensive monitoring. Yet this may well mean that the deterioration developed before 1985, and was not given due prominence by the limited monitoring on which the survey for that year was based. Another influence, this time well beyond NRA control, was low river flows during the drought that persisted through much of the survey period (and was not confined to these two regions).

These results have two implications. First, complex as it may be and certainly awkward for purposes of public information, the methodology of the survey work and the weather and flow conditions prevailing when local measurements are taken are liable to influence the results of one survey and comparisons with those of others. To that extent, maintaining consistency and seeking greater accuracy may work against each other: assessing water quality is a complex matter of accuracy and statistical procedures, subject to variations which may arise from method as much as from actual change. Hence the defining of RQOs for the future and statutory obligations to ensure they are achieved may be vulnerable to confusion or controversy among those involved. How then is information for politicians or the general public to be made accessible and meaningful?

Secondly, there are notable differences between the two regions manifesting the large changes. Thames is densely populated and intensely developed around a river heavily used for multiple

Table 10.1 Water quality in England and Wales, 1958–90

Former classification 1958–80 surveys

Non-tidal rivers and canals

Class	1958 km.	1958 %	1970 km.	1970 %	1975 km.	1975 %	1980 km.	1980 %
Unpolluted	24,950	72	28,500	74	28,810	75	28,810	75
Doubtful	5,220	15	6,270	17	6,730	17	7,110	18
Poor	2,270	7	1,940	5	1,770	5	2,000	5
Grossly polluted	2,250	6	1,700	4	1,270	3	810	2
TOTAL	34,690		38,400		38,590		38,740	

Tidal rivers

Class	1958 km.	1958 %	1970 km.	1970 %	1975 km.	1975 %	1980 km.	1980 %
Unpolluted	1,160	41	1,380	48	1,360	48	1,410	50
Doubtful	940	32	680	23	780	27	950	34
Poor	400	14	490	17	420	15	220	8
Grossly polluted	360	13	340	12	280	10	220	8
TOTAL	2,850		2,880		2,850		2,800	

New classification 1980–90 surveys

Freshwater rivers and canals

Class	1980[1] km.	1980[1] %	1985 km.	1985 %	1990 km.	1990 %
Good 1a	13,830	34	13,470	33	12,408	29
Good 1b	14,220	35	13,990	34	14,536	34
Fair 2	8,670	21	9,730	24	10,750	25
Poor 3	3,260	8	3,560	9	4,022	9
Bad 4	640	2	650	2	662	2
X	–	–	–	–	39	–
Unclassified[2]	–	–	–	–	17	–
TOTAL	40,630		41,390		42,434	

Estuaries

Class	1980[1] km.	1980[1] %	1985 km.	1985 %	1990 km.	1990 %
Good A	1,870	68	1,860	68	1,805	66
Fair B	620	23	650	24	655	24
Poor C	140	5	130	5	178	7
Bad D	110	4	90	3	84	3
TOTAL	2,730		2,730		2,722	

NOTES
1. For the 1980 survey, results were expressed in two ways: consistently with previous surveys, and on the basis to be adopted in the future
2. Unclassified river

Table 10.2   Length of rivers, canals and estuaries assigned a different quality in 1990

Type of water	Length assigned a higher quality in 1990 from that in 1985 (km.)	Length assigned a lower quality in 1990 from that in 1985 (km.)
Rivers	4,444	5,886
Canals	179	371
Estuaries	18	83

Table 10.3   Percentages of river length changing class, 1980–90

Region	1980 to 1985			1985 to 1990		
	Up	Down	Net	Up	Down	Net
Anglian	21	13	+ 8	9	11	− 2
Northumbria	4	1	+ 3	2	5	− 3
North West[1]	4	12	− 8	7	11	− 4
Severn-Trent	10	7	+ 3	10	9	+ 1
Southern	19	20	− 1	23	16	+ 7
South West	4	45	− 41	18	40	− 22
Thames	15	18	− 3	19	33	− 14
Welsh[1]	22	21	+ 1	20	18	+ 2
Wessex	27	10	+ 17	4	3	+ 1
Yorkshire			+ 2	4	9	− 5
England and Wales	12	14	− 2	11	15	− 4

NOTE
1. Figures for 1980–85 are for both rivers and canals

purposes. The dominant influences may be said broadly to be urban. By contrast, the South West region is more rural, with few large towns, much coastline, and considerable appeal for holiday visitors. In bald terms, the inclusion of this region in the two showing major levels of deterioration suggests strongly that pollution from diffuse sources in agriculture and other activities not special to urban settings is causing more damage to water quality. This indeed may be more difficult to quantify and relate to its sources, and then to reduce, than the more obvious effects of direct discharges from factories and sewage works. This problem is again not special to particular regions: it is showing up as a new

Table 10.4   River quality in 1990 by NRA region

	Good			Fair	Poor	Bad		Total
				Good and Fair			*Poor and Bad*	
Region	1a	1b	2	1a, 1b and 2	3	4	3 and 4	(km.)
Anglian	8	49	35	92	8	0.3	8	4,328
Northumbria	60	26	11	97	3	0.2	3	2,801
North West	45	14	20	79	16	5	21	5,323
Severn-Trent	15	40	32	87	11	2	13	5,721
Southern	23	47	22	92	7	1	8	2,185
South West	17	35	30	82	17	1	18	3,037
Thames	16	45	32	93	7	0.3	7	3,530
Welsh	54	32	8	94	5	1	6	4,647
Wessex	28	32	34	94	5	1	6	2,622
Yorkshire	39	33	14	86	11	3	14	5,767

Sources for Tables 10.1–4: NRA, *The Quality of Rivers, Canals and Estuaries in England and Wales*, December 1991

concern of pollution control agencies in many countries. It is yet another instance or consequence of the propensity of water already mentioned to pick up contamination as it moves through the river basin, its natural territory.

The limitations of these surveys of river-water quality have to be kept in mind, but this subject is so central to this and other chapters that some figures must be quoted here. Tables 10.1–10.4 indicate longer trends since 1958 (subject to changes in categories used), the scale of change 1985–90, and the situation in 1990.

Coming Clean on the Beaches

The regard that millions of people have for water almost certainly comes as much from their identifying it with leisure and relaxation as with its usefulness to them in the kitchen or the bathroom. So now that travel is so much easier than a half-century or more ago, and tourism and holidays have become big business for many places with picturesque settings to draw visitors to them, water sparkling in the sunshine is one of the key attractions – even if full-time exposure to strong sunlight is now being regarded as a possible hazard.

The role of water as a magnet for visitors is of very widespread significance. As Chapter 3 noted, many people who live near the Baltic may nevertheless aim to take their holidays around the Mediterranean. Often coastal areas – such as Cornwall, in Britain, and southern Italy – have much less industry than other areas and fewer alternative sources of employment. Thus attracting visitors, even if many of the extra jobs that creates are only seasonal, becomes more important for these regions. In such cases, questions about whether or not pollution is really damaging hardly need to be asked. Pollution of bathing waters and of beaches by litter, dog excrement and other debris can damage the business prospects of many places that do not have other sources of employment and income to turn to readily. People may accept levels of pollution at work and where they live largely because they are so familiar; but on holiday, in an area for which they have high expectations, they are not so accepting. Tourism is indeed one of the major practical spurs to protecting the local environment.

But tourism has a broad focus. Many people want to go each year to somewhere they have not stayed before, so they seek information about what facilities are on offer. As many holiday brochures become more standardized, so that pictures of Portugal look much the same as those of Greece, people turn to other sources of information too, such as travel agents, newspaper and magazine articles, and so forth. This whole trend, to easier travel, a wider choice of holiday destinations and more concern to make informed choices, has led to two major developments central to the processes of coming clean. Much more effort is being put into reducing the pollution of coastal waters where traditionally sewage was discharged almost in its raw state in the belief that dilution would abate its effect on the environment. Secondly, much more effort is also being put into providing easily accessible information regarding the reduction of pollution in bathing waters and beaches. This is standard-setting and monitoring in its most practical application – producing data that people are keen to have.

The EC made standards for bathing water the subject for one

of their earlier Water Directives (76/160/EEC). This lists nineteen parameters for physical, chemical or microbiological quality, some of which are mandatory requiring compliance while others are only intended as guidelines. The two key ones are total and faecal coliform bacteria, which are related to the presence of sewage discharges (for which treatment facilities may be barely adequate when peak numbers of visitors arrive to stay in caravans and campsites as well as at hotels and guest-houses). Bathing beaches to which the Directive applies have to be designated by the governments of member states, by reference to bathing being traditionally practised there by large numbers of people.

National governments also have to organize the necessary monitoring of water quality to obtain a suitable number of measurements to assess compliance throughout the season. The number of beaches identified for this Directive can be increased each year. Britain has had to add a great many beaches in this way because, perversely, when the Directive first came into force, the British government maintained that only 27 beaches need be considered. Or maybe it was shame at the likely results that prompted this blatant fudging. By 1988, it was recognized that 360 beaches came within the scope of the Directive, and by 1992, 416 (England 365; Wales 51).

The achievement of compliance has also improved, from 56 per cent in 1987 to 78 per cent in 1990 and 1992. Variations in temperature and other natural factors can lead to numbers of beaches being on the borderline; meeting the mandatory standards in one year but not for two years together. An encouraging improvement is evident in three-year results: 57 per cent of beaches in England and Wales had no failures in 1988–90. Only 12 per cent of designated beaches failed in all years of this three-year period.

In the important task of making information accessible, the Marine Conservation Society and the Coastal Anti-Pollution League led the way in Britain by jointly preparing and publishing their *Good Beach Guide*. This was an independent voluntary initiative of real benefit to holiday-makers and many coastal towns – as well as a spur to improvement elsewhere. Since then, the Foundation for Environmental Education in Europe launched

129

in 1987 (with EC sponsorship) a Blue Flag campaign for coastal areas. Non-commercial ports can seek citations in this in a separate category from beaches. For the beaches, the criteria are wider than the specific water-quality parameters of the EC Directive, but compliance with some of the EC requirements is a necessary qualification to take part. Moreover, standards for Blue Flag citations are being progressively tightened in respect of water quality, though deficiencies in the monitoring at some locations may make some of the results open to doubt.

The NRA publishes its own report, *Bathing Water Quality in England and Wales.** This gives far more detailed information than any award scheme (dependent on applications from local communities) could aim to do. It lists more than forty locations where schemes are in progress, and details in the Bathing Water Quality Survey have changed since the report for 1990. Generally, all bathing waters are intended to comply with EC requirements by 1995, but the EC has itself been reviewing the Bathing Waters Directive. The more recent Directive on Urban Waste Waters Treatment (91/271/EEC) will bring improvements generally to present methods of sewage disposal to coastal waters.

The NRA report also includes information published by the EC on comparisons of sampling frequency of coastal waters by member states. The UK is one of only two states achieving the monitoring required of all relevant bathing waters: France, Italy and Greece, which each have between 1,000 and 4,000 sampling points compared with the UK's 453, each have between 60 and 90 areas where sampling is carried out with inadequate frequency. Subject to this and other qualifications on sampling, UK compliance with the mandatory coliform standards of the Directive (by values of '1') is 76 per cent: other member states, with the exception of Germany, have produced results between 85 and 90 per cent, with Ireland in the lead at 97 per cent.

In 1992, the Blue Flag scheme required for the first time compliance with a Directive standard of guideline and those of mandatory status (for coliform bacteria) and in 1993 this applied

* No. 8, report for 1991, published June 1992; no. 11, report for 1992, published May 1993.

to the guideline standard for faecal streptococci too. This tightening of standards for Blue Flag qualification has reduced British participation. In 1991, 63 applications gained 35 citations. In 1992, only 17 beaches were entered. These were all successful, but more than 100 beaches did in fact have water quality of Blue Flag standard. The 1993 results show 20 applications made and gaining citations, but this is still lukewarm in comparison with Greece, Spain and Italy, each having more than 200 beaches with Blue Flag awards in 1993, and France with just under 200. Among countries with more northerly coastlines, Denmark has 122 beaches with awards, Ireland 61, UK 20 and the Netherlands 19. No British non-commercial port even applied.

In Britain, the progress may be confused by the Tidy Britain group (which administers the Blue Flag scheme in Britain) inventing new award schemes for British beaches alone. Their awards may have other useful demarcations, for example between Resort Beach awards, involving twenty-eight land-based criteria, and Rural Beach awards, based on eight land-based features. But these new 'Britain only' awards, also divided into Seaside Awards and Premier Seaside Awards, are more complicated, though requiring lower degrees of compliance with EC Directive standards than the now stricter Blue Flag scheme demands. The land-based criteria are easier to monitor reliably than water-quality criteria, but it can be said also that people are better able to judge land-based facilities for themselves. Thus the new award scheme of the Tidy Britain group has some tendency to play down the factors on which independent reliable information meets a need (though the group also argues that many people on the beach do not really go in the water anyway). In 1992, about 50 beaches gained Seaside Awards in the resort category and another 50 in the rural category, but only 36 beaches in both categories secured awards in the Premier class, more rigorous with regard to water quality (and close to the Blue Flag criteria).

The talk from ministers and others who have encouraged these new awards about them being 'complementary' to Blue Flag assessments is hardly convincing. At best the new scheme is a distraction; at worst it may undermine the interest of British resorts participating in the EC Blue Flag campaign. That could be damaging to British tourist appeal if it happened. As coastal waters around Britain become less polluted as a result of continuing investment in enhancing sewage treatment works near the coast, far more British beaches are already eligible to enter for and achieve the stricter Blue Flag standards.

Moreover, this is not only a matter for visitors from Europe or elsewhere overseas. People living in England and Wales may be asking more sharply what benefits they can expect to see from the greater spending on sewage disposal that drives the domestic bills for water services yet higher. Several hundred cleaner beaches may be a vivid and practical part of the answer to such questions which are relevant to far more families than just those who live near the coast. The value people place on good water quality for recreation and leisure may well be at least as high as the rating they might give to it in use at the workplace or at home. But how cost-benefit studies may deal with the economic worth of water quality for holiday resorts or leisure pursuits will probably continue to be subjective and open to question.

Sludge Disposal

Sludge is the mixture of wastes left after the treatment of sewage and the discharge of the liquid effluent. Again, the key questions concern quality (what is in it?) as well as volume (how much is there to dispose of?). Broadly, the more hazardous the substances discharged to sewers from industrial processes and other sources, the more likely they are to appear in the sludge, and to make it less suitable for disposal to farms. Regarding sewage treatment as a process of rendering discharges less damaging, the sludge is at risk of still containing damaging substances, so where sludge should go becomes an awkward question. One of the purposes of integrated pollution control (to be discussed later) is to ensure that discharges of hazardous substances, where they cannot be eliminated, are well controlled wherever they go.

The basic alternatives for sludge disposal are to land, preferably with benefit to agriculture or other parties as 'solid' waste; by

Table 10.5   Disposal of sewage sludge, 1991 (000 tonnes dry solids)

Region	Farmland	Landfill	Sea	Incineration	Other	Total
Thames	118	0	86	0	23	227
Severn-Trent	65	41	0	29	30	165
Yorkshire	67	28	9	26	0	130
England and Wales	479	108	206	68	84	945
Percentages	51	11	22	7	9	100

Source: Waterfacts, 1992

dumping at sea; or incineration (with appropriate technology and controls to limit air pollution). The Netherlands, one of the few European countries more densely populated than England and Wales, has been experiencing difficulties, as the quality of its sludge (containing more heavy metals, etc.) makes it less suitable for disposal to farm land. The phasing-out of disposal to sea has also been discussed at conferences by countries bordering the North Sea. Indeed, the British government has undertaken to end sludge dumping in the North Sea and elsewhere by the end of 1998. The methods adopted for sludge disposal in 1991 are shown in Table 10.5, with figures for only three regions which together generate more than half the total output of sludge in England and Wales.

Thus Thames will have the largest adjustment to make as disposal to sea is ended, but currently it makes no use of landfill or incineration. In Scotland, almost four times as much sludge is disposed of to sea as to farmland, but that is still only about three-quarters of the disposals to sea from the Thames region.

Through the North Sea conferences – representing a wider meeting of littoral neighbours than the EC does, though there is much overlap between both institutions – the British government is also committed to reduce inputs to the North Sea of specified dangerous substances via rivers and estuaries by 50 per cent between 1985 and 1995. This highlights the importance of continuing to measure these inputs reliably and accurately, as well as of controlling them tightly enough to secure this reduction. The dangerous substances (constituting what is known as the 'Red

List') are those to which IPC is being applied urgently. They include heavy metals such as mercury and cadmium, chlorinated industrial chemicals and solvents, and some pesticides. Polychlorinated biphenyls (or 'PCBs') will be phased out earlier, by decision of the 1990 North Sea Conference, which also agreed to aim to halve the volume of seventeen dangerous substances reaching the North Sea via air pollution.

Pollution from Intensive Farming

Water is polluted by what it picks up and what reaches it from its surroundings, which are basically land and air. Thus land use in general and the methods of intensive agriculture in particular are significant influences on water quality. Moreover, intensive agriculture with its dependence on fertilizers and other chemicals, and with much larger and more intensive holdings of livestock, is an innovation of the last half-century or so. Many of the British still hold to such a bucolic view of farming methods that they possibly find it difficult to see agriculture as posing probably greater threats to the water environment by the nature of its activities than it has ever done before when it was both less specialized and less intensive. Maybe even some farmers find it difficult to come to terms with this, if they see the intensification of farming methods as little more than helping along processes and activities which are basically part of the natural order. The natural order depends on balances being sustained by agricultural practices; intensification distorts them.

Unlike the waste generated by people, the treatment of animal waste is hardly practised anywhere; yet farm livestock widely produce three times the amount of waste that human populations do. Almost all of this is spread in an untreated form on land, so that the chances of pollution from some of it reaching watercourses through rainfall run-off and in other ways obviously increase. The more livestock, the more of their waste to store and spread. Many incidents of pollution arise as a result of slurry and other wastes escaping from store: 12 per cent of reported incidents of pollution arise from agriculture, and there are probably more unreported ones. Animal wastes can be 100 times more polluting than raw sewage, and silage 200 times more so. Some farms may have half a million gallons of slurry towards the end of a winter, a formidable source of potential pollution.

Progressive farmers and MAFF, with its information and advisory services, are trying hard to improve the care and knowledge which farmers apply to working with such hazards. But economic pressures on the profitability of farming hardly help progress in this, and policies of set-aside, in particular, do little to reduce the intensity of use in the remaining areas of land. Intensive stocking also tends to promote the use of more fertilizers, especially nitrogen on grassland. But even the ploughing of long-established pastures may increase nitrates in the soil, which may have some effect on nearby streams or on underground aquifers. One of the initiatives specifically to counter effects of nitrate pollution on underground water (often used for drinking water) has been to designate Nitrate Sensitive Areas, where use of fertilizers is regulated, and Nitrate Advisory Areas, where campaigns to achieve voluntary restraint by farmers are organized. More generally, nitrates along with other substances such as potash and phosphorus can have bad effects on water by enriching nutrients which may lead (especially in stiller waters) to eutrophication and the growth of algae blooms, some of which are toxic.

Because agriculture presents such a threat to water quality, the NRA has changed its tradition of concentrating on discharges as they reach receiving waters. In recent years, it has undertaken visits and inspections at more than 10,000 farms, 60 per cent of them in the South West region. Over 4,300 of this total were found to be already causing pollution or at high risk of doing so. In four regions – North West, Severn-Trent, Anglian and Welsh – the percentage of farms found in this category in the course of visits was between 54 and 69 per cent.

Against such problems, to refer to MAFF promoting the development of Farm Waste Management Plans risks sounding inadequate and bureaucratic. But the structure of farming businesses, with many farmers working alone or with only limited help, and without the range of specialized advice often available to factory managers, makes action to increase awareness of the potential hazards of waste disposal a matter of real value and urgency. MAFF has introduced pilot areas for implementing farm waste plans, which have proved very effective, and the NRA has launched similar plans linked to regulations for the storage of silage, slurry and fuel oil. Over 1,000 farms have already adopted these. The number of major incidents of pollution from farms has fallen substantially in 1991 and 1992.

Fish farming is another artificial and very intensive method of managing food production in water. It has also given rise to problems of pollution beyond the confines of the farms, some of which have occupied inappropriate sites. Where fish farms take a high proportion of river flow through abstraction and discharge points at some distance apart, the river flow may be seriously depleted for a kilometre or more, and, in conditions of low flow, the consequences can be very damaging. In the return effluent, the polluting load – including chemicals and pharmaceuticals used to promote fish growth and health, along with wastes high in phosphorus and nitrogen – can have a strong (and often somewhat uncertain) effect on the water quality of the natural flow it rejoins. Any view on the part of fish-farm customers that the fish are reared under natural conditions resembling the habitats of wild fish is likely, at least in England and Wales, to be widely mistaken.

One source of industrial pollution with links to farming practices (not always within the UK) is effluents discharged from tanneries and woollen mills processing hides and fleeces which have been treated with pesticides or other chemicals in earlier stages. Pesticides also get into watercourses as a result of their use by local authorities in the management of grass verges beside roadways and by British Rail in the maintenance of long strips of land. Disposal of residues of such chemicals to sewers can have bad effects on the very processes on which good sewage treatment depends.

It should be emphasized that these problems are in no way special to Britain. In almost every country, farmers are trying to increase the production of food from whatever land they have, and governments are widely encouraging them to do so. While the use of pesticides may appear helpful for this purpose, experience in rice-growing countries such as Thailand and Indonesia shows that use of general-purpose insecticides may in fact aggravate the pest infestation of tropical rice. The pests and their predators such as spiders are killed, but the pests re-establish themselves more quickly. Japan has caused much misgiving among bodies such as the International Rice Research Group by recently issuing free of charge quantities of pesticides to Cambodia. Cambodia's farmers have little experience in using such chemicals, and no system of controls on their use has been set up there.

Yet the chemicals that Japan has sent to Cambodia are banned from use in Indonesia. They can also be toxic for fish and crabs, which often form an important source of protein in the diet of villagers. Responding to criticism of this very two-edged gift, Japanese spokesmen say that they have given a smaller range and quantity of pesticides than they first had in mind. Whether this is capitalism trying to establish new markets for the products of the chemical industry, or real generosity to help a long-suffering and poor neighbour country in south-east Asia, it is very ill-judged. The worst feature of it is perhaps that the Japanese must know they do not have to cope with the consequences of their action – the basis on which so many polluters act against the welfare of other people and the environment as a whole. One shred of comfort to be derived from this very unpleasant episode is that future prosperity will lie very much with the chemical companies doing effective research on less damaging types of products which may achieve the desired results in far more acceptable ways: agricultural biotechnology is beginning to produce biological pesticides and pest-resistant strains of crops.

Pollution of Ground Water

While pollution of rivers and other surface waters is often difficult to identify at first sight, threats to ground water are assuredly invisible. They may arise from substances leaching through the strata from activities far more varied than those of farming. A late 1993 decision on a case of pollution from spillages of perchloroethanes at a tannery near Cambridge shows the difficulties. The pollution began before 1976 and before the underground water was used for public supply. The source was 1.3 miles away, and the standards which made the polluted water not fit for use only came into force later. But even with the main facts not in dispute, the issue of liability was argued through three levels of courts: the water company (and its customers) were granted more than £1 million damages in the Appeal Court, but the recent House of Lords decision held the polluter not liable.

In general, this is not as comforting for polluters as it sounds. For cases based on the law of nuisance, absolute liability still applies as before, with no need to prove negligence, though a 'natural' use of land may still be a defence. But the key new point in the final decision was that the damage must be reasonably foreseeable for absolute liability to be enforced. On the facts of this case, it was judged too remote.

The disturbing feature, however, is that, in relation to groundwater, damage is rarely straightforward to foresee, because pollution and water move slowly through strata over a wide area. Moreover, for a case in nuisance, the damage has to happen and be shown before action can begin. Thus, perversely, the law that now emphasizes damage being foreseeable nevertheless gives no scope for preventive action to be insisted on.

Thus the safeguarding of groundwater from pollution will depend more heavily on rules, powers of entry and liability for funding preventive or remedial work being clearly provided in legislation, and on agencies such as NRA being vigilant with enough local staff for effective enforcement. Industrial lobbies may not like this, but groundwater provides about a third of public supply, and the seriousness of damage to it does not depend on its being foreseeable, even when the judges make liability depend on that.

Pollution from Mineral Extraction

Another example of land use that generates problems of river pollution is mineral extraction and quarrying. Tin mining and china-clay workings contribute to some extent to the problems in the South West region, already noted as prominent in interregional comparisons. Elsewhere, coal mining enjoyed for a long time exemption from the controls by discharge consents that applied to virtually all other industries. Far from government giving a lead in accepting the disciplines of pollution reduction in respect of nationalized industries under its supervision, these privileges were only ended for new discharges in 1983. This was another case of delay suiting ministers left to implement change, as the relevant legislation – with that for the ending of concealment in discharge consents generally – was passed in 1974. Moreover, that decision only ended the exemption for new discharges of mine water; discharges of mine water from before 1983 were not brought under control until 1986. As one present at the DoE meeting in the early 1970s when representatives of the (then) National Coal Board were told of the intention to end their exemptions from river pollution controls, the author of this book still remembers the mixture of grievance and dismay with which they responded to the ending of the privilege. Monopoly in public ownership had made them hardly different in their level of sensitivity from the private mine-owners of the 1920s.

A special difficulty regarding pollution from discharges of mine water is that it is often less damaging while mines are still operating than when they are abandoned. At the closed Wheal Jane tin mine in Cornwall, very severe pollution developed in 1991, and it was doubtful whether anyone other than the NRA could be made to fund the emergency and remedial work needed. Mine discharges including high concentrations of dissolved iron, especially in the form of ferrous sulphate, can produce very damaging effects on the watercourses they reach. The water is turned to a vivid orange colour as the iron is oxidized by the dissolved oxygen in the water and then precipitated as hydrated ferric oxides. As a result, the stream is likely to become devoid of fish as well as wretched in appearance, the river bed being coated with iron oxides and unsuitable to support the organisms on which fish depend for food.

In the Yorkshire region alone – before the list of extra mine closures now threatened or being implemented – 36 significant discharges from disused coal mine workings were polluting some 40 km. of river. Techniques are certainly available to deal with effluents from working mines and, finance apart, these could be applied to some of the problems arising from abandoned ones. In 1981 a special commission on coal and the environment, led by Lord Flowers, made two constructive recommendations. First, discharges from old mines already closed should be regarded as a form of dereliction, for which remedies would be funded by central government (which had owned and operated most of the mines for part or all of the preceding thirty-four years). Secondly, when future closures were decided on, British Coal should assess and provide for the costs of taking action necessary to prevent or remedy potential pollution arising from the closures.

Amid recent widespread concern about mine closures threatening the economic and social welfare of mining villages, there may have been understandably little emphasis on the threat to the local landscape and streams. Yet if many of the miners may not find regular employment again, the setting for so much enforced leisure certainly deserves attention. The Coal Board had indeed done much good work in the 1960s and 1970s in lowering and grassing over the contours of colliery waste tips which had long overshadowed the windows of many houses in mining villages. But the Coal Board nevertheless continued to hang on to its privileged exemption from water pollution controls until well into the 1980s. Even then, the problems of pollution from already abandoned mine workings were not seriously addressed.

An underlying difficulty in pollution from mineral working and quarries is that such industries use the natural environment very directly – as farmers do. Thus it may seem that the pollution arises from the mineral composition of the land being mined or quarried rather than as a result of interference with the land. But a relevant test is whether the activity has consequences that go beyond leaving the natural environment undisturbed. If it does, those who conduct the activity must surely be brought to accept fuller liability for the consequences of their own actions. As environmental understanding grows, alibis such as not intending to bring about the results that occurred, or failing to foresee them, become less and less acceptable, especially in areas where good water is becoming scarce and many activities crowded together. Many incidents of pollution take place because of lack of care and planning.

Polluting Incidents

'Organized pollution' may seem an inappropriate term, but communities have always had liquid wastes to dispose of and rivers and coastal waters have always offered some natural capacity to absorb and purify them through dilution. The really awkward problem in practice is keeping the total load of pollution within acceptable limits, when there is such a wide range of people, companies and activities ready to contribute to it, deliberately or accidentally. Regular dischargers, subject to control by consents, fall into the 'organized' category, because they can be identified as discharging at known places. More difficult in terms of control or prevention are the unpredictable incidents of pollution, that may happen anywhere and at any time.

As previously mentioned, such pollution is often called 'diffuse' or 'non-point', as such incidents are scattered. They are diverse, too, some with sudden effects, the rest generally slower. Sudden pollution arises from accidents such as spillages and leakages from industrial processes or storage, or accidents to road tankers and mishaps during fire fighting or other emergencies. It may happen close to watercourses so that the polluting substances readily reach the water, or further away where rainfall drains may carry the pollution to a stream. An example from a few years ago is the fire at the Sandoz chemical plant in Switzerland, where fire-fighting action flushed much pollution into the River Rhine and some Dutch towns far downstream had to close their incoming water supply. The Swiss and the Dutch had hardly thought of themselves as neighbours in this way.

Soon after the NRA was launched, a real effort was made to arrest the upward trend of polluting incidents in England and Wales, which had been very marked during the 1980s. Between 1981 and 1989, the total number of reported incidents of pollution more than doubled, from 12,600 to 25,500. This increase reflects greater public alertness to pollution, although some incidents were counted twice. By 1992, 31,680 incidents were reported, of which 23,331 were confirmed, an increase of 4 per cent on the confirmed figure for the previous year. The rising trend still persists, but the rise is slowing.

141

Some 28 per cent of confirmed incidents occurred in relation to water and sewerage services, many of them from combined sewage and rainfall overflows; incidents which could be reduced by improving the capacity or operation of sewerage networks. Another 26 per cent involved leakage from industrial processes, storage or the use of fuel oil. These incidents are increasing, with diesel identified as the most common type of oil involved, the Severn-Trent, Thames and Anglian as the regions most affected.

The figures are more revealing for 'major' incidents. At just under 390 in 1991 and 1992, these have been reduced by more than 40 per cent from the years just before that. The other striking outcome of the NRA's efforts was that it made 297 prosecutions against those responsible for incidents of pollution occurring in 1992, and secured convictions in 290 of these cases. Fines imposed for these offences were mostly below £15,000. Magistrates courts may impose fines up to £20,000 now (compared to £2,000 under earlier legislation) but Crown courts have no limits to the fines they can issue.

Pursuing figures for incidents of pollution and their prosecution may not seem a matter of priority, but, although greatly reduced in 1991 and 1992, major incidents are still taking place at the rate of more than one every day each year. Such figures may be taken as a sign of how crowded the country is, or of how vulnerable rivers are to the consequences of the unexpected or of careless behaviour in a community committed to modern industry and agriculture. The South West region (already prominent as showing marked deterioration in river quality) had an incident of farm pollution in 1991 for every 4 km. of river (compared to other regions having averages no worse than one in 10 km.). In 1991, Southern region had the highest density of oil-related incidents, also averaging one for every 4 km. of river, but in 1992 these were very greatly reduced. In several other regions, however, they rose markedly. Tables 10.6 and 10.7 show the sources and regional distribution of all substantiated incidents of pollution in 1992 and of major incidents in 1991 and 1992.

Table 10.6 Total number of substantiated incidents of pollution by pollution source category, 1992

Region	Agricultural	Industrial	Sewage and water	Other	Total	Percent
Anglian	283	584	657	938	2,462	11
Northumbria	51	169	457	441	1,118	5
North West	417	279	1,051	1,523	3,270	14
Severn-Trent	320	715	961	2,424	4,420	19
Southern	71	236	446	336	1,089	5
South West	686	434	730	968	2,818	12
Thames	91	351	373	1,140	1,955	8
Welsh	446	864	858	630	2,798	12
Wessex	225	219	289	727	1,460	6
Yorkshire	180	658	598	505	1,941	8
TOTAL	2,770	4,509	6,420	9,632	23,331	100
Percent	12	19	28	41	100	

Table 10.7 Total number of category 1 (major substantiated incidents of pollution) by pollution source category, 1991 and 1992

Region	Farm		Industrial		Sewage and water		Other		Total		Percent	
	1991	1992	1991	1992	1991	1992	1991[1]	1992	1991	1992	1991	1992
Anglian	3	3	4	6	1	1	3	8	11	18	3	5
Northumbria	5	1	2	2	6	2	5	4	18	9	5	2
North West	10	10	11	9	17	19	18	23	56	61	15	16
Severn–Trent	27	17	35	43	23	15	37	76	122	151	32	39
Southern	3	1	2	1	0	4	2	1	7	7	2	2
South West	25	13	4	7	6	9	13	6	48	35	12	9
Thames	2	0	1	3	1	1	7	0	11	4	3	1
Welsh	4	10	4	5	4	5	3	8	15	28	4	7
Wessex	3	7	1	4	0	7	5	6	9	24	2	6
Yorkshire	17	5	19	22	38	16	15	8	89	51	23	13
TOTAL	99	67	83	102	96	79	108	140	386	388	101	100
Percent	26	17	22	26	24	20	28	36	100	100		

NOTE

1. Including incidents of pollution by oil

Source for Tables 10.6 and 10.7: NRA, Water Pollution Incidents in England and Wales, no. 13, report for 1992, published September 1993

Chapter 11

Struggling to Limit Pollution

The sources of pollution threatening water quality are wide-ranging and diverse, as the previous chapter showed. Equally, despite many of them being in some sense unintended or accidental, these polluting activities are exacerbated by the use of modern technology and by the market economy. Thus those seeking to limit or reduce pollution often find themselves in the situation of climbing up a downward-moving escalator, which is itself accelerating. The public agencies charged with controlling water pollution have to work very hard not just to stand still, but to prevent the situation getting worse.

This problem is now recognized more clearly than it was twenty years ago. But one of the difficulties is that, when the government responds to evidence of deterioration by proposing new agencies and new laws, the first effect is often uncertainty and a focus on reorganization, whatever advantages may follow later for the real task of pollution control. Moreover, pollution involves thousands of vested interests in all types of businesses (and their trade associations): they have to improve their supervision of effluent discharge to some extent if pollution is to be reversed. Even when such interested parties do not resist change, believing it to be unnecessary in their case (implying that the relevant effort to achieve change must all be made by others, or not made at all), they understandably require time to make the necessary adaptation. They generally have other pressing problems to attend to, and giving more attention to waste disposal rarely seems a high priority. The EC has been notable for the long time it has usually taken in settling the terms of its Water Directives and for the further long period before implementation is mandatory. Even then, less than complete compliance is tolerated as long as progress towards it is being made with real commitment.

This is, in effect, an issue of momentum and motivation. The accelerating growth of pollution in the aggregate has to be arrested at least to the point where measures to constrain or prevent it can get into the lead and hold it – by a reliable, even if small, margin. In England and Wales, surveys of river-water quality conducted between 1958 and 1980 suggested that this was being achieved. However, as the previous chapter described, similar surveys in 1985 and 1990 indicate the balance tipping the wrong way: the level of deterioration has been overtaking the level of improvement for a decade or more, though now the balance may be changing once more for the better. In so many ways, human communities make progress unsteadily, the bad times alternating with better periods. Unfortunately, in the case of pollution in the closing years of the century, so much of the capacity of the water environment is already committed and being used, in some instances beyond its powers of renewal, while there are currently too few moderating factors to check its momentum. The NRA strategy statement on water quality, published in August 1993, gives a good overview of the NRA's intended policies and remedial actions.

Well-defined limits and obligations are important influences in this context. Bear in mind that no limits, once introduced, should be expected to remain static: as we have seen, all the processes involved consist of interactions between human activities and river basin regimes, together with the marine environment. The speed of the downward-moving escalators that modern communities have to climb to get better water quality is in reality varying unpredictably. Consider also that, as the public generally become aware of this and increasingly concerned about it, they may lose confidence in the quality of tap-water, when generally very successful efforts are being made to sustain it. Or some of them at least may find increasing water bills harder to pay, for example during recession or in retirement. In the South West, the K price-cap factor has been raised from 6.5 per cent, as set initially, to 11.5 per cent for several years. This must seem very burdensome, and back-bench MPs are said to be uneasy as they receive letters of complaint from constituents. Yet the South West has been repeatedly one of the regions most prominent for the deteriorating quality of its river water and its beaches. With the decline of mining and of other local industry having a marked effect on unemployment – not completely offset by the seasonal tourist business – the necessary investment should, arguably, be funded at a national level, rather than leaving an already ailing region to carry the costs entirely by itself. Sewage pollution remains a social and political issue as much as a technical and economic one, even when government no longer operates the sewage service. Moreover, the option of letting pollution stabilize at present levels is hardly available even if some advocate this. The quantity of pollution discharged will gather further momentum unless very positive efforts to change the outputs from point and diffuse sources of pollution are put into effect.

Different Types of Limits on Discharges

Two technical points on how limits on discharges are actually expressed should be briefly noted here. First, limits may be expressed as uniform emission standards (UES) or environmental quality standards (EQS). The uniform standard would say, for a whole nation or region or river basin, that no effluent discharge to water must contain more than, for example, 10 parts per 1,000 of this or that substance. The EQS system would set limits in individual permits for each discharge in its specific location, taking account of the level of dilution available in the river or estuary flow and the quality of water already prevailing there. In economic terms, the EQS system has the advantage of flexibility: if the river can dilute more pollution without ill-effects, it is offering a natural opportunity that the community may reasonably decide to make use of. However, this EQS system may come under pressure when later would-be dischargers want larger shares of capacity that is already reduced by permits granted to others. Moreover, when permits are negotiated individually (and concealed as they were until 1985), a discharger may feel there is little wrong, or little chance of exposure, in frequently breaching the limits.

The second technical difference is in the legal and practical effects of how the limits (in UES and EQS formats) are actually expressed. If the limits are absolute – as for example, the 30 mph speed limit is on roads where it applies – any exceedence of the limit (that is, a statistical measure beyond a limit) is readily recognizable as an offence, though no prosecution may follow. Most statutory limits are expressed in absolute terms because certainty is important for social as well as legal reasons. But limits may be expressed in percentile terms. This has the effect of allowing exceedences of the stated limit for a proportion of a stated period, or, more precisely, in a proportion of the sampling checks made in that period. Percentile limits may be useful in indicating the standard that must be achieved 'on average', or most of the time, which can be significant for measuring continuous discharges of effluent and their impact month after month. However, these limits have the drawback of setting no limit to peak pollution loads in the x per cent of time or samples outside the percentile limits. For example, peak levels of pollution can cause fish to be killed which will not be revived by establishing lower levels of pollution afterwards. Thus a percentile limit applying (say) to 95 per cent of samples may sound almost as tough as an absolute one applying at all times. The key difference, however, is the absence of any limit for some of the time.

A further drawback is the increased difficulty in identifying when an offence (as distinct from an exceedence) is committed. If 5 per cent of samples are allowed to exceed the 95 percentile limits specified in any given period (say twelve months), no single sampling result can be said to show a breach of the permit until it is known whether other samples have failed often enough to use up the quota of allowed exceedences. This depends on the number of samples taken as well as the number failing. Thus uncertainty prevails much of the time: enforcement proceedings cannot begin until results are accumulated to show the full number of samples beyond the limits. For some purposes it is helpful to set absolute and percentile standards together. In any event, EC Water Directives do not prevent local standards being set more tightly where necessary. But to be easily understood by dischargers and the public, and for enforcement procedures such as warnings or prosecutions to be issued appropriately, percentile limits can be very confusing.

A Biased Relaxation of Limits

The use of different ways to express limits helps to explain one of the worst episodes in the government's administration of water pollution controls in recent years. In 1985, ministers finally moved to end the concealment of the findings of the discharge consent system, prevailing since its inception in 1951, and to establish public registers of the discharges, the relevant consents and the sampling results for which Parliament had legislated in 1974. Belated as it was, this could still have represented an important step: a public much more concerned about the natural environment, and water pollution in particular, was for the first time to be offered access to the relevant data. As so much environmental protection depends on the everyday awareness of all sorts of people, this would be an obvious opportunity for a constructive exercise in public information at a suitable moment.

But instead, Whitehall was more worried by the public seeing just how many sewage works were operating illegally beyond their pollution limits. Moreover, much of the poor performance was attributable to restrictions on capital expenditure imposed on the water authorities by Whitehall, or to manning of sewage-works being too sharply reduced. Yet ministers and civil servants chose this time – even after an eleven-year delay – to alter the consents of the larger sewage works operating under absolute numerical limits, so the public could not see the illegalities. The key change, made to consents for sewage works operated by the water authorities and no others, was to substitute percentile limits for the absolute ones. Thus illegality was to be veiled in statistical obscurity. No one could tell without a so-called 'look-up table' showing how many exceedences were allowed out of any given number of samples taken, or without records how many had occurred.

This was a sort of environmental betrayal. It sought to outsmart the public by obfuscating the very facts they were to be given for the first time. Moreover, it had no other countervailing advantages: its only effect was to make the illegal operation of sewage-work discharges less obvious and thereby less embarrassing to the DoE. Indeed, it set back respect for the pollution control system which the NRA would have to rebuild, along with all its other tasks, when it was launched a few years later. Until then, the all-purpose water authorities would not only be poachers and gamekeepers at the same time, but their 'poaching' role, which could no longer be completely concealed, would be obscured by statistics.

This biased relaxation of restrictions came, however, to have a new significance as preparations for privatization gathered pace from 1987 onwards. For flotation, a prospectus would have to be prepared for each company, showing all information would-be investors might regard as material to their decision to invest or not. Thus evidence of recurring illegality in sewage-works discharges could hardly be left unclear. Yet as the change to percentile limits left many of them failing to meet even these lower standards, it could hardly be exposed either. Hence it was decided that the all-purpose authorities should apply for further relaxation of numerical consents sufficient to bring even the poor performance of their troubled sewage works within the bounds of legality. The scale of such breaches – even on the basis of percentile limits – is shown in Table 11.1, reducing between 1986 and 1988 as performance perhaps improved and as consent limits were generally eased.

An independent report of how ministers set about legitimizing this situation was provided by the respected ENDS Report (no. 171):

In 1988, the number of non-complying works fell to 751, or 17 per cent of those with numerical consents. But improvements are not being achieved at anything like the rate necessary to bring all works into compliance by the November deadline. Last November, the DoE therefore encouraged the authorities to apply for relaxed consents, on an interim basis pending completion of improvements or on a long-term basis for smaller sewage works.

[At mid-April 1989] a total of 1,033 applications has been submitted,

Table 11.1 Sewage works in breach of consent

| Water authority | 1986 | | 1988 | |
	No.	%	No.	%
Anglian	309	40	210	27
Northumbrian	37	19	26	15
North West	62	14	43	10
Severn-Trent	179	23	116	16
Southern	54	19	41	15
South West	55	29	68	29
Thames	67	18	60	16
Welsh	112	17	110	15
Wessex	39	14	16	6
Yorkshire	88	23	61	17
TOTAL	1,002	23	751	17

Source: ENDS Report, no. 171, April 1989

but the number is likely to rise well above 1,100 ... The number is significant because the DoE told the authorities in January that the government wished 'to restrict relaxations below 1,000', no doubt because it is keen to avoid embarrassment as the Water Bill continues its passage through Parliament.

The large number of applications will also pose extreme difficulties for HMIPs water branch [the part of DoE dealing with applications] which is short of support staff but must take decisions before August when its work passes to the NRA.

The proportion of sewage works for which relaxations were requested ranged from 3 per cent in the Southern region to 22 per cent in Yorkshire and Thames, and 24 per cent in Anglian (national average, 16 per cent). The ENDS Report quoted industry sources as indicating that applications were even being made (and turned down by Her Majesty's Inspectorate of Pollution [HMIP] where works were not at risk of failing consents – but where relaxations would still be welcome. These were refused as were relaxations in cases where excessive trade effluent loads were being accepted – described as 'taking money fraudulently at the expense of the environment'. Thus, as a part of the DoE due to emerge with a wider gamekeeper role, HMIP had an awkward task to perform. It began imposing absolute limits again, and it agreed with the NRAAC rather than the discharging authorities in arguments about how low those limits should be.

Discharge Consents under Review

Putting the system of discharge consents back on a basis that could command some respect thus became one of the NRA's most urgent tasks as soon as it was launched in 1989. The DoE invited the NRA to get on with this quite independently, on agreed terms of reference. But the Review of Discharge Consents and Compliance had more significance than that. It would be the first review of the discharge consent system since concealment was ended and public registers established, as well as the first open independent review for twenty years. Thus the Compliance Group* could seriously consider the system for the first time as a means of communication and accountability between dischargers, the NRA and all sorts of other interested parties such as anglers, landowners and amenity groups, locally and nationally. Not only the work of the NRA as a pollution control agency but the dischargers themselves would be subject to far more scrutiny.

The Compliance Group's recommendations, which were open to some informal consultation before being settled within six months of the work starting, concentrated on four main matters:

1. The wording of application forms, consents, and the way limits and conditions were expressed, to make them easier to understand and less ambiguous.
2. The limits that consents specify for compliance; absolute limits would be retained as the key controls, plus percentile limits where relevant. Limits on ammonia would be included more widely and consistently.
3. Proposals for more effective sampling and monitoring, including scope for automatic monitoring where practicable (and what

---

* The report of this group (published in July 1990 as *Discharge Consent and Compliance Policy: A Blueprint for the Future*) is often referred to as the Compliance Report or the Kinnersley Report, as the author of this book acted as chairman of the group.

changes in parameters might facilitate that in the longer term). Self-monitoring by dischargers can hardly be relied on as a main method while the courts resist convicting defendant companies on their own evidence, but self-monitoring can be welcome as a real sign of dischargers' being committed to supervise their effluents.

4. The motivation of dischargers, to provide up-to-date information on effluents to the NRA and to allocate clear responsibility for the supervision of discharges to named managers. This could improve internal and external liaison and accountability without making individuals liable to prosecution, rather than the company.

The Compliance Group could only pave the way for improvement in the statistics that NRA inherited about discharges. At the time of the review, the best figure available for the number of consents in operation (at nearly 140,000) turned out to be over 50,000 higher than the total reliably established by mid-1991 at 86,000. Achieving greater accuracy of pollution control data may be seen as a result of there being a single national body focused wholly on river basin functions, replacing ten regional bodies with a dominant interest in water utility services – and perhaps another benefit of the ending of concealment. But it follows, of course, that accuracy and openness require more effort, and more resources in staffing and information technology are needed for that effort to be translated into effective action.

A Positive Commitment from Dischargers

The public agencies concerned with water pollution control and prevention were by no means alone in setting the pace of change or adapting to it in the period when the NRA was being formed. Some very positive support from industrial and other interests was emerging too. The Compliance Group was particularly struck by the constructive responses it received, especially from some leading companies, when the group's provisional conclusions were made open to informal comment. A meeting with such companies (in March 1990) proceeded far better than would have been expected ten or even five years earlier.

In part, this changed spirit was no doubt due to many interested parties feeling more comfortable with the separation of river basin functions – especially pollution control – from the utility ones. In part, the good spirit was due to the fact that participants were from leading and progressive companies rather than from the more numerous laggards whose attitudes were not yet changing greatly. But a third important element lay in the new perceptions about pollution control and its costs. These costs were no longer being seen as an extra burden added to all the other costs of production. As reduction in the generation of waste and methods for suppressing pollution were increasingly built into production processes, the 'extra' costs involved became less and less prominent because other benefits also arose from the changes made. Moreover, while investment in integrated production and pollution control technologies might be for a while the concern of only a minority of companies, nevertheless emphasis on innovation, quality assurance and other influences arising from changing technology and competition were all helping to shorten and speed up investment cycles, and thus the wider integration of pollution control in new production routines.

The DoE had commissioned a study by Ecotec Research and Consulting of Birmingham and Brussels, which reviewed the costs to industry of pollution control in very positive ways (published in August 1989 as the NRA was taking up its full duties, but covering more than water pollution). Among a mass of comparisons between different industries in the UK and between the UK and some European countries, this report estimated financial gains from pollution control to the companies concerned, as well as costs. Nearly 120 companies took part (by interview as well as questionnaire) from seven major industries including engineering, chemicals, metal manufacturing, paper and pulp and food processing. At 1986 prices, the net costs of pollution control were estimated at between 0.3 per cent and 1.4 per cent of turnover. For four out of seven industries, the figure was less than one per cent.

The same sort of practical change was evident elsewhere. A leading chemical company had installed at one of its plants a new control room with sophisticated technology monitoring and transmitting to central control displays most or all of the key production processes operating in the plant. Thus any process showing irregularities could be picked up, and the relevant operating staff alerted. The company found that this improved production performance in various ways that made its installation all worthwhile. The notable feature, however, was the company had included effluent discharges from the plant as a process with much the same scope for central monitoring as the production processes. The extra cost was relatively modest: the gain in supervision of any variations in the discharges and what was giving rise to them was considerable. This is pollution control rising from its status as a neglected 'add-on' to be of equal concern as quality or cost control.

In this positive vein, one other incident also deserves notice here. Following a severe spillage from an oil pipeline in the River Mersey in 1990, Shell UK was fined £1 million, after pleading guilty. The judge observed that, but for the company's public-spirited record in many other areas, he would have imposed an even larger penalty. Some months after this, the company arranged a meeting with the NRA chairman to explain that it had thoroughly reviewed some of its pollution control facilities and procedures, with the result that it would be investing an additional £30 million in raising the standards of its processes overall in order to help reduce the level of pollution produced.

It is sometimes suggested that prosecution can only bring more conflict and encourage negative attitudes to prevail. The NRA has hardly any incentive to prosecute save as a last resort, as prosecution is generally a slow and costly process. But, as this episode shows, it can bring constructive results as well as signalling that compliance is being seriously and widely enforced. Directors in company boardrooms need to be aware of this and of the state of their production processes, as do the middle or junior technical staff actually operating the effluent discharges. The Compliance Group's report discussed how such awareness at the highest levels of company management could be fostered. The then managing director of Shell UK also confirmed to the author how the company's reaction to this incident fitted in with promoting greater attention to good operating routines and maintenance of existing plant – and less haste for making extra capital spending the only priority. As a result, the company has gained in efficiency and profitability.

HMIP reports similar experiences in its dealings with integrated pollution control (IPC) in relation to water. Operators of some production processes involving discharges of cadmium are ending them because of more stringent requirements, but others are incorporating new equipment. Cost savings arising from recovery and re-use of metallic cadmium and from reduced water consumption then help to offset the costs of new systems installed. HMIP has been involved also with companies which formulate pesticides, including prescribed substances. Results include minimization of waste production at source and new emphasis on better handling procedures for materials in order to avoid spillages. For the dangerous prescribed substances, every reduction in the generation of waste helps towards achieving a real improvement in standards.

Integrated Pollution Control

IPC includes several interlinking approaches. For substances prescribed as dangerous for disposal to air, land and water, in three separate lists, generation of wastes is to be brought to nil or as close to that as possible. This is to be done by using the 'best available technology not entailing excessive cost' (BATNEEC), and clear guidance about what this means can be provided. More than one 'best' technology may be available and suitable: 'best' essentially means most effective in preventing, reducing or making harmless polluting releases to any medium – land, air or water. 'Available' means able to be obtained, possibly from suppliers overseas if need be – as long as it is regarded as generally accessible. The more sensitive point may be that of cost. The greater the potential damage from polluting releases, the higher the costs may be before they are judged excessive. Lack of profitability of the specific business involved will not affect the judgement on what is excessive. If serious harm from releases is still in prospect after BATNEEC considerations, the permit requested for the process can and probably will be refused. The assessment of BATNEEC may differ, obviously, as between existing and new processes.

As a measure of how long innovations in pollution control take to be adopted and put into operation (never mind becoming fully effective), IPC was put forward as necessary in 1976, in the 5th Report of the RCEP. The emphasis here was on selecting the media in which a hazardous release would be least damaging (the 'best practical environmental option') and on minimizing each release wherever it was going. Ten years later, a Cabinet Office review confirmed the need for IPC. HMIP began to be formed as the executive unit for this in mid-1987; legislation followed in the 1990 Environmental Protection Act; the first processes were brought within IPC in April 1991, and the later stages of the programmes to bring thirty-three processes within it run until late 1995, with applications required by January 1996 – almost twenty years from the date of the RCEP report urguing the necessity for establishing IPC.

HMIP is still (1993) part of DoE, and its staff civil servants linked to ministers. The NRA, which has a fifteen-member board appointed by ministers but is otherwise far more independent. As with the NRA, the arrangements for staffing HMIP have always appeared grudging, though recruitment of suitable technical staff has been difficult – at times because the personnel needed, who are much in demand elsewhere, were offered unrealistically low levels of pay. An initial complement of 199 staff in April 1987 (with 66 posts then unfilled) had only reached 212 (with 40 posts unfilled) a full three years later. In a further two years, nearly a 100 more posts were approved, and by then unfilled posts had been reduced to 26, or less than 10 per cent of total. For five years of progress, this record suggests at least ambivalence among HMIP's departmental masters. When a new agency and system take this long even to get staffed and organized, the periods which it quite rightly allows for adaptation and implementation by the companies to be regulated can make the total time required to get the new system fully under way very long indeed. If the applications for early 1996 take a year or so to work through to approval, those approvals will have been settled (for the first time) a full decade after HMIP was set up.

One other feature of HMIP's work deserves comment here. Under the relevant legislation, applicants can request exclusion of their prescribed processes and authorizations from public registers on grounds of commercial confidentiality. The devotion to secrecy clearly lingers on more strongly among the applicants than within HMIP. Of 67 applications for concealment in 1991–2, 40 were refused in part or wholly, and 3 others withdrawn. Indeed, in their *Practical Guide to Integrated Pollution Control*, the DoE quotes one of the main objectives of IPC: 'to maintain public confidence in the regulatory system through a clear and transparent system that is accessible and easy to understand, and is clear and simple in operation'. A worthy objective indeed, acknowledging the current public concern for effective control of pollution. But can this be the same department that delayed introducing public registers of river discharge consents for eleven years after Parliament legislated for this, and then obscured the compliance of sewage works by changing the relevant consents to percentile standards? Have politicians and civil servants capacity for corporate repentance, and how can one tell whether their welcome new commitment to openness and accessibility is more than skin deep? The total of applications granted concealment may be edging towards 100 by 1996; if non-compliance arises in some of these cases, will that be subject to concealment too? Confidentiality should be made terminable at once if the pollution control required by the authorization becomes deficient.

Purity at the Tap

To ensure rigorous independent supervision of drinking-water standards following privatization, the government provided for a whole new inspectorate to be created (with modest staff numbers of 27 in 1991). The Drinking Water Inspectorate applies standards set for it by legislation: the relevant EC Directive (80/778/EEC) sets maximum allowed concentrations and minimum mandatory concentrations for more than forty parameters and UK regulators add eleven more. Water-supply companies have legal duties to monitor their own supplies, subject to additional independent checks by local authorities and the DWI. In 1991, more than 2.6 million determinations of drinking-water quality were made. Only about 1.6 per cent of these (about 42,000) were found to exceed values set for them (the equivalent percentage for Scotland was 3.1). Standards based on the EC Directive are set for the level of pesticides in drinking water. Of some 450 substances used in pesticides, 34 were identified during 1991 in public water supplies in excess of the relevant standard but still at levels well below those known to be harmful. Of 800,000 samples taken in this context, only 3 per cent exceeded the standard. Applying this measure of drinking-water quality, Scotland did better, recording nil exceedences in 1990.

Innovation lies not only in the formation of the DWI, but in the revolutionizing of the way in which legal requirements are stated and in the refinement of sampling procedure. It is not so long since the legal standards were expressed using words such as 'wholesome' rather than precise limits based on forty or fifty specific parameters. Thus company standards of monitoring have changed from being more rigorous than the law required to having to be even better conducted to match the legal requirements. Part of this change is due to technological advances enabling trace elements to be measured more accurately; part of it is due to action by the World Health Organization and the EC in ensuring that precise numerical limits are increasingly adopted.

The water and sewerage companies seem at times proud of their record in this highly sensitive field and yet disconcerted by the pressures it imposes on them. In October 1991, the chairman of the Severn-Trent company told a conference that the industry would be spending £12 billion by the end of the century on improving the quality of the very few samples that fail to meet standards but that are still judged safe. This may well represent over-investment relative to the risks remaining, but it reflects the chairman's deeper worry that, while drinking water, bathing water and sewage treatment had all improved, public satisfaction with them seemed to have fallen. Amid other influences beyond the industry's control (such as the presence of lead pipes in some houses), he felt the public wanted water to taste and smell better. Chlorine, he suggested, was both the public's guarantee of safety and the reason why it did not like the taste of water.

Another influence to which he may have given less weight than he should is widespread public feeling that polluters are still having a detrimental effect on water quality. The water-supply companies seem not to have made common cause with the NRA (responsible for protecting water quality from all types of pollution) as much as might have been expected.

Yet there is an irony in this state of affairs that preoccupies the water industry so expensively. As tap-water is the subject of massive investment and much more thorough and precise independent monitoring than before, the British have taken to drinking bottled water on a scale hardly imagined earlier. Moreover, they do so at supermarket prices which, litre for litre, costs more than 1,000 times the price of tap-water. At least for some part of the population, this says something about what people are prepared to pay for water with a taste congenial to them – and to carry it home. Among analysts of consumer taste, the sparkling bottled waters are regarded as competing mainly with other soft drinks, while the still ones are bought as alternatives to tap-water. As the market matures, the expectation is that sales of the sparkling water will be more likely to decline. The public confidence in bottled waters does not seem to have been diminished by the contamination that hit Perrier, the market leader with more than a quarter of the UK market. In fact, bottled waters are subject to far less independent monitoring: maybe the illusion that they come almost direct from the spring into the bottle is part of their powerful attraction. The water industry still seems far from sure how, if at all, attitudes to bottled water and tap-water are linked; this might be worth more thorough study than has been so far published.

Charges for Discharges

As households and business premises pay for conventional sewerage services, so industry has to pay extra for discharge of so-called trade effluents to sewers – with a permit system to exclude effluents that damage sewage treatment processes. But for those dischargers given consents to put effluents directly into rivers and coastal waters, access to natural capacity to absorb wastes has been a really free gift: no charges have applied, as if, say, land could be specially rent-free for waste disposal.

Rivers have limited capacity for self-purification, and polluters incur costs to make their discharges match the standards that consents specify. But free use of natural capacity would be logical only if the resulting pollution load were close to nil. The real problem has been old-style attitudes regarding the water environment as a natural asset and sink which even intensive users in industrial countries need not pay for as there is enough of it for all users and it never wears out. Such attitudes were shown to be out of date forty years ago when discharge consents were introduced: and out of touch with reality far longer ago. The need has been to give dischargers the motivation to reduce the loads of pollution for which they seek and hang on to consents: applying annual charges as well as legal consents to direct discharges (the classic carrot as well as stick) is the way to do this, as has long been done for water abstractions (see page 45).

Thus one of the significant changes in the 1989 Water Act little noticed at the time was that it provided for the implementation of charges for discharges. The NRA followed this up and after some consultation, were introducing charges within three years. This was a hectic effort in the circumstances, but it was also severely hobbled. The legislation and its implementation were not only 10–20 years behind the practice of several of the UK's European competitors and neighbours, but they confined the level of charges to such a total as would cover only the cost of administering the discharge consent system and related monitoring. In principle, then, the natural capacity of the river to absorb pollution would still be offered free.

This is not a matter of ignorance. Britain has provided some of the leading consultants in Europe on these matters, often preparing reports for the EC and indeed for the DoE when it shows interest. Mr Ridley's political leanings were clearly sympathetic. But asked privately why he introduced such a weak use of pricing to help reduce river pollution, he claimed that he had to proceed gradually. With other European nations well ahead, inertia in the DoE as well as some resistance from business interests probably contributed to his untypical hesitation. This kind of charging needs to be fully understood, of course, by HMIP and NRA staff who would have to apply it. But how are they to learn if legislation fails even to provide for the style of charging required?

The style of charging required is known as 'incentive charging'. It will recover the costs of running the discharge consent system plus an 'extra' element. The extra element has three purposes. First, it should reflect the value to would-be users of the river's natural capacity to absorb pollution. It makes economic sense that the cost savings they make by discharging authorized levels of pollution should not be free, because in so doing they impose costs on others by limiting alternative uses of the water – the so-called opportunity costs. Secondly, in response to incentive charges being applied at a given level, some dischargers will find it cheaper to reduce the amount of pollution in their discharges, while others will choose to continue as before. This has the great economic advantage of getting companies to make reductions where these can be achieved at lowest cost – information otherwise almost impossible to obtain realistically by independent bodies. Finally, the surplus income that incentive charges produce (over costs of running the system) can be recycled in once-off capital grants to motivate further reductions in pollution-generating processes or activities, from point or diffuse sources. In so far as the grants are focused on point discharges, the dischargers as a group face no extra cost-burden; the element of charge beyond cost-recovery becomes a transfer payment from those who want to go on polluting to those willing to reduce the pollution they generate.

Thus incentive charging is not really a pollution tax, but an inducement to change within a permit system. It is hardly prudent to look towards free trade or auctions in water pollution permits (as the Americans are exploring in the case of air pollution) because discharges to water are far more dependent on a particular location. A given pollution load cannot be switched from an estuary to an upstream length of river with much less flow to dilute it, as if the two locations were much the same.

The RCEP's 16th Report, *Freshwater Quality*, has a substantial chapter on market instruments, including far more comparisons with the German, Dutch and French systems than can be included here. The RCEP acknowledges the case for introduction of changes to be phased, and makes a positive proposal for this:

We recommend that the level of charge should be comparable to those in the Netherlands and Germany. It should be set initially such that the total income generated should be roughly similar to that generated under the NRA's cost recovery scheme, then increased in annual steps according to a published predetermined programme to reach the desired level over a period of five years.*

Some indications have suggested that the government will legislate soon for some progress on these lines, but this seems in doubt now as the resolve of ministers to do anything controversial seems to grow pale. Yet, for them, incentive charging should hardly be radical or awkward to implement. It brings in more powerfully the market forces they favour. Why should anyone be permitted to use the natural capacity of rivers rent-free? Moreover, and more significantly, it moves away from a situation where the legal consent controls of water pollution and the economic factors are pulling in opposite directions – for restraints in the use of capacity that has been offered for so long with no price tag, and is still under-priced. As a check to the accelerating level of pollution, the introduction of incentive charging is urgent now.

Incentive charging would also help OFWAT in its concern about the cost to the water utilities of achieving higher standards of river-water quality. At present, OFWAT tends to argue that all possible improvements must be costed in advance – difficult to assess effectively as knowledge about which of all dischargers (not just sewage works) can achieve reductions of pollution at least cost is so scanty and hard to obtain reliably. Incentive charging, producing surplus income to be recirculated as 'once-off' capital grants, could bring benefits to some sewage works able to offer low-cost reductions, and advantages to OFWAT in opening up the information available about options for improvement and their cost far more successfully than theoretical debate about uncertain cost-benefit calculations ever could. OFWAT could then begin to be far more constructive about environmental

* RCEP 16th Report: paragraphs 8.52 and 8.53 and Recommendation 77.

improvement than its narrow (but understandable) concerns, as they are currently expressed, often make it appear.

River Quality Objectives

Unusually, the government went further than they were pushed in one innovation in the 1989 Water Act. This provided for River Quality Objectives (RQOs) to be set for lengths of river by the Secretary of State, instead of being set informally by NRA or its predecessors. He would do this on advice from NRA and with wide consultation: NRA would then have the explicit duty to secure achievement of the RQOs by stated dates. This would give the NRA's work real and broad extra clout: but it can be seen as DoE also keeping control while NRA took most of the responsibility – especially to find the least-cost routes to the reductions in pollution decided on.

These new powers could be used only to improve or maintain water quality: setting RQOs lower than the status quo was ruled out. But one dilemma was how great an increase in water bills the privatized companies might demand for increased investment in sewage works. Another problem was how to secure reductions in pollution from diffuse sources, often elusive or intractable as already noted: some of these might offer some least-cost reductions.

A sensible intention to introduce statutory RQOs in pilot areas has now become entangled with Europhobic and other worries about the Municipal Wastewater Directive coming into effect. DoE have quoted first £2bn and later £10bn as estimates of what this might cost, when they might have seen both figures as unconvincing. To meet possible RQOs, NRA sees improvement necessary at 131 sewage works at a cost of £700–£800 million. The Directive offers alternative ways of assessing compliance, and the ENDS report (No. 228) suggests that the DoE are now hoping that spending linked to it may be £8bn or less. However, more in the spirit of restricted spending on sewage works in the early 1980s, they are also asking how much achievement of RQOs would result from spending only £250 million.

Before it is complete, this episode shows again how slow practical adaptation is to better environmental protection even after Parliament has legislated good intentions. Repeatedly ministers hesitate to follow through forcing action on new policies (as with the ending of concealment, see page 8). A power similar to that which sets RQOs was given in 1963 to ministers to set Minimum Acceptable Flows to guard against excessive abstraction, and was indeed never used (with consequences noted in Chapter 8). In the role of OFWAT, even an independent regulator does not seem to stop ministers worrying about increased water bills losing them votes. In these ways, privatization seems to have changed remarkably little.

An Environment Agency

The concept of Integrated Pollution Control discussed earlier had not drawn much attention to possible mergers of relevant agencies, but Mr Major as Prime Minister saw the creation of a new Environment Agency (Envage) as possibly giving his election manifesto a green flavour. In July 1991, therefore, he suddenly announced (while opening an exhibition) a decision to do this, with no preparation and less than a week's notice to the agencies involved. The complexities were hardly recognized, and yet more legislation was suddenly projected, in contrast to the hesitations in following through the 1989 Act just described.

Then, much more wisely, long consultation took place about a central issue – should river pollution control be transferred from the NRA to the new agency, largely disrupting the coherence of river basin management as reflecting a natural unity between water resources and water quality? Alternatively, should the whole NRA be merged into the new agency, making it larger and more difficult to manage, with a wider range of environmental concerns? This dilemma was firmly resolved in favour of the second option, so Envage would become a merger of HMIP, the NRA and the waste regulation agencies. HMIP would bring in its fledgling work on IPC and its longer tradition of minimizing pollution in the actual production processes.

The legislation was expected then to be prepared in time for the 1993–4 session of Parliament, but this will now be only a 'paving' Bill leading to full legislation a year or so later. Explanations include the projected volume of 'law and order' legislation and the view that environmental problems are slipping down the political agenda from the 'white heat' they seemed to generate a few years back. Possibly more preparations will be helpful. As both the NRA and HMIP have had such difficult launch periods, any further restructuring of agencies coming so soon will somewhat disrupt the work of each of them just as it begins to proceed more effectively. Moreover, some of the differences of method between them may be handled more positively now. The NRA, at least in its farm visits, has been able to go beyond identifying the discharge point to establishing the real sources of pollution. HMIP may now be accepting that monitoring cannot all be left to operators once the processes are approved (and perhaps that attitude was, in any case, a by-product of extreme staff shortages). More generally, a constructive difference is perhaps developing in that pollution prevention in processes and discharges of all sorts may be seen as at least having a separate thrust from controlling diffuse sources and the monitoring of water quality in inland and coastal waters.

The strains and hazards of this difficult reshaping of pollution control agencies are also being aggravated by so-called 'market-testing', a steam-roller process going through units of government to see how cheaply private companies might do their work on short-term contracts by some form of tendering and notional quality control. At a time of less insecurity and anxiety for NRA and HMIP staff, this might be a good idea, but in a broader sense, this is not the time to press it in environmental regulation. All sorts of dischargers and polluters need to be given chances to understand the control systems and ways of working Envage will establish: IPC itself is still only in course of being introduced up to about 1997 (see page 157). Reduction of pollution often involves investment, taking time to plan and longer still to show results. Moreover, if the legislation provides as it should for incentive charges to be applied to all effluent discharges, staff experienced in the current consent system will need to work closely with suitable consultants in environmental economics to cope with the special tasks of implementing new charges and legal consents in parallel. In regulatory work, both integrity and accountability remain critical. The polluters need to see how policy is developing, and everyone else needs to see that relationships and decisions are open, consistent and well-explained.

The European Community

The EC has made itself one of the most positive influences on the environmental standards and progress of our off-shore island in the last ten years or so. Thus to comment on this at the end of a long chapter, almost in the form of a postscript, risks seeming ungracious and misleading. Yet there are reasons for doing so. The editorial one is that the scale of EC's Water Directives and their impacts and complexities could easily take most of a book rather than part of a single chapter. The deeper reason is that, in several ways, the EC's environmental concerns are much affected by the circumstances and attitudes of governments and peoples in each member state.

As evidence of this, new Directives are prepared with long and careful consultation. Decision on methods of implementation and monitoring are very largely left to member states. The Directives certainly include specific standards which become mandatory from specified dates, but, even so, there is tolerance about delays in achieving full compliance. Repeatedly the British tend to suggest or think that the rules are not enforced elsewhere, but this is hardly so. According to 'Parliamentary Answers', quoted in *Waterfacts*, in the years 1988–90 inclusive, 50 cases came to the European Court of Justice, only 2 of them from the UK. Non-compliance is not passing unregarded. In recent years, France and Spain have carried through major revisions of their water legislation, as Britain has already done for England and Wales, and will likely do for Scotland soon.

In Germany, which already has some of the highest bills for water services among EC member states, some DM 100bn (£40bn) was spent by local authorities on extensions, renewals and upgradings of sewerage and sewage treatment plants. In the next few years, projections suggest another DM 10bn to be spent on this in the former West Germany, and four times that amount in the eastern part now unified. Charges to industry trebled between 1981–91 and may double again by the end of this decade. If Italy makes less progress than this, it may well be due to the limitations and confusions of its public-expenditure and price-control arrangements. The commitment of many of its water professionals to overcome the pollution in the northern Adriatic is very clear, and political and public backing for it is not lacking. The tourist income dependent on reversing present levels of degradation in the marine environment is a significant influence even for the most hard-headed business and civic leaders, and this applies more widely than to just Italy.

The environmental concerns of the EC member states are in effect those of neighbours who have to share the larger rivers and adjacent seas. Aware that the interactions of the environment go beyond sovereign boundaries, each country, while indisposed to sacrifice its own interests, is none the less keen that its neighbours uphold environmental standards – so that no member-state business is exempt from practising 'greener' policies, and no beach from 'coming clean'. As among any group of neighbours, they make fair assessments of each other, as well as harbouring prejudices and forming misjudgements due to lack of information. The part the British government played in dealing with the early stages of the Bathing Waters Directive was hardly likely to show commitment or gain trust. The Urban Waste-water Treatment Directive may well carry the water and sewerage companies in England and Wales further in some respects than they had thought of going. Arguments about specific standards will recur.

The characteristic of pollution is, however, that people and public bodies and companies generate it essentially to the disadvantage of others, who mostly have to put up with the damage and loss of amenity it causes. Where rivers cross political boundaries, as they do in Europe, even sovereign states are in this situation. The EC's work on water and other environmental Directives represents a real attempt to provide external standards to counter this. An island people understandably becomes uneasy at times that its neighbours should be setting standards for it, but this is the essence of a neighbourhood. Moreover, Europe, from the Mediterranean to the Baltic and beyond, has only one environment to share as neighbours. So this is no mere postscript. The EC is a major constructive influence in achieving the transition to better management and conservation of the water environment, but it recognizes that each member state must do for itself most of the adaptation that the transition requires.

Chapter 12

Regulator in Charge?

The Thatcher government busied itself at first with privatizing state-owned units that already were in or could be put into competitive markets as private companies. But, from 1984 onwards, as it came to the big utilities – telecommunications, gas, water and electricity – it had to address issues of monopoly as much as those of privatization. Thus it came to put regulation centre-stage.

The political purpose of regulation was and still is to sanitize the replacement of public monopolies by private ones. Its economic purpose is to discipline the new monopolies while still enabling them to draw in the capital required from private investors on a sustainable basis. In this setting, water supply and sewerage were to prove specially awkward. Yet paradoxically, in water supply a tradition of private monopoly regulated by old-style dividend limitation had been familiar and accepted. As mentioned in Chapter 6, so-called statutory water companies, each operating under their own 'private' Acts of Parliament and supervision by Whitehall, had been providing water supply (but not sewerage services) to nearly a quarter of the population in England and Wales for more than a century.

Why then was new-style regulation of water supply and sewerage as monopolies to be so fraught with difficulty? In principle, it should have been relatively easy because the regulator, though more burdened by having nearly forty companies to regulate, counting ten water and sewerage companies and the water-only companies together, would be able to make comparisons between them and use competition to help improve their performance. Yet these companies are in a capital-intensive service, and one with little volume growth in prospect compared to, say, telecommunications or gas. Moreover, water supply faces increasing problems of defining and meeting quality standards (see page 158 about the work of DWI). As a natural resource dependent on locality, water, even after treatment, is much less of a standard product than a unit of gas or a connected telephone call. Worse than that, for a non-growth industry, huge additional capital investment was required. As Chapter 6 showed, the ministers who launched the flotation had to set not annual price caps below the rate of inflation and push for efficiency gains but price rises regularly above inflation (see Table 6.2 for the detailed figures). In addition, the physical assets of companies providing water and sewerage services – namely, water pipes and sewers – mostly have long working lives and many of them are buried underground. This protects them, but also makes deterioration and leakage somewhat more difficult to observe.

Thus OFWAT has to maintain an elaborate supervision, through selected independent consultants, of the so-called 'asset management plans' of companies and their investment spending. The K factors are only justified by the projected capital pro-grammes: if spending on them falls behind, the K factors or other adjustments governing price increases can and should be clipped back too. This is heavy-weight regulation indeed. It reflects the extreme security the companies have in their area of monopoly from owning all the relevant assets. In the French water-supply industry, about three-quarters of the population are served by large companies operating under local contracts. When a local contract expires, the assets all revert to public ownership, and the executive mayors of local councils – usually in touch with voters as water users – have a major influence on whether or not the company gains a renewal of its franchise. The arrangements in England and Wales provide for appointments to be terminated (on ten years' notice, not to be given before fifteen years have elapsed); but with the assets in company ownership, termination and transfer would be hugely complicated. In this respect, the companies feel very secure in their area of monopoly. Such anxiety as they have about the regulator's powers relates largely to its control over prices for their core services as water utility operators. Even in this context, moreover, they can draw a good deal of comfort from the price caps being set five to ten years ahead, and OFWAT having a specific obligation in the legislation to secure that companies 'are able (in particular by securing reasonable returns on their capital) to finance the proper carrying out of their functions'.*

OFWATching the Water Companies

These arrangements require OFWAT to be in touch with the companies a great deal, getting them to provide a mass of detailed information about their own operations and costs, and consulting them more generally and formally on some issues. As others have observed, this is a costly form of regulation. OFWAT costs are about £6 million a year, with about 130 staff at March 1992. But in total the companies also employ significant numbers of highly qualified staff in regulatory departments to respond to OFWAT and anticipate its next moves.

An example of the progress being made is that OFWAT has moved some of the industry's traditional physical accounting from volumes of water put into supply (15–25 per cent or more of which may be lost before it reaches the boundary of the customers' properties), to volumes of water delivered. In an industry with little metering of domestic users, the losses through leakage should continue to be monitored. Much additional leakage is believed to occur within the user's property, for instance in pipes running through front gardens, which it is the consumer's responsibility to maintain, not the company's. But in the absence of metering, consumers have no incentive to attend to this.

On a larger and more complex issue, OFWAT issued a consultation paper, *The Cost of Capital*, a key issue in a capital-intensive industry now driven by the need to reward investors. To respond to this, the two associations, of water and sewerage companies and of water-only companies, the WSA and WCA joined together to produce a formidably co-ordinated reply, running to 150 pages of main report and nearly 90 pages of largely mathematical appendices. This might be described as the theology of price-cap regulation, but it may come, thereby, to face again some

* Water Act 1989, S5, consolidated into Water Industry Act 1991, S2.

problems of old-style regulation of return on capital. One of the issues under debate is how the cost of capital should be assessed for a conspicuously low-risk utility business, currently with most consumers paying bills in advance of usage and calculated on a property tax base, without reference to consumption. This makes prospective income remarkably secure and predictable compared even to that of other utilities, let alone businesses run in competitive conditions. The rise in the share price since flotation, especially through the recession, shows that some investors at least find water company shares rewarding to include in their portfolios. OFWAT somehow has to ensure that they are not over-rewarded for a part they take so readily at evidently low risk.

The water companies vary in the relations they cultivate with OFWAT. There are occasional confrontations, sometimes perhaps from misjudgement rather than by design. One water and sewerage company was so disposed to discriminate in the charges to some of its sewerage customers supplied by water-only companies that it only backed down when OFWAT sent to it informally the official enforcement letter to be despatched the next day. The company had left it till the last moment to blink in face of OFWAT's ultimate power.

Generally, OFWAT has more power to stop companies doing something (seen as breaching their obligations) than to make them do what they are not disposed to do. With NRA support for areas where water resources are under strain, OFWAT has been trying to promote the spread of metered charging for domestic users. This would assist the management of water resources but would probably be unhelpful for company finances. Thus now the accountants oppose it as much as the water engineers used to do, as it would make company income less predictable. At least OFWAT has persuaded a number of companies to lower the higher standing charge many apply to metered properties. Although Anglian Water has made bolder long-term plans than others, no company appears yet to have broken ranks to the point of a whole-hearted effort to show how efficiently metering 20–40 per cent of households could be done.

In other ways, the companies may find themselves in a sort of trap. By law, they have to abandon charges based on old rateable value or derivatives of it by the year 2000. Although this legislation was passed in 1988, the companies have hardly moved even 5 per cent of households away from rate-based bills. If they try now to base charges upon the new-style council tax instead, they will face all sorts of rebates and exemptions included in that tax scheme to reflect personal circumstances. But if they try to set up other property banding schemes for water bills, they risk causing confusion with the council tax bandings. In short, having done so little to address the need for change in charging methods, through at least fifteen years of intermittent discussion, water companies now face far more awkward conditions for implementing it. The rateable value system of charges incorporates all sorts of inequality and cross-subsidy, the changing of which would produce losers and winners at a time when water bills are rising sharply and customers are expressing their dissatisfaction about them.

It remains to be seen whether and how OFWAT may feel able to push companies on this issue. In a sense, that should not be the regulator's task. Its main remit is to guard against monopoly abuse. But as privatized companies hang on so devotedly to a billing basis last updated twenty years ago for council taxation and now abandoned even for that purpose, when does such inertia, which suits their own finances and maintains many inequities, begin to be close to abuse?

OFWATching Consumer Interests

OFWAT has a general concern with the levels of service provided under price-capped charges and a specific interest in consumer-related issues. For the latter purpose, it has a network of regional customer service committees. To gain a wider audience, it has recently invented a national body as well on which chairmen of regional councils sit. In their regions, these committees seem to have a constructive dialogue with most companies: for example, monitoring the flow of complaint letters and how they are responded to, and discussing codes of practice which companies have to put forward and publish. Compensation is being made routine for specific deficiencies of service.

173

OFWAT and its regional service committees have rightly given much attention to debt and disconnection procedures. After two years of totals below 10,000, following privatization, the total number of disconnections rose steeply, dropping to 18,000 by 1992–3. In half the cases of cut-off in 1991–2, supply was restored in forty-eight hours or less. Only one in five cases was left without supply for a week or more. The rate of cut-offs varies notably between companies. The average rate is under 10 per 10,000, but a rate half as high again as this was recorded in no less than fifteen companies.

The issue here is not so much whether cut-off is a proper response to non-payment after suitable reminders, but how much is done to facilitate and encourage regular payments, however small, by customers who get into difficulty, even with the standard payment-by-instalments offered by virtually all companies. Cutting some 10,000 households off and reconnecting them within forty-eight hours is a waste of effort if payment can be obtained without it. Over several years the East Midlands Electricity Board seems to have achieved very high standards of attention to individual customers, bringing various internal gains too. On the basis that they will not cut off customers who keep in touch about outstanding debts, they are reducing the number of disconnections in their service to below 1,000 a year. Perhaps due to its local authority traditions, the water industry has generally shown little progress in treating customers consistently well as individuals, and maybe this is a challenge it should address. The experience of East Midlands Electricity – attributable perhaps to very determined policy-making in this respect at the top – seems to indicate that, after a process of change that may be arduous and take time to gain full internal acceptance, really high standards of attention to customers may not add much to costs, but add greatly to internal efficiency and staff commitment.

OFWATching the Water Environment

Since water supply and sewerage operations have considerable impacts on the water environment, the companies conducting such activities are inevitably subject to the same special regulations intended to limit and prevent damage to river basin resources and capacity, as apply to all other industries and to agriculture. This exposure presents OFWAT with several dilemmas. Given that the cost of upholding environmental obligations may lead to higher water bills, should OFWAT intervene in the decisions made to enforce such obligations? Arguably, wage rates and salary levels of water company personnel combine with other costs to influence charges too, but is OFWAT to call publicly for restraint when pay negotiations begin or when the salaries of company chairmen are reviewed?

It seems that OFWAT has given itself a role to comment on environmental policy, and now tends to do so with little recognition of how these environmental matters go far wider than its own concerns with utility costs. Here OFWAT deserves some sympathy too. As noted earlier, environmental agencies and policies have long suffered from lack of progress or even interest in making more use of economic analysis and instruments. As the RCEP report showed (page 163), there are effective pricing methods for river basin resources in use in Europe which the UK has been slow to adopt or even learn from. OFWAT is caught in a situation where application of such methods and policies would be a great help to it, but it is unable to do much about it, save, for example, to encourage the sort of comments made by the RCEP.

Thus OFWAT calls for what sometimes sounds like a halt to any setting of higher standards for anything, from the quality of drinking water to that of river water. These calls for restraint are made partly in the name of water customers quoted as unwilling to face yet higher bills, and partly on the grounds that only improvements subject to elaborate (but largely hypothetical) cost-benefit analysis with favourable outcomes should be put forward. Whether OFWAT would require the same imaginative rigour in dealing with proposals to lower some standards is not clear.

In this context, OFWAT is a victim of circumstances. Water consumers are getting restless about the increases implicit in K factors set by ministers at the time of flotation, as they go on building up year by year. In the case of the South West regional company, OFWAT itself saw that the system established for massive private investment required the K factors to be lifted yet further, especially to make adequate progress in reducing beach pollution, and approved this in 1991.

In conventional markets, producers are often described as price-takers (who have to accept prices set by the market) or as price-makers (meaning they have enough power to dominate market prices in their own interest). Applying the same labels to environmental standards, OFWAT appears now to be claiming that the water utility companies or their customers, or OFWAT as a proxy for them, should be standard-makers, rather than accept the standards set by others. This has been the style of overweening monopoly down the ages. The exposure of water utilities to environmental constraints and obligations is a serious factor as it is more important for them than for many other industries. But neither they nor OFWAT should expect or claim a dominant role in this policy area.

The 1994 Review

One reason why OFWAT's concerns are now being so strongly expressed is that in 1994 it is to conduct a periodic review of K factors that may change those already set for the next five years and look further ahead. This brings out a feature of the system perhaps not revealed earlier.

Water supply and sewerage services are generally not foreseen as showing much growth in volume terms in the next few years. Industrial demand has been falling, and domestic demand is rising only slowly. Moreover, growth in demand for water or in sewage loads would hardly be welcome, least of all in the south or east of England. In this setting, the companies' main route to growth in the core business is in effect via increased investment in improving the quality of tap-water or sewage discharges. If they have to invest more, OFWAT is obliged to see they get an appropriate return on their investment. Thus the companies have some vested interest in capital investment persisting at high levels – subject to being sure that the rewards in income will be reliably available.

But OFWAT's growing concern about consumers resisting paying yet higher water bills may well lead it to press downwards on investment plans as well as on the return companies are to expect on their assets.

Two ironies are evident in this situation. First, OFWAT sounds at times as if it wants to recreate the attitudes and policies of the early 1980s which privatization was intended to get away from. At that time, the water industry said more investment was essential, and Whitehall frustrated its efforts to achieve this. Now investment is going ahead on a substantial scale, and OFWAT seems extremely anxious about the consequences for some low-income water users of rising bills.

Secondly, spokesmen for OFWAT seem increasingly to slip into the language of consumer choice such as is applied to conventional goods and services that households buy on an individual basis. Yet water supply and sewerage are essentially collective standardized services. The consumer cannot choose the supplier or standard of service. Moreover, in the absence of metering, water consumers cannot even influence the size of the bill by moderating their own usage: indeed, extra usage is generally free as the bill is fixed by property values.

In a press release publicizing his recent annual report (1992/3), the director-general of OFWAT, Ian Byatt, rightly takes credit for several achievements – including price limits about 2 per cent lower than previously allowed by 1994–5. But he also said: 'I am addressing some fundamental issues within the industry. The challenge facing me . . . is to achieve prices which reflect the right trade-off between quality and price.' He stated later in the same announcement: 'I believe that customers . . . would be unhappy with increases which exceed the likely rate of growth of average household income – which would be in the region of 2 per cent.'

These comments may be very largely directed to subduing company ambitions ahead of the 1994 review, and taking a strong negotiating position at an early stage. Such motives are understandable and legitimate. However, comments of this nature risk misleading public expectations if they gain much attention, because they do little or nothing to recognize that the dynamics of the water environment and the relationship of water users to it are only partly under official control or influence. The mechanisms of privatization and regulation (by the NRA, HMIP and DWI as well as OFWAT) were intended to enhance the community's understanding of the different factors at work in the water environment and the impact people have on it. If OFWAT sees it as its role to deal with environmental standards (and sometimes it is unclear whether what OFWAT means by quality is that of tap-water or of the river basin resources), it would be better if it could regard itself or the utilities less as standard-makers, and more as standard-takers. At least this would have the merit of acknowledging the wider and interconnected influences on the water environment, as well as helping the public to understand these issues.

Most recently, the regulatory situation has been further complicated by a report from OFWAT entitled *Paying for Quality – the Political Perspective*. This runs together arguments in favour of relaxing some aspects of the long-standing EC Drinking Water Directive (specifically very strict limits on pesticides) and arguments for slowing down implementation of the recently agreed Urban Waste Water Treatment Directive. The reason for wanting to reverse commitments already made is mostly presented as the burden higher water bills threaten to bring to households, especially those with low incomes. One press release from OFWAT suggests that average annual bills of £190 in 1994–5 could rise by a further £54 in real terms by the end of the decade; this is following increases of 25 per cent since privatization.

OFWAT's report and more colourful press releases may have two effects. Although OFWAT has worked with the NRA, making use of the latter body's greater expertise on environmental matters, OFWAT is in effect bidding for a leading influence on environmental standard-setting. At one level, this may give the Opposition scope to embarrass the government all over again about the consequences of water privatization. At another level, it may encourage consumers to believe that increases in water bills can and will be halted to a greater extent than is likely to happen.

In broader terms, OFWAT's work for consumers is showing the hazard of the price-cap formula for water services created by institutionalizing repeated annual increases above the level of inflation. The whole success of the flotation had depended on this: it largely offset the concern that investors would take fright at the prospect of the water companies' need to fulfil environmental obligations. Now OFWAT is emphasizing that it is the customers who will take fright – a more explosive political issue for a government feeling insecure on a small majority. This is a sad new round of confusion to bring to the cleaning up of our rivers and beaches.

1994 will be the time for a fuller assessment of how price-cap regulation has worked in the special case of the water industry. Two points in particular are worth focusing on. First, as a recent article in the *Financial Times* showed, the companies are arguing for a return of something like 9.5 per cent on investment while OFWAT is considering 5–6 per cent as possible. With so much capital spending involved, where OFWAT draws this line is the key issue for 1994. Second, the rise in share prices relative to the FTSE (100) Index is a good marker of how investors see the situation. Since the flotation of water shares (late 1989 to early June 1993), the FTSE (100) Index has risen 22 per cent. In the same period, shares in half a dozen water and sewerage companies have risen by between 85 per cent and 135 per cent. It looks as if the shareholders are the reverse of worried about the spending on improvements in quality and the 25 per cent increase in charges.

Chapter 13

Water in Development

Most of the preceding chapters have concentrated on the latest stage in the long-run effort in Britain since 1945 to achieve a better-balanced relationship between people and their water environment. To repeat at this stage the point that this effort has been taking place under simplified conditions, owing to the absence of significant schemes for irrigation or for generating hydroelectric power, may seem almost perverse, given the complexities now indicated. Yet there is no ignoring the situation overseas. As soon as attention turns to countries in the early stages of development, the dominant impression, accurately enough, is not only of problems on a larger scale, but of hazards and obstacles which are inter-active, cumulative and self-reinforcing. This is an immensely important issue – and a largely underrated one – applying to international affairs generally. It is relevant also to the difficulties which industrialized countries encounter in their own water sectors and to the deeper argument that the transition to a market economy more attuned routinely to take full account of environmental costs and constraints will take a long time yet.

The difference in perspective is partly due to climatic and other natural factors, as well as their economic implications. In the absence of a temperate climate, national policies for encouraging self-sufficiency in food production or agriculture in adverse settings become tied to irrigation, which can be costly and of dubious benefit. Those nations that are energy-poor rather than oil-rich also find the prospect of generating hydro-electric power very attractive if river profiles are suitable and the government not already too indebted to borrow more money for such projects. Giving priority to irrigation and hydro-electric power can be enough to distort the water policies of nations at any stage of economic development. Irrigation and hydro-electric power not only require enormous amounts of money and water for use in projects usually controlled in a very centralized manner; they often have the consequence of absorbing money (and sometimes good-quality water) desperately needed for improving water supply for the everyday use of households with insufficient or no access to it.

In a large group of low-income countries, the domestic sector is estimated to take only 4 per cent of total water withdrawals and the industrial sector 5 per cent, while agriculture takes 91 per cent. The equivalent figures for high-income countries are 14:47:39. Because agriculture is such a powerful vested interest, often resisting change, this dominance of water resources by irrigation can be a considerable brake on getting more water for other purposes unless significant uncommitted resources are within reasonable reach of where they are wanted.

But the claims of irrigation and hydro-electric power are by no means the only major factors preventing developing countries from finding paths to economic progress and a better balance between communities and their water environment. A brief bleak catalogue of other influences would have to include the following:

1. Collective poverty, especially where governments are already in debt. Water projects of any sort almost always involve collective action (and potential benefits) and hence collective finance. Scope for individual initiative or private financing is rare and usually impractical.
2. Actual shortages of water and deterioration of its quality due to abuse of river catchments and salinization as well as more conventional forms of man-made pollution.
3. Pressures of increasing population, especially in urban settings in future.
4. Lack of health education and, more widely, of better opportunities for women to gain longer and fuller schooling.
5. Lack of effective institutions and political will to create or sustain them strongly enough to facilitate better use of water resources and readier access by the people to larger volumes of clean water and to healthy sanitation.

The Hazards of Water Scarcity

Although temperate countries suffer drought – in the sense of rainfall well below average – natural sources do not often dry up completely. Reservoir storage can be a robust defence against extreme scarcity. Water loss due to evaporation will usually be less than that in hotter climates. In much drier climates, drought will often be far more severe and possibly more prolonged too. For example, in the Sahel, south of the Sahara, rainfall in the 1970s was only about half that of the 1950s. From 1970 to 1990, every year has recorded less than the 100-year average for rainfall (in 1738–56 and the 1820s and 1830s similar long, dry periods are known to have occurred, half the population having died in the first period). The contours and geology of Africa offer less scope for small-scale reservoir storage than do most other regions, and irrigation is provided for only 3 per cent of Africa's farms, against some 30 per cent in Asia. Cutting down forests and over-grazing also aggravate soil erosion. The desert is spreading southwards and, some say, even northwards to southern Italy.

Poverty and drought can be a specially harsh combination, because poverty tends to imply a lack of any reserves of money, food or stored water to fall back on. Those farmers who can afford to do so may try to carry extra cattle as a sort of insurance against hard times, but if they hang on longer as drought takes hold, their over-grazing (especially of areas around waterholes) may damage the pasture and soils permanently. This will be to the disadvantage of neighbours, as in the 'tragedy of the commons' discussed in Chapter 7.

Dam Projects Challenged

Even where reservoir and dam projects are feasible, they give rise nowadays to far more controversy for the social and environmental damage they may inflict. This is sometimes argued to be so adverse as to make the potential benefits either unlikely to be achieved or not worth having. In Chile, such strong opposition

has arisen against the Pangue dam project proposed by the privatized ENDESA electricity company as the first of a sequence of
six dams, that progress with the other five can hardly be expected
to be straightforward. This was a relatively small project, involving the flooding of only 400 hectares and the displacement of
fewer than sixty people, but its dependence on borrowing from
the World Bank's private-sector arm (the International Finance
Corporation) gave the opposition to it more leverage than it
would have internally. Lack of consultation was one of the main
complaints. The IFC arranged for an independent consultant to
make an environmental evaluation which had not been done
adequately before, and even then ENDESA tried to prevent that
assessment being made public. In many other settings, serious
assessment of environmental consequences and open disclosure of
such information has to be fought for. It cannot be taken for
granted, and powerful independent lending agencies have significant roles in securing it by their financial 'clout'.

In Maharashtra state in India, however, a larger dam project
has proved even more contentious for almost everyone involved.
Discussed first in 1946, with a foundation stone laid fifteen years
later, this project only gained World Bank loan approval for an
initial US$450 million (out of a project cost of probably US$3
billion) in 1985. One main reason for this delay was disputes
between Maharashtra and two other states which share the River
Narmada, the basis for the whole project. But by then, the Indian
prime minister, Rajiv Gandhi, was among those acknowledging
the disappointments and frustrations built into many such projects
in India: 'Perhaps we can safely say that almost no benefit has
come to the people from these projects.'

Thus there were firm intentions to do better next time. An
environmental master-plan was to be prepared, and the three
states were to pay compensation to the people displaced (the
project would flood the land inhabited by nearly a quarter of a
million of the poorest people of India). But as protests built up,
the World Bank became so troubled that an independent report
was again called for, which confirmed many of the points made
by those opposing the project for environmental and social reasons. Again, the outlook is bleak for other projects outlined to

follow along the Narmada River. But one outcome in this case was that, rather than comply with the approach the World Bank was insisting on for the resettlement of villagers and more adequate study of environmental consequences, the Indian government withdrew its application even for the rest of the money sought from the World Bank for this project. One of the saddest features of this whole saga is that the project was intended to provide drinking water for many millions of people, as well as to generate massive volumes of hydro-electric power. Yet as this and similar episodes have shown, as a way of getting more water to more people, this must be among the slowest and most costly methods available.

Conflict can arise around natural waters (as well as man-made systems of storage) where water is not plentiful enough for all the purposes required. Ironically, internal disputes in Sudan, Uganda and Ethiopia have held back projects for making more water available, and there are demands for increased access to Nile waters that could well give rise to wider conflicts. The Nile has been Egypt's main water source, providing 90 per cent of its needs for time beyond recall. The benefits which Egypt has had from the flows of the Nile have been partly due to upstream countries taking relatively little (the head-waters of the Blue Nile, which provides a large share of the Nile flow, are located principally in Ethiopia, and the river then flows through Sudan to join the White Nile before reaching Egypt). Now several upstream states, including Uganda, in which the head-waters of the White Nile are situated, expect notable increases in population, and hence will need to draw more water in the very period when Egypt may have to do the same.

Elsewhere in the Middle East tensions are arising about the sharing of water sources and rivers. Allocation of water rights has become a matter for a special programme of meetings in the course of the multi-lateral Arab–Israeli peace talks. Israel currently draws a substantial part of its water supplies from territory where its occupation is under challenge. Whatever concessions Israel may be willing to make on territory, it might not be able to do without the water it gets from this area.

The basins of the rivers Euphrates and Jordan are also the scene of rivalries and counter-claims. In January 1993, disputes about water were yet again a possible source of difficulty in talks between Turkish and Syrian leaders when other aspects of their relations seemed to be taking a turn for the better. Syrians want durable guarantees of water, which is crucial for more than half of the country's power generation. They claim that the Turks earlier held out prospects of a long-term settlement once their new Ataturk reservoir was filled. Turkey, by contrast, talks of yet more irrigation using water that would otherwise flow downstream to Syria. Increases in population and the need to feed more mouths aggravate these competing claims. Moreover, tendencies to greater salinity when flows are lower add to the mutual suspicions and anxieties.

The familiar view is that oil is the resource on which much Middle Eastern political and economic rivalry focuses, with military rivalry only just below the surface. But the sharing of water may become a subject for conflict and give rise to natural hazards too. These harsh issues of water scarcity and the tensions arising from it get sharper in many countries, and are a painful start to what should be progress towards economic development by improving water use in ways that are equitable and do not harm the environment. Such issues demonstrate how water is world-wide essentially a localized or regionalized resource, and the river basin is an arena for sharing, sometimes between reluctant neighbours. This is so partly because water goes its own way across man-made boundaries, and is costly to divert by artificial means. But tensions also arise because there is little readiness or scope to trade in water, whereby those claiming increased withdrawals might compensate those reducing their claims to necessarily shared rivers. Indeed, the status of water as a free, scarce, endlessly renewed natural resource is just what may lead people to fight about it. They may see this as their only way to get more of it, or even to hang on to the access to it that they have at present.

Floods

The localized character of water as a natural resource and the variations in its patterns of circulation would be inadequately presented if examples of water scarcity were not followed by some mention, however brief, of the effects of flooding.

China has been preoccupied with water and hydrology for thousands of years. It is now building hydro-electric power stations along the River Yangtze on a scale never attempted before. At the same time, the Yangtze is one of China's greatest sources of flooding (in contrast to regions further north where water is less plentiful). Thus transfer schemes to carry water north have also been in preparation, partly based on using for this purpose the 1,500-year-old Grand Canal. Even so, none of these interventions in the flow of the powerful Yangtze river are likely to tame completely its tendency to flood.

In mid-1991, floods swept across the countryside of Jiangsu and Anhui provinces, causing the deaths of over 1,400 people. Water from eastern China's largest lake, Lake Tai, rose above its embankments, forcing some 300,000 people in or around the city of Wuxi (with a population of 4 million) to abandon their homes temporarily. The losses to crops were very great – 'three years' income has just disappeared,' as one local mayor expressed it – in one of the most fertile areas of China.

About a third of the mulberry trees crucial for the culture of silkworms were damaged, and many fish-farming structures washed away. The damage was probably the more widespread as the Grand Canal passes through much of the area affected and has networks of sub-canals linked to it. Dysentery and cholera were spreading through some flooded districts – another aspect of water's potential to threaten as well as support human life.

China not only possesses much respected hydrological experts, based at universities and in specialized institutes; the vast majority of the people also have a great awareness of water as many of them work and live on China's rivers and canals that are always busy with boats (in a country otherwise rather short of transport systems). Add to that the routine commitment to growing and eating rice and China becomes probably one of the modern world's most water-oriented economies. But, as has been illustrated, the very resource which is such an asset can turn very destructive, despite the skills and huge communal effort put into restraining it.

Urbanization and Women's Access to Schooling

The encouraging evidence for the years ahead is that world population is growing at a somewhat slower rate than it has done in recent decades. Yet the rate of growth is still high, especially in many of the low-income economies where some 3 billion of the present 5 billion total world population struggles to keep going.

In 1990 it was still true that more of the world's people lived in rural areas than in towns, but this will not remain the case for much longer. A levelling-out of rural populations is now in prospect, but the future concentration of population growth in urban areas will probably make it seem as if the overall situation is getting worse. In the middle of this century, just over half the people in more developed regions of the world (54 per cent) lived in urban areas. Now that figure is over 70 per cent, and in another thirty years it is expected to be over 80 per cent. Thus in much of the more developed parts of the world, well-established cities will be exposed to far more congestion, and hence far more strain on their present services – water supply and sewage disposal, housing, public transport and systems of traffic control. Coping with this increased congestion within existing towns will cost a good deal more in terms of capital investment. Taking a population of 8 million as the definition for a 'mega-city', London and New York were the only two among the more developed countries in 1950, while, in the closing years of the century, there are now six.

But in the less-developed economies, the acceleration of urban growth is far more marked. The proportion of population in urban areas, only 17 per cent in 1950, was 37 per cent in 1990. It is forecast to be 45 per cent in 2000, and 58 per cent in 2020. Moreover, the less-developed regions have fourteen mega-cities already, and are likely to have twenty-two by the year 2000.

Such a concentration of population growth, happening at such a pace, has formidable implications. In probably as many as ten of these mega-cities, the services of water supply are already inadequate for present numbers, and those of sewerage even poorer. Across Latin America, scarcely more than 2 per cent of sewage is treated before discharge. Across India, hardly anywhere has a regular, 24-hour water supply. Mega-cities can hardly expect to gain overriding priority in project design or funding. Yet if present water and sanitation services are not transformed, what spread of disease may the greater crowding threaten, and with what wretched economic consequences? In Mexico City (forecast population 25 million in the year 2000), pumping of ground water is already being increased at rates 40 per cent faster than that of natural recharge. In Bangkok, subsidence of buildings is widespread, largely due to over-pumping of ground water. In a lengthening list of big cities, losses from the supply system not accounted for suggest that almost half the water put into supply may be lost before it reaches registered consumers.

This begins to raise questions of how well or badly facilities already installed for water supply are being operated. But there is a wider – and more difficult – issue to be considered ahead of that, also related to the pace of population increase. This is the role of women and the opportunities they have for more schooling and for developing their potential. The situation differs in each country depending on economic and cultural circumstances. In parts of Zimbabwe, women spend a fifth of their time collecting wood for cooking. Across much of Africa and Asia, women also do a large share of the cultivation of crops (though the herding of cattle is more generally men's work).

But women are still held back by unequal provision of schooling or in other ways. Banks are on the whole reluctant to provide business loans to women in developing countries. When village leaders (all men) are consulted about the siting of a new pump, for example, they may well reach a decision without even asking for the views of women, who are the main water users and carriers. Most significantly, careful studies across several countries indicate that, where women are largely excluded from secondary education, average family size is seven children. Where even 40 per cent of women can continue to secondary schooling, average family size reduces to three children.

As well as being wasteful of talent, it is a striking irony that, while water has to be fetched and carried home probably every day, this drudgery is almost universally women's work. But when water is distributed by pipes, this is called engineering; it involves money and some power; and it becomes predominantly a matter for men. This applies in the case of irrigation too. Yet in some places this situation is changing. In Bangladesh, Kenya and Lesotho, for instance, women have gained roles as caretakers for handpumps, and in Mozambique they work alongside male engineers and mechanics.

The need, however, is to give women far more scope at local level to lead and influence community initiatives, in the shaping of services that families want, as well as in business. To achieve this – throughout South America, Africa and Asia – longer schooling for women is a necessary and urgent step. Nor must the pressures of increased population in the mega-cities swamp and frustrate this aim. Given more chances to develop their potential, women can moderate those pressures in direct ways. The moves to involve more citizens in consultation, more involvement of non-governmental organizations, and the sheer wastefulness of excluding women must surely all bring much more change on this front in future. The water sector could provide one of the best springboards for such change.

At the same time, much more needs to be done to spread health education and remedy the causes of infant mortality. The assurance that more children will survive childhood is a key element in families deciding how many they should plan to have. Moreover, this is not just a matter of relative national income levels. Brazil's income per head has been about six times that of Sri Lanka, but its mortality rate for children under age five is three times higher. Among the poorest countries with average incomes per head of less than US$500 a year, infant mortality varies widely between 20–160 per 1,000 live births. The quality of water and its accessibility to families living in harsh circumstances would doubtless be part of the explanation for these differences, but so will a cluster of other social and cultural influences. Perhaps the most compelling point is that, if there is to be a major increase in numbers of people living in crowded urban settlements, new ways of organizing all sorts of services using paid employees and regular voluntary workers will be necessary, and women must be allowed to play a full part in making such changes effective.

Water Pollution

That excellent weekly the *Economist* hardly has a pro-environment bias, so when it says that Asia has 'bought economic growth at the price of ecological devastation' (6 October 1990), clearly some very serious mistakes have been made. Moreover, pollution in Asia means degradation of urban and rural areas, and attendant hazards, for almost half the world's population. Industrialization is racing ahead in many places. More than two-thirds of industrial firms in the Philippines are located in Manila, where almost all of their wastes discharged into rivers and the sea are untreated. In Taiwan, less than a million out of 20 million people are served by sewers, and the country has one of the highest incidences of hepatitis in the world.

For all its respect for water and rivers, China has allowed a huge volume of pollution to build up, both in the water and the air. Hong Kong hardly does better: would-be swimmers have been finding many of its beaches closed due to pollution. About a third of people living in Manila, Kuala Lumpur, Bangkok, Jakarta and Dacca are estimated to occupy informal settlements with little or no access to sewerage systems or, in many cases, even clean water. Experts made a survey of river-water quality in parts of the River Ganges and found it good apart from bad patches near major cities. Nevertheless, they added that the river was vulnerable to extensive damage if pollution loads increased significantly. Indeed the river was actually protected by the lack of mains sanitation which, combined with inadequate water supply in most of the large conurbations, prevented extra loads of pollution from reaching the river.

These problems are not special to Asia, however. Amid Egypt's extreme dependence on the waters of the Nile there is recognition that pollution is now reaching drinking-water sources and contaminating fish. In South America, too, a sophisticated city such as Buenos Aires, whose water services operated well when the city was smaller, now fails to provide sewerage services to about half the 10 million population in the urbanized area. With a serious recent outbreak of cholera in Peru, the buses in Buenos Aires have already been carrying posters urging that it must not be allowed to spread to their city. In Rio de Janeiro, a project has been finalized for loan approvals to reduce by 30 per cent the volume of sewage discharged without treatment into Guanabara Bay, at a cost of some £430 million. But this is only part of a much larger programme (costing £2–3 billion) to restore the condition of the bay as a whole. The Japanese are offering to help, following their experience in cleaning up the Bay of Tokyo (four times the size of Guanabara's 380 sq.km.), which took thirty years.

This project in Rio de Janeiro has presented a dilemma: whether to extend sewage-collection systems to more of the population living around the bay, or to provide more treatment for the volumes of sewage already being collected but far from adequately treated. This is a classic instance of the double aspect of water infrastructure discussed in Chapter 2: it can provide services which will improve amenities for water users, and it can also improve the relationship of the community with its water environment. But to enable it to do both can require considerable investment in improving sewer networks and sewage-treatment capacity. This may take years, and considerable political will-power in providing public information. But unless a well-balanced result is finally achieved, much of the effort and money spent on investment will appear to have been wasted.

These indications of how cumulative the dangers of pollution can be, and how policies must address coherently issues which are political, economic, social and technical, may read like a catalogue of misery. In large part it cannot avoid being that. Water can be a threat instead of a support to health if its quality is not protected from degradation by pollution. A great deal of remedial work is currently under way in the preparation of projects, seeking international loans and establishing better local tariffs. There are of course obstacles to overcome, and not just financial ones. Central to such work is the formation and sustaining of effective agencies that can carry through the wide-ranging changes that are essential and operate the expanded services reliably afterwards. Yet the capacity to cope with problems that have not been experienced or addressed on this scale before can rarely be created quickly because it involves the whole community.

For the better sharing of water the problems are clearly multiple, so the remedies must be multiple too. No one of the several factors necessary for success should be taken in isolation as a magic or all-purpose key to achieve better progress. Poverty and indebtedness are an underlying problem, especially because organizing water services at any level tends to require investment and the availability of money 'up front'. So international aid and lending programmes are very important. When the inequality of wealth is so marked, it is the more harsh and deplorable that governments of relatively rich countries keep their aid budgets at such modest levels. Only five of the richest countries provide aid at the target level widely recognized as 0.7 per cent of gross domestic product. In 1992, debt repayments and interest had the effect, intended or otherwise, of transferring US$50 billion from developing countries to the industrialized ones. Thus the poverty that holds back the poor so much from helping themselves is aggravated by what they still have to pay the rich.

Water Institutions

Even so, money in large amounts would not on its own solve the problems of the 1 billion people without access to clean water. As previously stated, the other necessary element is establishing appropriate and effective institutions: suitable water-management agencies, relevant and up-to-date legislation, arrangements for finance and charges for water, the gathering of staff with flexible skills, plus a political and managerial framework to bring these ingredients together and make them work with sustainable policies.

In both industrialized and developing countries, it is assumed that government would provide all these components. Central or local governments have done this and, to a large extent, still do. But now this is increasingly seen as having disadvantages that become more serious handicaps as the whole task gets larger. The problem stems from the fact that government imposes its authority as it were from the top downwards. Yet administration of water supply and sewerage networks demands a participatory approach.

But in standardized water services decisions still have to be made, yet the idea of government getting in touch with water users, and consulting their preferences, is not widely recognized as desirable or worthwhile. It is generally presumed that the public will put up with a system of water supply and sewerage if the technical people provide what they regard as the best service possible in the circumstances, depending on local conditions.

This 'top-down' methodology has other implications. The technology involved is often large-scale and sophisticated. Little attention may be given in designing a system to the need for maintenance to be reliable and requiring only local materials and skills much of the time. The administration of a small loan or project is almost as much trouble as for a large one, so small projects are played down. Perhaps most damaging of all, where the projects are set up by government, the intended charges for water are often distorted. This is, ironically, specially evident in the case of irrigation, even in prosperous countries. Residents of Phoenix, Arizona, pay twenty-five times as much per cubic metre of water as nearby farmers do. In parts of China, cheap water sources are used for irrigation of low-value crops, while water for the towns is brought at great cost through transfer schemes from other river basins.

The multiple changes required to achieve a better balance consist primarily of implementing more rational policies and establishing better controls in the allocation of water resources. There should be more attention to and consultation with water users about the standard of service that suits their needs; and much greater recognition that water has to be paid for at realistic prices, which many people are ready to do if they get the service they want. Yet as soon as these requirements are spelt out, they can be seen as the type of changes that governments often find uncongenial and difficult to introduce. They require collaboration with people and voluntary groups in ways in which civil servants may have little experience. The politicians may feel that such methods may erode their influence on voters, because it often suits them if water becomes a political issue locally. But even in Britain, which has a long tradition of water services being organized in a heavily 'top-down' style, one can observe a powerful trend towards involving and consulting water users. Two of the main forces driving this trend are recognition that water supply is becoming more costly, and public interest in water quality and environmental issues. The desire of users to be involved will be all the stronger where the change is from carrying water home to installing a few pumps, wells or taps within easier reach, and paying for the first time modest amounts for their maintenance.

The scope for voluntary initiative and the involvement of local people is far greater than is realized by many civil servants and water professionals, and crucial to promoting the safer use of water through health education. At the same time working with volunteers or local groups requires sensitivity and patience. As a way of organizing water supply for people without it, this may seem time-consuming and not very efficient. But as a way of achieving community development through improved water supply, it provides added value in various ways. As well as gaining experience of organizing their own affairs, the people acquire some sense of ownership of the project, and become far more committed to look after it. In many places across the developing world, water schemes put in by contractors or consulting engineers have fallen out of use, because local people did not have the necessary spare parts or the commitment to keep the system going. They may not even have been consulted about where pumps or taps should be located, as such decisions are often viewed as technical (and taken by outsiders, usually men) rather than social (taken by local people, including women).

Since its formation in 1981, the British voluntary body WaterAid has gained much experience in enabling local people to complete their own projects in some of the poorest communities in the world. Improvements on which WaterAid has worked with local partners have now benefited nearly 2 million people, usually at an external cost of £10 or less per person, and hardly ever more than £20. This is mostly for raw materials such as cement and transport: local people themselves do as much of the work as they possibly can (typical investment per head in water supply and sewerage services in England and Wales has long been about £500 per person served, and in the period to the end of the century, this is likely to have almost doubled). WaterAid gets its funds from a wide range of personal donations from water users, from tireless support from water company employees, from Rotary, church and other interested groups and from charitable trusts, the Overseas Development Administration and the EC.

To give some insight into the ways such bodies operate with local partners, three short statements from WaterAid's annual review of 1992, are printed in the Appendix, p. 213. WaterAid and other voluntary bodies are finding that work done in this way can be very effective (at intervals WaterAid takes opportunities to send review teams back to projects completed several years ago to learn how they are going). But much more generally, people with low incomes want better water and sanitation and will pay towards this. They pay quite a lot to water vendors where there is no alternative supply. In Kumasi, Ghana, for instance, people are willing to pay 2 per cent of income for better sanitation. WaterAid is currently looking into how local people may pay user-charges to keep systems operating efficiently long after WaterAid has finished providing the modest level of help it gives them.

The challenge for the future, however, is how public agencies and voluntary bodies can develop equally effective methods in urban settings (almost all WaterAid's projects have been rural). Governments must concentrate on finding 'enabling' roles in place of direct operational roles, and consultative procedures in place of 'top-down' decision-making. This will require giving the professional staff training and time to work in this way, even if it is a slower process. The sense that people are getting the service they want will also be crucial to their readiness to pay for it.

Many of the points made here may be briefly recapitulated in terms that link them more to other chapters. One main theme outlined earlier was that industrialized countries with well-established water services still have a long and costly task to make those services better attuned to the protection of the river basin environment. Developing countries should therefore beware of following the approaches and technologies adopted in rich countries and finding themselves caught later with needs for far more expenditure for the same reason as industrialized countries. They need to find methods of providing and improving water supply and sanitation for their people that will not abuse or overload the capacity of the water environment. Westernizing or privatizing water services in developing countries should not be seen as the only way forward. The industrialized countries still have a long way to go in their own adaptation of the market economy to reflect environmental costs and constraints. Repeating in developing countries the European experience of urbanization in the nineteenth century may not be the only or the best way to cope with the global problems of the twenty-first century.

Chapter 14

Could Do Better?

The widespread and persistent rise in concern about the natural environment over the last thirty years or so is much more than a passing fashion or a campaign by short-lived, single-interest pressure groups. It is one of those profound changes the full effects of which take some long time to work through or gain complete acceptance. Possibly the exceptional progress in transport and communications throughout this century would be an equivalent change, or, more appropriately, all that flowed in terms of a new understanding of the natural world from Darwin's *Origin of Species*. Darwin published this in 1859, after years of anxiety about the disruption it might threaten to established institutions and the existing political order. It did indeed force powerful bodies such as the Anglican church and universities then widely occupied with theology as much as science to modify and adapt major parts of their well-established attitudes and practices. But it did not generate serious political disruption. The capacity to adapt to new insights offering a different perspective on the natural world and the place of humankind in it was robustly there to be drawn on; indeed. the adaptability of species, including humans, was one of Darwin's key themes.

In much the same way, the rise of environmental concern need not be seen as threatening the survival of the market economy. The challenge is essentially to achieve a further major adaptation – one that somehow should make it possible to cope with the allocation and protection of natural resources even in a world becoming still more congested due to effects of economic growth as well as a sharply increasing world population.

This adaptation will build up through different stages, as it has to go all the way from introducing new ideas and attitudes (as it did in the 1960s, almost exactly one hundred years since publication of Darwin's radical book) to seeing those perceptions fully adopted and institutionalized. They will then be routine features of what may well be termed, some time in the next half-century, the sustainable market economy. However strange or unlikely some people may still find that prospect, it will probably turn out to be, in its very gradualness, less different than they anticipated. In essence, it will be the market economy with new instruments and procedures for letting environmental constraints and costs be reflected far more fully in everyday prices and transactions. This will greatly reduce the scope for the real and recurring costs of the depletion of natural resources to slip unnoticed and uncounted into externalities which damage the interests of neighbours, and ultimately our own interests too.

Several influences, such as more education and more leisure time, better global communications and higher standards of living will contribute to this adaptation. But it will be compulsory rather than optional to achieve such an adaptation, and irreversible. In some crowded areas at least, it is clear now that the capacity of natural resources – even where they are endlessly renewed as water resources are – is becoming so overstretched as to have serious practical consequences. In one sense, what were margins of reserve capacity, so to speak, are now being committed, such as the level of flow streams need to maintain their own ecological health. In bolder terms, water is becoming in some areas 'quality-scarce', whatever its physical availability. Rivers become unfit for use as drinking water; some land-locked seas become practically devoid of fish.

Increasingly in industrialized countries, river basin capacity on which the community depends so heavily, for effluent disposal as well as water supply, is becoming congested and more costly to use. The aggregate claims being made on it are overloading it, and still growing. Matching these claims to the capacity available – during drought, flood or average climatic conditions – can no longer be reliably achieved or sustained. Some forms of rationing – by permit and/or price – are becoming not only necessary, but are being put under greater strain where they have already been introduced.

Yet the seeds of change have already been sown. In industrialized countries, the public is beginning to demand more consumer-oriented policies to be put into practice by corporate business and government. People are increasingly questioning whether suppliers of goods and services are providing what consumers really want, whether enough choice is available at prices that offer value for money. Increasing public interest in environmental issues is also having an effect. Although some of the most forceful environmental campaigns have somewhat abated now, the scale of real changes becoming well established in industry and business, and sometimes even in government, can none the less be seen as substantial.

Business Adapting to the Environment

California, the eighth biggest economy in the world, has provided itself with some of the toughest environmental rules. On the one hand, this has led many manufacturers to move out to nearby states such as Nevada and Arizona – quoting having to abide by the stricter regulations for the 'greening' of California as their reason. But as these businesses have gone, California has shown how much the environmental services industry can grow. In 1991, this was already worth US$130 billion a year. Defence companies, engineering and big utilities are all fitting in constructively to what they see as opportunities as much as liabilities. Both the Congress in federal legislation and other states, notably in the north east, are following California's lead in some of their new standards for controlling air pollution.

Companies based in California gain competitive advantage in return for their early adaptation. By the end of the 1980s, for instance, Bechtel had annual earnings of nearly US$1 billion from environmental projects in the USA alone. California is well ahead in the generation of electric power from wind and sun. With 3 per cent of all the cars in the world in this one state, the car industry is watching very keenly the emission standards being set there for the early years of the next century. The utilities are even competing in their pace of adaptation, Edison trying to overtake Pacific Gas and Electric in this instead of trying to resist new standards limiting pollution.

The attention leading companies pay to reporting their progress in moderating the environmental impact of their businesses is making great strides too. A Dutch information-technology company has published a set of environmental accounts with its annual report. This gives a total for all environmental damage it does, from car emissions and processes such as incineration and power generation conducted by others to supply its needs. The cost is taken as the marginal cost of reducing emissions to the cross-over point where the marginal benefits of doing so equal that. In the USA, the large chemical company Monsanto has published annual environmental reviews (as British Gas has done in Britain). The Monsanto reports give details of the main releases of hazardous wastes and where they go. The company recognizes that its own employees are one of the most significant audiences for this sort of information, especially those under forty. The standards Monsanto is setting itself – to reduce by 90 per cent world-wide emissions to air of more than 300 chemicals – has pre-empted much of its potential improvement in profit margins, but strengthened its position against less progressive rivals as stricter standards become compulsory. As the balance swings to the leaders who go beyond the mandatory standards, the laggards are likely to be squeezed by competition and legislative pressures together.

This kind of effort nevertheless needs to be made by the suppliers to a company too, and there is evidence that this is happening. In Britain, the retailing chain of do-it-yourself materials B&Q has been planning not to stock timber from unknown sources, and has ceased to buy peat from sites of Special Scientific Interest – thereby making a great impression on environmentalists. There has been much innovation too in 'green' labelling. Since 1978, Germany has been running a 'Blue Angel' scheme, and a poll taken ten years later showed that nearly 80 per cent of consumers recognized its label. The Japanese Eco-Mark scheme gave some 850 labels to 31 types of product in its first two years or so of operation. Schemes of this sort may extend to some products where the way they are used is as significant as how they are made. Criteria for some labels may be open to challenge. But the key point is the commitment to communicate standards in ways that are not just special to one company, and enable comparisons to be made. This gives consumers an extension of choice by providing fuller information for making choices.

The notion of environmental audit is taking hold as a continuation of the assessment of impact to the environment already familiar and applied to many one-off projects. A British Standard (7750) has been prepared and published for what it defines as environmental management systems. In an initiative significant for its authority and its cross-disciplinary character, the Institute of Chartered Accountants in England and Wales published last year a thorough 120-page report entitled *Business, Accountancy and the Environment: A Policy and Research Agenda*. This covered disclosure as well as auditing methods, because audit and disclosure are each of little point without the other. In the annual reporting cycle, this report recommended that companies should publish the identity of the director with overall responsibility for environmental issues, and express their environmental objectives in ways open to measuring performance, with details of expenditure on specific objectives and other data, plus measures of compliance with regulations and relevant guide-lines.

This kind of openness on the part of companies also influences the ways in which bankers, insurers and investors look at businesses. It is becoming increasingly clear that the ability to take on tougher environmental commitments, and publish measures of performance in them, says something about the competence and self-confidence of management as well as about the objectives the company sees as achievable in its own competitive setting. Investment trusts concentrating on 'green' products and companies do not necessarily gain from the 'greenness' itself, but may well do so from the skills and styles of management and marketing associated with it. Moreover, as environmental liabilities from the past worry lenders and insurers, companies that show themselves to be thoroughly aware of their environmental impact are likely to win the confidence of bankers and others much more readily.

These instances have mostly come from recent business-news reports, taking examples from different contexts and countries. Far more could be found more systematically presented in books such as *Changing Course*, published by the Massachusetts Institute of Technology, with the Business Council for Sustainable Development helping in its preparation. The range of businesses included in the case studies that occupy its last seven chapters is specially notable.

The Greening of Government

The adaptations which leading companies are seeing as in the interest of their own future profitability to achieve are at the moment probably more significant than the changes that government itself is building into its own ways of working (as distinct from particular lines of policy). At present many governments are trying to learn more from the world of business and markets than they have been used to doing. Yet it could be argued that, relatively early on, governments had already made two 'green' adaptations.

The first of these, especially notable in Britain where there has been such a potent culture of government concealment, is the adaptation to openness in environmental regulation and monitoring, and indeed in the field of environmental policy also. The publication of official reports such as *This Common Inheritance* and *The UK Environment* represents a huge change from what was available a few years ago, even if some of the commentary is still rather bland and uncritical. The necessity for openness in environmental matters and moves towards it partly set the title for this book.

The second main adaptation by governments has been in taking a positive attitude (even if sometimes slowly) towards international agreements and the setting of standards and target dates in environmental matters. This has developed not only through the United Nations but among member states of the EC and states bordering regional seas such as the Mediterranean, the Baltic and the North Sea. The programmes agreed upon for these seas require substantial reductions of in-country river pollution as well as in effluent discharges and sludge disposal to the seas themselves. Moreover, the scale of international tourism has promoted the state of the water environment as a matter of international concern, with progress reports and monitoring data widely published.

In another direction too, innovations are being made in that most traditional role of monarchs and governments, the resolution of disputes. The rise in congestion and in public concern about the environment has been threatening to make conflicts even more intractable, but work done in the USA on alternative ways of resolving conflicts by Professor Larry Susskind and others has been encouraging. These methods focus much less on legal precedents, adversarial processes and courtroom procedures than British public enquiry procedures have tended to do. They aim rather to foster a spirit of equality and recognition of mutual interests between the different groups involved, on the basis that a solution has to be found. The option of every community wanting the new waste dump located on somebody else's doorstep is not a realistic one.

These procedures can also incorporate on occasion an element of bargaining, not so much with regard to cash compensation but to the provision of other constructive amenities – new facilities for recreation or education, for example. This can help to work against the chain of adverse influences when, once an area gets a bad reputation for lack of amenities, new business investment and new public projects may be more and more steered away from it. If a new waste dump and a new leisure centre can be established in the same area, the standard of care in waste dumping will probably be raised as well as other standards. The underlying thrust of this method of seeking alternative solutions to conflicts is, so to speak, the insistence that the adaptation any community is called on to make should not be expected or shaped to be repeatedly in a negative or adverse direction. Scope should be deliberately made to introduce and create positive innovations as well. This will usually have economic as well as other advantages.

Uneven Adaptation in the Water Sector

Compared to some of the industries just mentioned, one might expect progress in the water sector to be more evident because it has such direct and close dependence on the water environment. In Britain especially, if the water utilities do not come to terms constructively with the limits in capacity and the dynamics of the river basins on which public water supply and sewage disposal have substantial impacts, who else can be expected to do so? But a contrary argument is that the changed situation and prospects threaten the water utilities with such unaccustomed stress and difficulty that their adaptation should be expected to be slower, or less coherent, for that very reason. Not surprisingly, progress so far in the water sector in England and Wales may be best described as patchy. In the utility sector, in the river basin functions and policies, and in central government, there are major gains and major gaps. But such gains, however welcome or impressive, cannot really compensate for the gaps: the process of adaptation needs, above all, to become more coherent.

In the utility services, almost certainly the most significant gain is the formation of clearly defined units for water supply, sewerage and sewage disposal services, supported by adequate financial investment, and monitored by OFWAT and the NRA as independent agencies whose roles as monopoly regulator and environmental watchdog are expected to develop strongly. This could be a framework in which water utility privatization comes to be seen as sustainable, so that neither the next government nor the next generation comes to wish that in our time we had done it differently. For all the seeming logic of the now reversed reorganization of 1974 (perhaps too strong on internalizing conflicts better kept in the open), the gain now seems to be as much in clarity of purpose in the different agencies as in private financing being more flexible and substantial than finance under Treasury control could be in the late 1970s and much of the 1980s.

Yet with this real gain comes disappointment and signs that in some ways change has been limited or superficial. The water utilities appear to be very isolated, especially from effective dialogue with their customers, a situation that is eased only a little, if at all, by sophisticated but remote systems of enquiry or complaint. This state of affairs has arisen because, as long as things do not go wrong, the customers need hardly be in touch with the service providers except for the payment of bills. Wessex Water has recently made an imaginative move, beyond the general practice of occasionally opening sewage works to the public, by opening some sixty plants in the same week. It even had picture postcards for sale, which visitors could send to their friends. This might signify a real change in attitudes, but, on its own, it is still lightweight. Gas and electricity companies have high-street shops in many towns and often launch major programmes of advertising and corporate communication because there is competition between fuels in the energy sector and they want to promote sales of their product. These utilities also still send meter readers to call on customers at home, even though many bills are estimated. The water companies' problem is due more to inherited than recent factors, although changed attitudes might have been expected after privatization. Even so, it would not be desirable, on the whole, to promote increased use of water, and the companies by and large do not want to bother with charging most customers in any individual way on the basis of how much (or little) water they use. In this respect, one implication of the bill as it reaches domestic consumers may be that in their eyes the service may have hardly changed since it was run by the local councils in the 1960s (except that the bills are much higher).

Assessments of consumer attitudes in surveys that OFWAT has commissioned tend to confirm this sense of isolation. These actually summarize attitudes towards the water and sewerage companies as 'rather negative'. Another view consumers tend to endorse is that the companies 'should be making those improvements anyway, given the profits they are making'. One question still open is whether OFWAT, despite its customer services committees and its persuasion of companies to reflect customer opinion in their business plans, may almost be adding to this isolation. OFWAT cannot really produce a substitute for the across-the-counter or face-to-face interaction most conventional businesses have with their customers, and the water companies need to find one for themselves if they can. They may be perhaps focusing too much on OFWAT as regulator instead of on the customers, because they see OFWAT as having more impact on their profits and the prices of their shares.

Breaking through this isolation will be all the more important for the water utilities in view of the pressures that lie ahead. Over a period of ten years, if not five, charges for access to river basin capacity, only just introduced by the NRA on a restricted cost-recovery basis, will almost certainly be sharpened to a so-called 'incentive' basis, as in several other parts of Europe. Companies improving their sewage discharges may gain some capital grants by the recycling of revenue from these charges, but generally, as water and river basin capacity become better valued as economic resources, this will put pressure on the water utilities. In addition, they must be more positive on new charging methods, as well as achieving more reduction of pollution within tighter price-caps. OFWAT cannot shelter them from these, nor can the NRA, which has to deal with a far wider group of all businesses using river basin resources or capacity. In the 1994 review of K-factor price limits, which will take place in the setting of inflation and interest rates at or close to their lowest levels for many years, OFWAT will have little choice but to push price limits down to levels that the water companies can hardly bear, knowing that they must not lose the momentum of their programmes of improvements.

Indeed, the NRA and OFWAT may be seen as having a joint task, which is to ensure that river basin capacity is not degraded or used to provide additional profits for utility company shareholders or an implicit subsidy for their customers. Their recommendations should not be regarded as hostile to the water companies themselves, but as possibly the only foundation on which, amid circumstances and public attitudes that have already changed greatly and will continue to change, they can expect to build the new, positive relationships with their customers that they will need to have in the early years of the next century.

River Basin Adaptation Achieved and Neglected

Beyond question, the key adaptation achieved in river basin management has been the ending of concealment in pollution control and the commitment to openness in the NRA – and even to some extent in Whitehall. Other chapters have made sufficient reference to this to make further emphasis here unnecessary. Another important gain – though it could have gone wrong – has been in forming one effective river basin agency at national level, with serious effort devoted to keeping its regional work and liaison well linked to local interests. If it can avoid becoming remote or isolated from its river basin 'grass roots', the NRA's influence as a national body dealing with Whitehall and national trade-associations will be far greater than that which could be achieved by ten regional agencies. The further upheaval threatened by plans to create a new environment agency may yet bring some disruption in this focus and local liaison. How marked this becomes will largely depend on the staffing levels and budgets projected for the new agency, matters that were such a hindrance initially to HMIP and the NRA as they were launched. Surely Whitehall can avoid a third repetition of such a blinkered approach?

In the context of river basins, the major setback has been in the government neglecting to make more postive use of market instruments in its management of the water environment. Sharper use of pricing with legal permits could help to stimulate action where benefits could be achieved with the least cost and delay. Such improvements need not always be a matter of much extra expense or investment. Careful operation of existing facilities and the sort of improvements that many farmers are making with MAFF and NRA encouragement can make a lot of difference. But industry and agriculture, as well as NRA staff, need to become familiar with the economic rationale underpinning the policies, seeing that practical steps are taken at a pace and in directions that are well judged and clearly articulated, thereby holding public support. Through fuller understanding and commitment and through providing incentives throughout industry and agriculture, many businesses can come to recognize the benefit to them of reducing some of the adverse impact they have on river basin capacity, and then to include such insights in their own business decisions or in dialogue with the NRA or HMIP.

The processes of adaptation call for continuing new effort. In the last ten years or so, business has been sharpening its attitudes in many other directions, and this would have been the moment for more change. The concepts are not just theoretical, or even new: in France at least, British companies operating there have been well aware of them and responding to them for almost twenty years. Reluctance among ministers and civil servants to push for sharper pricing has contributed to the delay, but the 16th Report of the RCEP puts the case for action beyond question. All that is in doubt is the political will-power to put this into practice, an odd outcome after ten years or more during which the public has become notably better informed and more vociferous about the environment generally and water pollution in particular.

The Confusions of Adaptation

The situation just described might be seen by some as typically British. The changes needed are understood, by ever wider numbers of interest groups, companies and individuals; but somehow they do not get done even when other huge changes, such as water utility privatization, are promoted with strong emphasis on the benefits they could bring to the environment. The isolation of the water utilities is similarly paradoxical, considering how the river basins in which they operate are among the most crowded in the world. Perhaps there is a tendency to see large changes as once-off or self-contained – as if each is not one of a sequence of responses to circumstances which are continuing to evolve, in social, economic and physical terms. It is as if the British, crowded as they are on their own island, expecting and attaining ever higher disposable incomes, cannot accept that unless they keep reducing levels of congestion and pollution, they will themselves devalue the very benefits they have achieved.

In the water sector, a century or more of mostly local authority control had much to its credit. This style of management was, moreover, democratic in political terms. Yet in other ways it was not participatory and increasingly lost respect as people's expectations changed. In public services and the sharing of common resources, the role of government as reflecting the community's will with authority remains important. Nevertheless, in the last fifteen years or so, other changes include more attention to citizen and consumer opinion, and the opening up of environmental information in response to increased public concern.

Together, these changes surely suggest that there is scope now for new understanding among the public about routes to life-styles with less pollution. The best means to achieve this is in specific sectors — such as roads and transport, or water and the way it is shared and managed not only here but in Europe and elsewhere. But adaptation is often a confusing process. New arrangements and old ones may not fit together very well, and it may be understandable to blame the new ones for this rather than the old ones. In the water sector in Britain, some good adaptations have been achieved recently but they are still nowhere near coherent.

We need perhaps to re-read the story of Darwin's *Origin of the Species* and its consequences. As we have seen, that new view of the natural order, strange and disruptive as it seemed to be, became coherent and well established over a few decades, so that its being strange or new is hardly recalled now. Likewise, a new constructive view of our relationship with the water environment still has to gain acceptance and become routine — a process that may also take several decades.

Global Prospects

Over the next twenty years, many developing countries are bound to face very severe difficulties in their dealing with water. Present levels of indebtedness and capital scarcity make it hard to provide almost all families even with basic facilities such as a safe, easily accessible water supply and simple forms of sanitation, such as latrines. The trends towards rapid urbanization — usually associated with later stages of economic development — will probably aggravate the hazards as much as the sheer increase in numbers of people. Claims on water resources and waste-disposal capacity will be intensified in relatively small areas. Congestion and pollution are likely to be close to or beyond the levels at which the threat to health becomes greatly magnified. Easier travel, immigration and tourism may yet add to the potential hazards, somewhat subdued in recent decades.

Previous chapters have shown how industrialized countries are becoming much absorbed by the problems of improving their own capital-intensive infrastructure in the water sector. But even if

209

they were not so absorbed, it is not clear how much help they could offer in ways that would be appropriate and sensitive to the individual circumstances of developing countries.

Only one main comment is therefore offered here. Following the UN Drinking Water Supply and Sanitation Decade, which ended in 1990, much more priority still needs to be given to this aspect of the water sector. It has often had a sort of Cinderella status relative to irrigation and hydro-electric power, with damaging consequences both socially and to people's health, and thus often in economic ways too. Even though it may not be appropriate to replicate western-style capital-intensive systems in developing countries, for utility services to seek to provide what users show they want will be crucial. Where budgets are limited, efficient use of human and physical resources, the reliable collection of revenue and the control of leakage all demand coherent attention and management. NGOs may have a greater role to play in these activities, as women generally will have if they can be given better opportunities including further schooling.

In developing countries, which lack the filters and other defences against water-borne disease provided by the water services in more prosperous countries, there are direct links between the state of the water environment and the health of the people. Thus attention to the protection of that environment, especially water quality, is hardly the optional extra that many countries becoming industrialized a century or more ago then took it to be. The greatest goal that developing countries could aim for is to find new, sustainable ways of limiting the impact of an increasing population, concentrated in the towns, on river basin resources at less cost than richer nations are having to pay. The interaction of bad water and poor health, often accounting for high infant mortality, must be overcome by every effort that can be put into it.

The natural renewal of water is endless, due to its own circulation. But this has long invited a sharing of water that is careless and open to damaging conflicts, especially as vested interests in it become established and inflexible. Thus, slowly, we have put the process of natural renewal under such strain that the amount of water available has become insufficient or unsuitable even for our own purposes. For all the technological skills and capital wealth of our age, the sharing of good-quality water can no longer depend on yet more or better technical fixes. We have to effect a transformation in our economic and social institutions – one that respects the dynamics of the natural environment – however long this may take. Moreover, we have to work at this as individuals and communities, and as good neighbours. The sustainability of the river basin habitats, on which we and future generations will depend, is still being put in peril.

Appendix

Extracts from WaterAid's 1992 Annual Review

Practical Solutions

By funding projects using simple and appropriate technologies many villages throughout Africa and Asia now enjoy the benefits that safe water brings.

Sam Mwanja is a practical man. As an engineering technician working on WaterAid-funded projects he helps villagers in the Butagaya District of Uganda to transform unprotected springs into safe sources of water. Sam offers technical advice on how to protect springs and how to install sturdy and long-lasting rower pumps to withdraw the water. The villagers take on the hard construction work, but their efforts and patience are rewarded by a safe supply of water.

Elsewhere remote springs and streams are harnessed to bring safe water into the heart of the community. In Sierra Leone, such sources of water are in abundance yet they are often far from people's homes involving long, arduous journeys. Damming these springs and streams enables villagers to pipe water, often over long distances, to within a few metres of their homes. The technology may be low but the effort is high. In one of the world's poorest countries, where life has been disrupted by civil war in neighbouring Liberia, the villagers still continue their work. They must, because in a country where one child in three dies before its fifth birthday, there is no choice.

In Zimbabwe, too, local people, using practical technologies can dramatically improve their water supplies. Many farmers have dug their own wells. Once they have lined them to prevent collapse, funds from Water Aid enable village masons to cap them and so prevent contamination. A windlass rope and bucket provides a cheap and convenient way to draw the water. Such simple improvements, while involving much hard work, have lasting benefits for everyone.

Working Partners

WaterAid's aim is always to work with local people and their organisations to support their own projects. Those partnerships take many forms.

In Nepal, for example, at national level, we work alongside the Social Services National Coordinating Council (SSNCC). By providing funding and technical advice, WaterAid is able to support the efforts of the SSNCC to reach many Nepali villages so that they have the chance to improve their own water supplies and sanitation.

In other parts of the world our partners are similar to ourselves in both structure and aims. The Kenya Water for Health Organisation (KWAHO), with its roots in Kenyan society, works directly with the people who fetch, carry and use water most – women. Through village-level women's societies, like the Makwasinyo women's group, KWAHO can channel the real dynamism that exists towards improving water supplies. The women of Makwasinyo took the lead in improving their water supply and as a result of their efforts they now pay as much in a month for almost unlimited water as they used to pay for a single bucket during the driest parts of the year.

At whatever level such relationships exist, our true partners will always be the ordinary men, women and children who benefit directly from safe water. In the village of Kullampatti in Tamil Nadu, India, men and women now realise the full impact of improvements to their water supplies. One of the handpump caretakers, a young woman called Siurambeyer, points out that none of the water from their new tubewell is wasted. 'Look at this coconut tree,' she says. 'When it is full grown we will be able to get 1,000 rupees from the sale of the coconuts. We have papaya, lime, mulberry and banana plants, too.'

By taking control of their water supply women like Siurambeyer have a chance to influence their own destiny. Water is not the end of the story; it is the beginning.

Lasting Development

Practical technologies and hard work, vital though they are, are not enough to ensure that the benefits of safe water will be felt for years to come. Skills, in engineering and in health education, must be shared to ensure that safe water supplies have the maximum impact on people's lives.

In Ghana funds from WaterAid enable many graduates undertaking compulsory national community service to become involved in rural water and sanitation projects. With training in the methods used in hand-dug wells, the most common source of water supply in rural Ghana, the young graduates are able to accelerate the Government's programme to help villagers construct their own wells. Having completed their national service, some of these young graduates have chosen a career in rural development work, so sharing their skills with others.

While graduates in Ghana assist in the development of a national water programme, in the capital of Ethiopia, Addis Ababa, young community workers, mainly women, work on water and health projects in the city's slums. Organised by WaterAid's partner, the IHA-UDP, these 'Yellow Girls', as they are known because of their brightly coloured coats, pass on vital health messages about clearing the slums and improving sanitation. And in Tanzania other young women take on the task of passing on crucial health messages to others in the village. Women like 21-year-old Janet Kusenha who, in common with the other women in her village of Sagara, has to spend hours each day fetching and carrying water.

Yet her commitment to improving her and her family's health and that of her neighbours is such that she finds the time to help at the local dispensary, talking to the village women about health-related matters. 'I am happy,' she says, 'to have gained knowledge that helps both my family and my neighbours and I feel I have gained both confidence in myself and other people's respect.'

WaterAid's funds help ensure that such commitment is not lost.

Country	Expenditure 1991/2
Uganda	£338,048
Sierra Leone	£254,737
Zimbabwe	£62,908
Nepal	£276,979
Kenya	£320,774
India	£306,184
Ghana	£301,813
Ethiopia	£372,818
Tanzania	£316,554

WaterAid's address is: 1 Queen Anne's Gate, London SW1H 9BT

Glossary of Acronyms

BATNEEC best available technology not entailing excessive cost
BWB British Waterways Board (established 1963)
CBI Confederation of British Industries
CPRE Council for the Protection of Rural England
DoE Department of the Environment
DWI Drinking Water Inspectorate (established 1989)
EC European Community
ENDS Environmental Data Services Limited
Envage Environment Agency
EQS environmental quality standard
FTSE (100) Index *Financial Times*/stock exchange 100-share index
GNP gross national product
HMIP Her Majesty's Inspectorate of Pollution (established 1987 by merger of several older units)
IFC International Finance Corporation: private-sector arm of the World Bank
IPC integrated pollution control
IWEM Institution of Water and Environmental Management
MAFF Ministry of Agriculture, Fisheries and Food
NGO non-governmental organization
NLF National Loans Fund
NRA National Rivers Authority (established 1989)
NRAAC National Rivers Authority Advisory Committee (active 1988–9 only)
OFWAT Office of Water Services (established 1989)
PCB polychlorinated biphenyl
PCE perchloroethane
RCEP Royal Commission on Environmental Pollution
RPI Retail Price Index
RQO River Quality Objectives
SAUR Société d'Aménagement Urbain et Rural
UES uniform emission standard
WAA Water Authorities Association (1984–9 only)

WCA Water Companies Association (those companies providing water supply only)

WQO Water Quality Objective

WRB Water Resources Board (active mid-1960s to mid-1974)

WSA Water Services Association (those companies providing water supply and sewerage services) (from 1989)

Further Reading

Cairncross, Frances. 1991. *Costing the Earth*. London, Economist Books

Conway, Gordon R. and Pretty, J. N. 1991. *Unwelcome Harvest: Agriculture and Pollution*. London, Earthscan

Department of the Environment (Welsh office). 1992. *Using Water Wisely: A Consultation Paper*. London, DoE

Department of the Environment (Welsh office). 1993. *Integrated Pollution Control: A Practical Guide*. London, HMSO

Department of the Environment Water Services Association and others. 1993. *Water Metering Trials: Final Report and Summary*. London, WSA

Haigh, Nigel, and others. 1986. *Water and Waste in Four Countries* (EC Environmental Policy in Practice, vol. 1). London, Graham and Trotman

Kinnersley, David. 1988. *Troubled Water: Rivers, Politics and Pollution*. London, Hilary Shipman

McDonald, A. T. and Kay, D. 1988. *Water Resources Issues and Strategies*. London, Longman (with John Wiley, New York)

National Rivers Authority. Annual reports and series of reports on water quality, including:

no. 1, *Discharge Consents and Compliance Policy: A Blueprint for the Future*, published July 1990

no. 4, *The Quality of Rivers, Canals and Estuaries in England and Wales*, report for 1990, published December 1991

no. 6, *The Influence of Agriculture on the Quality of Natural Waters in England and Wales*, report for 1991, published January 1992

Bathing Water Quality in England and Wales: no. 8, report for 1991, published June 1992; no. 11, report for 1992, published May 1993

Water Pollution Incidents in England and Wales: no. 9, report for 1991, published September 1992; no. 13, report for 1992, published September 1993

NRA Water Resources Development Strategy: A Discussion Document, 1992

Low Flows and Water Resources, 1993

The NRA also published in August 1993 a series of strategy documents covering water resources, water quality, flood defence, fisheries, conservation, navigation, recreation, and research and development

NRA head office address: Rivers House, Waterside Drive, Almondsbury, Bristol BS12 4UD

Office of Water Services. 1991. *Paying for Water: The Way Ahead*, and other publications from OFWAT, Centre City Tower, 7 Hill Street, Birmingham

Purseglove, Jeremy. 1988. *Taming the Flood: A Natural History of Rivers and Wetlands*. Oxford, Oxford University Press and Channel Four

Royal Commission on Environmental Pollution. 1992. 16th Report, *Freshwater Quality* (Cmnd 1966). London, HMSO

Economics and Privatization

Daly, Herman and Cobb, John, jun. 1992. *For the Common Good*. Boston, Beacon Press

Foster, C. D. 1992. *Privatisation, Public Ownership and the Regulation of Natural Monopoly*. Oxford, Blackwell

House of Commons Committee of Public Accounts. 13 July 1992. 7th Report, *Sale of the Water Authorities in England and Wales*. London, HMSO

Jacobs, Michael. 1991. *The Green Economy*. London, Pluto Press

National Audit Office. 14 February 1992. Report by the Comptroller and Auditor General, *Department of the Environment: Sale of the Water Authorities in England and Wales*. London, HMSO

Pearce, David W. 1993. *Economic Values and the Natural World*. London, Earthscan

Pearce, David W. and Turner, Kerry. 1990. *Economics of Natural Resources and the Environment*. London, Harvester Wheatsheaf

Vickers, John and Yarrow, George. 1988. *Privatisation: An Economic Analysis*. London, MIT Press

Development and Environment

Adams, W. M. 1992. *Wasting the Rain: Rivers, People and Planning in Africa*. London, Earthscan

Burton, Ian, with others. 1978. *The Environment as Hazard*. New York, Oxford University Press

Schmidhiny, Stephen, with the Business Council for Sustainable Development. 1992. *Changing Course: A Global Business Perspective on Development and the Environment*. Cambridge (Mass.) and London, MIT Press

UNDP/World Bank. Annual Reports on Water and Sanitation Programme and related Reports

White, G., Bradley, D. and White, A. 1972. *Drawers of Water*. Chicago and London, University of Chicago Press (classic study of domestic water use in East Africa)

World Bank. 1992. World Development Report. Development and the Environment. New York, Oxford University Press

Statistics

Department of the Environment and Government Statistical Service. 1992. *The UK Environment*. London, HMSO

Organization for Economic Co-operation and Development. 1991. *The State of the Environment*. Paris, OECD (available through HMSO)

Public Finance Foundation. *The UK Water Industry* (annually)

Water Services Association. *Waterfacts* (annually: an excellent source for figures on water utility services in England and Wales)

Classic Texts

Several texts which did much to launch environmental concerns in the 1960s and 1970s deserve a mention.

Carson, Rachel. 1962. *Silent Spring*. English edition: London, Hamish Hamilton

Mellanby, Kenneth. 1967. *Pesticides and Pollution*. London, Collins New Naturalist

Ward, Barbara and Dubos, René. 1972. *Only One Earth*. London, André Deutsch

Index

Discover more about our forthcoming books through Penguin's FREE newspaper...

Penguin

Quarterly

It's packed with:

- exciting features
- author interviews
- previews & reviews
- books from your favourite films & TV series
- exclusive competitions & much, much more...

Write off for your free copy today to:
Dept JC
Penguin Books Ltd
FREEPOST
West Drayton
Middlesex
UB7 0BR
NO STAMP REQUIRED

READ MORE IN PENGUIN

In every corner of the world, on every subject under the sun, Penguin represents quality and variety – the very best in publishing today.

For complete information about books available from Penguin – including Puffins, Penguin Classics and Arkana – and how to order them, write to us at the appropriate address below. Please note that for copyright reasons the selection of books varies from country to country.

In the United Kingdom: Please write to *Dept. JC, Penguin Books Ltd, FREEPOST, West Drayton, Middlesex UB7 0BR*

If you have any difficulty in obtaining a title, please send your order with the correct money, plus ten per cent for postage and packaging, to *PO Box No. 11, West Drayton, Middlesex UB7 0BR*

In the United States: Please write to *Penguin USA Inc., 375 Hudson Street, New York, NY 10014*

In Canada: Please write to *Penguin Books Canada Ltd, 10 Alcorn Avenue, Suite 300, Toronto, Ontario M4V 3B2*

In Australia: Please write to *Penguin Books Australia Ltd, 487 Maroondah Highway, Ringwood, Victoria 3134*

In New Zealand: Please write to *Penguin Books (NZ) Ltd,182–190 Wairau Road, Private Bag, Takapuna, Auckland 9*

In India: Please write to *Penguin Books India Pvt Ltd, 706 Eros Apartments, 56 Nehru Place, New Delhi 110 019*

In the Netherlands: Please write to *Penguin Books Netherlands B.V., Keizersgracht 231 NL–1016 DV Amsterdam*

In Germany: Please write to *Penguin Books Deutschland GmbH, Friedrichstrasse 10–12, W–6000 Frankfurt/Main 1*

In Spain: Please write to *Penguin Books S. A., C. San Bernardo 117–6° E–28015 Madrid*

In Italy: Please write to *Penguin Italia s.r.l., Via Felice Casati 20, I–20124 Milano*

In France: Please write to *Penguin France S. A., 17 rue Lejeune, F–31000 Toulouse*

In Japan: Please write to *Penguin Books Japan, Ishikiribashi Building, 2–5–4, Suido, Bunkyo-ku, Tokyo 112*

In Greece: Please write to *Penguin Hellas Ltd, Dimocritou 3, GR–106 71 Athens*

In South Africa: Please write to *Longman Penguin Southern Africa (Pty) Ltd, Private Bag X08, Bertsham 2013*

READ MORE IN PENGUIN

A CHOICE OF NON-FICTION

The Time Out Film Guide Edited by Tom Milne

The definitive, up-to-the minute directory of over 9,500 films – world cinema from classics and silent epics to reissues and the latest releases – assessed by two decades of *Time Out* reviewers. 'In my opinion the best and most comprehensive' – Barry Norman

The Remarkable Expedition Olivia Manning

The events of an extraordinary attempt in 1887 to rescue Emin Pasha, Governor of Equatoria, are recounted here by the author of *The Balkan Trilogy* and *The Levant Trilogy* and vividly reveal unprecedented heights of magnificent folly in the perennial human search for glorious conquest.

Berlin: Coming in From the Cold Ken Smith

'He covers everything from the fate of the ferocious-looking dogs that formerly helped to guard East Germany's borders to the vast Orwellian apparatus that maintained security in the now-defunct German Democratic Republic ... a pithy style and an eye for the telling detail' – *Independent*

Cider with Rosie/As I Walked Out one Midsummer Morning
Laurie Lee

Now together in one volume, Laurie Lee's two classic autobiographical works, *Cider with Rosie* and *As I Walked Out One Midsummer Morning*. Together they illustrate Laurie Lee's superb descriptive powers as he conveys the poignancy of a boy's transformation into adulthood.

In the Land of Oz Howard Jacobson

'A wildly funny account of his travels; abounding in sharp characterization, crunching dialogue and self-parody, it actually is a book which makes you laugh out loud on almost every page ... sharp, skilful and brilliantly funny' – *Literary Review*

A CHOICE OF NON-FICTION

Citizens A Chronicle of the French Revolution Simon Schama

'The most marvellous book I have read about the French Revolution in the last fifty years' – Richard Cobb in *The Times*. 'He has chronicled the vicissitudes of that world with matchless understanding, wisdom, pity and truth, in the pages of this huge and marvellous book' – *Sunday Times*

Out of Africa Karen Blixen (Isak Dinesen)

Karen Blixen went to Kenya in 1914 to run a coffee-farm; its failure in 1931 caused her to return to Denmark where she wrote this classic account of her experiences. 'A work of sincere power … a fine lyrical study of life in East Africa' – Harold Nicolson in the *Daily Telegraph*

Yours Etc. Graham Greene
Letters to the Press 1945–1989

'An entertaining celebration of Graham Greene's lesser-known career as a prolific author of letters to newspapers; you will find unarguable proof of his total addiction to everything about his time, from the greatest issues of the day to the humblest subjects imaginable' – Salman Rushdie in the *Observer*

The Trial of Lady Chatterley Edited By C. H. Rolph

In October 1960 at the Old Bailey a jury of nine men and three women prepared for the infamous trial of *Lady Chatterley's Lover*. The Obscene Publications Act had been introduced the previous year and D. H. Lawrence's notorious novel was the first to be prosecuted under its provisions. This is the account of the historic trial and acquittal of Penguin Books.

Handbook for the Positive Revolution Edward de Bono

Edward de Bono's challenging new book provides a practical framework for a serious revolution which has no enemies but seeks to make things better. The hand symbolizes the five basic principles of the Positive Revolution, to remind us that even a small contribution is better than endless criticism.

READ MORE IN PENGUIN

A CHOICE OF NON-FICTION

Bernard Shaw Michael Holroyd
Volume 2 1898–1918 The Pursuit of Power

'A man whose art rested so much upon the exercise of intelligence could not have chosen a more intelligent biographer ... The pursuit of Bernard Shaw has grown, and turned into a pursuit of the whole twentieth century' – Peter Ackroyd in *The Times*

Shots from the Hip Charles Shaar Murray

His classic encapsulation of the moment when rock stars turned junkies as the sixties died; his dissection of rock 'n' roll violence as citizens assaulted the Sex Pistols; superstar encounters from the decline of Paul McCartney to Mick Jagger's request that the author should leave – Charles Shaar Murray's *Shots From the Hip* is also rock history in the making.

Managing on the Edge Richard Pascale

The co-author of the bestselling *The Art of Japanese Management* has once again turned conventional thinking upside down. Conflict and contention in organizations are not just unavoidable – they are positively to be welcomed. The successes and failures of large corporations can help us understand the need to maintain a creative tension between fitting companies together and splitting them apart.

Just Looking John Updike

'Mr Updike can be a very good art critic, and some of these essays are marvellous examples of critical explanation ... a deep understanding of the art emerges ... His reviews of some recent and widely attended shows ... quite surpass the modest disclaimer of the title' – *The New York Times Book Review*

Shelley: The Pursuit Richard Holmes

'Surely the best biography of Shelley ever written ... He makes Shelley's character entirely convincing by showing us the poet at every stage of his development acting upon, and reacting to, people and events' – Stephen Spender

READ MORE IN PENGUIN

A CHOICE OF NON-FICTION

Riding the Iron Rooster Paul Theroux

Travels in old and new China with the author of *The Great Railway Bazaar*. 'Mr Theroux cannot write badly ... he is endlessly curious about places and people ... and in the course of a year there was almost no train in the whole vast Chinese rail network in which he did not travel' – Ludovic Kennedy

Ninety-two Days Evelyn Waugh

In this fascinating chronicle of a South American journey, Waugh describes the isolated cattle country of Guiana, sparsely populated by an odd collection of visionaries, rogues and ranchers, and records the nightmarish experiences travelling on foot, by horse and by boat through the jungle in Brazil.

The Life of Graham Greene Norman Sherry
Volume One 1904–1939

'Probably the best biography ever of a living author' – Philip French in the *Listener*. Graham Greene has always maintained a discreet distance from his reading public.This volume reconstructs his first thirty-five years to create one of the most revealing literary biographies of the decade.

The Day Gone By Richard Adams

In this enchanting memoir the bestselling author of *Watership Down* tells his life story from his idyllic 1920s childhood spent in Newbury, Berkshire, through public school, Oxford and service in World War Two to his return home and his courtship of the girl he was to marry.

A Turn in the South V. S. Naipaul

'A supremely interesting, even poetic glimpse of a part of America foreigners either neglect or patronize' – *Guardian*. 'An extraordinary panorama' – *Daily Telegraph*. 'A fine book by a fine man, and one to be read with great enjoyment: a book of style, sagacity and wit' – *Sunday Times*

READ MORE IN PENGUIN

A CHOICE OF NON-FICTION

When Shrimps Learn to Whistle Denis Healey

Taking up the most powerful political themes that emerged from his hugely successful *The Time of My Life*, Denis Healey now gives us this stimulating companion volume. 'Forty-three years of ruminations ... by the greatest foreign secretary (as the author quietly and reasonably implies) we never had' – Ben Pimlott in the *New Statesman & Society*

Eastern Approaches Fitzroy Maclean

'The author's record of personal achievement is remarkable. The canvas which he covers is immense. The graphic writing reveals the ruthless man of action ... He emerges from [his book] as an extrovert Lawrence' – *The Times Literary Supplement*

This Time Next Week Leslie Thomas

'Mr Thomas's book is all humanity, to which is added a Welshman's mastery of words ... Some of his episodes are hilarious, some unbearably touching, but everyone, staff and children, is looked upon with compassion' – *Observer*. 'Admirably written, with clarity, realism, poignancy and humour' – *Daily Telegraph*

Reports from the Holocaust Larry Kramer

'A powerful book ... more than a political autobiography, *Reports* is an indictment of a world that allows AIDS to continue ... he is eloquent and convincing when he swings from the general to the specific. His recommendations on the release of drugs to AIDS patients are practical and humane' – *New York Newsday*

City on the Rocks Kevin Rafferty

'Rafferty has filled a glaring gap on the Asian bookshelf, offering the only comprehensive picture of Hong Kong right up to the impact of the Tiananmen Square massacre' – *Business Week*. 'A story of astonishing achievement, but its purpose is warning rather than celebration' – *Sunday Times*